In Memory of

Charles B. Burdick

Other Books by JAMES P. WALSH

Legacy of a Native Son: James Duval Phelan and Villa Montalvo
with Timothy J. O'Keefe

The Irish in the West
with Timothy J. Sarbaugh

San Francisco's Hallinan: Toughest Lawyer in Town

The San Francisco Irish

The Irish: America's Political Class

Ethnic Militancy

SAN JOSÉ STATE UNIVERSITY

An Interpretive History
1950–2000

JAMES P. WALSH

San José State
UNIVERSITY

San José, California
2003

San José State University
One Washington Square
San José, California 95192

Book design by John A. Jensen, SJSU, BS, Graphic Design, 1979

Printed in the United States of America

Walsh, James P., 1937-
San Jose Staté University : an interpretive history, 1950-2000 / James P. Walsh.
p. cm.
Includes index.
ISBN 0-9741479-0-7.
1. San Jose State University—History—20th century. I. Title.
LD729.6.S4 .W35 2003   378.794′74—dc21

Table of Contents

Acknowledgments

THIS VOLUME BEGAN at San José State with a 1997 request from the president's office to the history department. President Robert L. Caret had exhausted the available supply of copies of the university history (*Washington Square, 1857-1979, San José State University*). His staff simply wanted more copies so that he might continue presenting them to friends of San José State. I recommended that the university not reprint the existing book, but rather commission a new work. My reasons were twofold. First, vast change had taken place at San José State during the concluding decades of the twentieth century. And, second, the then surviving co-author of the previous history had not been altogether pleased with that product. Charles B. Burdick suggested that if I ever had the opportunity to reassess the history of San José State, that I should do so.

Acknowledgments go first to President Robert L. Caret for the basic support that was necessary to research and to write this history. The most important component of President Caret's support was the freedom and encouragement of scholarly inquiry that became a characteristic of the university during the actual period under study. The help and encouragement of Janet C. Redding, assistant to the president, are likewise noted and appreciated. As this six-year project neared completion, editor Carol Beddo directed a dedicated team that included John Jensen (graphic designer), Lori Stahl-Bauer (copywriter and copy editor), Rebecca Morean (copywriter), Sylvia Hutchinson (communications director, San José State), Craig Kochersberger (graphics coordinator, San José State), Samuel J. Koplowicz (multimedia producer, San José State) and Robert C. Bain (photographer, San José State). Together the history project team improved the manuscript, largely by selective text reduction that allowed the addition of cameos and graphics. The process was intended to enhance reader interest and to maintain the interpretive integrity of the text. The original, uncut manuscripts are to be placed in the Dr. Martin Luther King, Jr. Library at San José State University, and The Bancroft Library at the University of California, Berkeley.

The pioneer scholarship of Professor Benjamin F. Gilbert, who completed the San José State College centennial history in 1957, is the basis for current understanding of the origins and developments of the first one hundred years. He and co-author Professor Charles B. Burdick extended that study to 1979 in a second volume, the one that this current work is offered as elaboration, interpretation, and extension. In creating this third volume of the history of San José State University, I found that the scholarship of Professor H. Brett Melendy served as a central source of data and insight. His numerous oral histories of former presidents, administrators, and faculty spanned most of the years covered by this book. Melendy's work was invaluable. A significant addition to the university oral history collection includes Charles B. Burdick's interviews with President John T. Wahlquist. For bringing these and a vast amount of other documentary sources to my attention, I am grateful to Cecilia Mullen, former head of library special collections, who was ably assisted by Michael Condon. For crime records and other law enforcement history sources, I am indebted to campus police chief Ric Abeyta and to Noemi Hinchberger.

The comprehensive files of the *Spartan Daily* constituted another vital source of primary information. Throughout the early years of this study, the student newspaper received recognitions as an outstanding example of the best in college journalism. Not only was the quality of journalism high, the coverage was broad and deep. While the *Spartan Daily* was an abundant source of historical material, its vastness and richness constituted a handicap in itself. The paper is in serious need of being indexed. In my case, I am grateful to historian Eric Narveson for sharing with me his personal index of the *Spartan Daily* relating to campus construction history.

Numerous others have contributed to what substance and value this current work may claim. Talented faculty and students have created an echelon of studies of departments, colleges, and other institutions within the evolving history of the university. Among them are Professor Theodore M. Norton's history of the Academic Senate, Professor Dolores Freitas Spurgeon's history of the journalism department, the account of engineering at San José State that Dean Jay D. Pinson initiated and Dean Donald E. Kirk shared with me, the story of modern women's athletics by communication studies student Suzanne Hughes, Professor Pete Zidnak's collected work on sports throughout the institution's history, and Ted Sielaff's biographies of retired faculty. These accounts are merely the more permanently available sources for scholarly inquiry and are supplemented by informal summaries of unit histories. The most abundant, but mortal, are the walking storehouses of facts and myths shared by emeritus faculty, alumni, and all others who have been observers or members of an extensive campus community. I express my gratitude to all of these remarkable persons, for without them this work would have been severely stilted. Besides, their interviews made my job all the more enjoyable.

My completion of the original manuscript coincided with my retirement from an abundant career at San José State. Throughout, I have enjoyed many campus friendships and satisfying professional associations. I regret the passing of those who served as my early models of the best in higher education. Others have remained as friendly and sustaining influences in what was, upon reflection, an ideal university career. First, I wish to recognize the late History Professor Gerald E. Wheeler for minding my academic well being until I became capable of doing so myself. History Professor Peter M. Buzanski served as a model senior colleague as did Professor Theodore M. Norton and the late Professor Roy E. Young from the department of political science. Professor George E. Moore provided this, too, plus an education in the cultures of modern Hawaii and Japan. I appreciate the work of the late John Galm and Burton Brazil, and of Carol Beddo, Hobert Burns, Nancie Fimbel, Bobbye Gorenberg, Lester Lange, Donald Ryan, St. Saffold, and Bernard Schneider, all of whom reviewed the early manuscript and offered me their insights and corrections. For why so many others and I are indebted to the late Professor Charles B. Burdick, readers may consult the concluding chapter, "The Reason for Being, Academic Life of the University."

Professor Charles Keserich's help fills a category of its own. Through more than three decades at San José State, Dr. Keserich helped me meet the academic challenges. In the case of this work, he read and improved the full manuscript over a period of two years. He did the same for previous books. His friendship and his commitment to scholarly improvement are among the prizes I have valued most during an academic career. Last, and certainly not least, I record my gratitude to my colleague and friend in academic administration, Professor Adnan Daoud. As associate dean and then as dean of the College of Social Sciences, Dr. Daoud made administration efficient and just, and conducted it with cultivated good taste.

Stability was my constant companion at San José State, and it allowed career productivity amid personal satisfaction. My spouse, Ann McKinnon Walsh, has assisted and supported me in every important undertaking. This began when as a teenager she corrected my spelling. Now it concludes amid information technology. Thank you, Ann, for the companionship and the help. I wish also to thank our children Eileen, Laura, and Daniel and to encourage our grandchildren Elizabeth and Alison Frost and Benjamin, Casey, and Shannon Lau. Now is their turn to engage the challenges and opportunities of California education.

James P. Walsh
San José State University
March 4, 2003

Introduction by Robert L. Caret

March 2003

Dear Reader,

As I look out the window of my office in Tower Hall,
I see San José State University's future. Our new Dr.
Martin Luther King, Jr. Library, a first-of-its-kind
collaboration between a major university and a
city, will open this summer. At the opposite end of
the campus, construction is proceeding on Campus
Village, an innovative residential complex that will
ultimately transform the southeast quadrant and
provide housing for 6,000 students and nearly 200
faculty and staff.

Well established as the Silicon Valley's Metropolitan University, San José State is
expanding its connections and creating new partnerships around the globe, in such
places as China, Taiwan and El Salvador. International students come to us from
more than 100 countries, and the new Global Studies Institute, established in 2002,
has awarded 10 fellowships to professors to pursue global studies projects.

While we work to build an ever-brighter future for SJSU, we take inspiration from
its past—a distinguished heritage as the oldest public institution of higher education
in the West. And we are grateful to those who have stepped outside the rush of events
and day-to-day activities to chronicle the university's remarkable history and development since its founding in 1857.

With *San José State University, An Interpretive History, 1950–2000*, History Professor Emeritus James Walsh takes a place of honor alongside previous SJSU historians Benjamin F. Gilbert and Charles B. Burdick. Based on research begun more than
five years ago, Walsh traces the university's progress from the 1950s to the end of the
twentieth century. He spotlights the university's leadership, faculty and students, as
well as the challenges and hot issues of those decades. Anyone associated with the
university during that time, as well as all who value history as a context for today,
will find this book interesting reading.

I am pleased to introduce and to commend to you *San José State University, An
Interpretive History, 1950–2000*.

Robert L. Caret
President
San José State University

CHAPTER ONE

Who Runs the University?
TRACKING THE MOVE TO SHARED GOVERNANCE

J OHN T. WAHLQUIST always knew who ran San José State in his day. From 1952 to 1964 he ran the college because that was his job, and he always did his job. Authority infused his 1940s concept of education leadership. Even at the moment of his elevation to presidential authority, he witnessed the imposition of unrestrained power by the outgoing president.

At the start of his San José State presidency in the summer of 1952, Wahlquist discovered that his appointment overlapped by 60 days the concluding term of outgoing President Thomas W. MacQuarrie. At Wahlquist's suggestion, the two men occupied separate desks in the same office until MacQuarrie recognized the inevitable and took sick leave until his own 25-year presidency concluded.

During this interregnum, out-going President MacQuarrie alerted Wahlquist to a few of his lingering concerns. Particularly, MacQuarrie warned Wahlquist that a former instructor would be calling for a letter of recommendation. This was a problem for MacQuarrie, who had fired the instructor in the hallway outside his classroom over an allegation of homosexuality. Clearly, what President MacQuarrie accepted as correct in 1927 still held for him in 1952. His action on his judgments was not subject to challenge or review. No appeal mechanism existed, and the customs of the day backed the president.

As the tenure of college presidents is measured, MacQuarrie's 25-year record was extraordinary. In 1927 he was well prepared when measured by the educational and administrative standards of his era. The eras of the Great Depression and World War II constituted the bulk of MacQuarrie's presidential administration, the longest in the institution's history since the time of his appointment by the California State Superintendent of Education. Slight consultation had accompanied his appointment then, and the narrow selection process had broadened only slightly by 1952.

Wahlquist's term was a long one as well, and though it was but half of MacQuarrie's, it produced accelerated change. Far more dynamic, the twelve-year Wahlquist era (1952-1964) began and ended in two different worlds of higher education. Wahlquist began by observing MacQuarrie exercise authority in an assured, arbitrary manner. But by the time Wahlquist's term ended, institutional revolt was underway.

Wahlquist's inauguration was civic pageantry planned to impress the San José of 1952. An academic procession from Washington Square to the downtown Civic Auditorium allowed the big college an opportunity to display itself to the small town. Wahlquist and Earl E. Warren, California Governor and later Chief Justice of the United States, led the line of marchers. Those who followed included delegates from 200 other colleges and universities, including 16 of their presidents. The full faculty turned out, robed in colorful regalia reflecting academic symbolism dating back to the Middle Ages. Next marched prominent alumni, student representatives, and a concluding escort of uniformed members from the Police School and the Reserve Officers Training Corps. All who participated did so with pride, a feeling that excited the cheering onlookers who lined San Carlos Street.

As president, Wahlquist ran the campus with a centralized, concise administration and reported to the State Department of Education via the superintendent, Roy E. Simpson. He selected his own managers and retained those who met with his performance standard. When he and his subordinates met, they discussed the issues he decided to discuss. Thereafter, he drew his conclusions, announced his decisions and initiated their implementation.

The conservative, small, public school-like faculty that Wahlquist inherited in 1952 was breathing its last. The academic standards associated with the explosive

From California State Normal School to San José State University

1857
George W. Minns founds California's first public institution of higher education, located in San Francisco.

1862
The Minns school becomes California State Normal School.

1871
The State Normal School moves to San José.

1881
A branch campus is established in Los Angeles. This branch later becomes UCLA.

1887
The State Normal School becomes San José State Normal School.

1910
Tower Hall (State Historic Landmark No. 417) and new facilities replacing those damaged in the Great Earthquake of 1906 are dedicated.

1921
The school is renamed San José State Teachers College.

1935
The college becomes San José State College.

1949
SJSC awards its first master's degrees.

1961
SJSC is incorporated into the California State Colleges (now the 23-campus California State University system).

1972
SJSC becomes California State University, San José marking the achievement of university status.

1974
CSU, San José, is renamed San José State University.

1990
The number of students tops 30,000.

1991
Campus reaches cultural pluralism, with no ethnic majority.

1994
San Carlos Street is closed, from 4th Street through 10th Street, unifying the campus.

1996
SJSU begins competition in the Western Athletic Conference. The city and the university celebrate the official opening of Paseo de San Carlos.

2000
Construction begins on the new joint city/ university library — the first such collaboration between a major city and university in the nation.

Harry Edwards

BA, SOCIOLOGY, 1964

APROMINENT SPORTS SOCIOLOGIST, social critic, activist, professor and sports consultant, Harry Edwards was once described by Maya Angelou as an angry man, but a man who could put that anger to work and get things done. A long-time professor of sociology at the University of California, Berkeley, and the author of such books as *The Revolt of the Black Athlete, The Struggle That Must Be, Sociology of Sport, Black Students*, and *Playing to Win: A Short Guide to Sensible Sports Participation*, Edwards is renowned for his outspoken and specific beliefs concerning how society needs to shift in order to cultivate and achieve an unbiased and just world. A long and distinguished career began with his aggressive stance on the rights of black Americans during the 1960s. He then went on to earn both a doctorate from Cornell University and accolades as a consultant to the NFL's San Francisco 49ers and the NBA's Golden State Warriors. After a 30-year career as associate professor of sociology at Berkeley, Edwards left to become director of the Department of Parks and Recreation for the city of Oakland. "I don't mind controversy. I was born in controversy, whether it was at San José State or Cornell. I think it's the biggest part of my personality."

On Campus: Led a black student protest against institutional racism in 1967.

post-World War II growth at San José State allowed the new president to enlarge, greatly upgrade, and professionalize his instructional staff. He personally hired most of the new faculty during annual tours across America when he traveled to major centers of higher education and attended numerous academic conferences. His objective was to hire those who already had teaching experience and the PhD or other appropriate terminal degrees. He sought such candidates who were graduates of prestigious universities. He also kept an eye out for those whom he considered to have special talents. Those with doctorates from Berkeley and Stanford were fine, but Wahlquist wanted greater intellectual diversity. He sought faculty from the Ivy League, the Big Ten, and throughout the Midwest and Northwest as well as from the South. However, his faculty selections often disregarded the departments' needs as the department members understood them.

Wahlquist's most senior and inherited faculty, long experienced in being told what to do, hardly complained. It was the very people Wahlquist hired by his more demanding standard who, once at San José State, found his methods unacceptable. The newly minted PhDs expected to be treated according to the standards of the mature graduate environments in which they had earned their degrees. While they hardly objected to their own personal selections by Wahlquist, these young professors, in time, objected to his methods and to his management style. As the new faculty became more comfortable in their positions and in their new tenure, many began to voice their convictions through the Academic Council.

As the years passed, Wahlquist's method of seeking counsel from his administrators within his authoritative management system enjoyed less and less acceptance among the faculty. In the end, afflicted with a bleeding ulcer, an unsympathetic new chancellor, faculty activism and unionization, the president who had built the modern campus became vulnerable. By 1964, at age 65, President Wahlquist understood that the time to move aside had arrived.

R OBERT D. CLARK (1964-69) came from a more open and interactive university background and was comfortable in soliciting faculty participation in the formulation of university policy. Clark believed that the new methods by which faculty and administrators consulted with each other and shared in the creation of college policy were the best way to advance a major public institution of higher education. This system was called "shared governance" by educational theorists. San José State, like so many postwar universities, had gathered an exceedingly large number of specialists with a great variety of transferable skills and expert knowledge. Clark felt that college policy creation would profit by their input, and he championed the concept of shared governance. For instance, Clark ended Wahlquist's hierarchical practice of appointing department heads. Instead, he approved the chairs recommended to him by their own department members. So intent was Clark on ending what he considered the permanent reign of "terrorizing chairs" over their departments, that he also instituted a five-year review policy. His initiative allowed the faculty to provide the most substantial input into a department chair's review. Additionally, Clark dealt with authoritarian-type administrators at higher levels by: removing the most intransigent; counseling or reassigning the more amenable; and recruiting a new wave of teacher-scholar-administrators for San José State's future.

This policy redirection profited greatly by the quality of his new academic vice president. Clark's selection for the new post was Dr. Hobert W. Burns, an academic philosopher with a thoughtful, friendly manner and a practical approach to management. Burns had worked with numerous university presidents before accepting Clark's offer to come to San José. He joined Clark's team, he said in his oral history, because the new president impressed him with his refreshing openness.

The campus body for the expression of diverse faculty opinion was the Academic Council. Clark respected the council and cooperated with its members in the creation of college policy. Together Clark and the council conveyed legitimacy to critical policies, which they jointly created. This became a critical feature of college management as the protest years emerged.

Clark came to San José State from the University of Oregon, where he had already gained considerable administrative experience. As a faculty member, he discovered that he liked to participate in policy formulation. He concluded, too, that faculty did a better job, and the college and students were better served, when faculty helped determine what policies would help them do their work. Clark made a great effort to know faculty personally, even on a campus with 18,000 students and more than 1,000 faculty members.

The image of an administrator as a redeployed academic evoked positive faculty responses, and Clark was the first San José State president to project this new image. Faculty members could more easily trust and respect other faculty on loan to administration than they could warm to a separate class of professional managers.

In Clark's case, the teacher-scholar appearance was the reality. He did not manipulate or try to enhance his image as a scholar even as he kept scratching away on his own research agenda. The newer faculty who were teaching full loads of classes while publishing or performing were reassured by Clark's ongoing private, unheralded, and uncompensated research scholarship. Few knew any details until his work surfaced much later with the publication of his biography of Thomas Condon, an Irish immigrant to Oregon who had served as a missionary and a geologist.

Clark had no problem, then, with a faculty seeking to engage itself in the remolding of California's first institution of public higher education. His problem was an inherited centralized administration that was more comfortable with the past than prepared for the future.

Dean of the College John W. Gilbaugh exemplified the old way of doing things. Instead of simply removing his predecessor's number two man directly and for all to see, Clark used the state college system's authorization of a new vice presidency to effect the task. San José State had tripled in size during the Wahlquist years, and the chancellor's office promised an additional vice president to Clark when he agreed to accept the presidency. Clark used his recruitment enticement to reorganize his administrative structure and to deal with Gilbaugh. On his newly designed organizational chart, Clark upgraded the structure to two vice presidencies and no Dean of the College. The position of Academic Vice Presidency was the new post, the one Clark would persuade Burns to accept. The Executive Vice Presidency already existed, and Clark retained its incumbent, English Department Professor William J. Dusel. Dusel was a flexible administrator, cooperative, someone who could fit Clark's new management requirements.

These were unhappy developments for Gilbaugh. He pressed Clark for a commitment toward his own appointment to the new and upgraded position; privately, Clark explained the new reality. He said that he would be able to support him for positions that might be more in keeping with his qualifications. Needless to say, Clark developed no such positions at San José State in the 1960s.

The Academic Council supported Clark's actions with a commendation for his achievements during the first 18 months of the new administration. The council passed its congratulatory motion over the expressed opposition of Gilbaugh, who was becoming the shrill voice of opposition to the updated academic order. Thereafter, Gilbaugh retreated to his tenured professorship in the School of Education and from there went public with a series of newspaper articles that criticized San José State and other colleges.

Robert Clark, his reorganized administration, and active faculty inaugurated a cooperative relationship to advance a growing, complicated educational undertaking. Among the numerous tangible changes was the creation of explicit standards for faculty recruitment, retention, and promotion. The president would no longer travel America each spring and hire new faculty in his wake. Professionalization and specialization went hand in hand with administrative decentralization; the Academic Council and the president's new team consulted and formulated the broadest range of policies. The basic undertakings of the institution, organizing and delivering instruc-

First ombudsman tackles institutional racism

A WHITE SOUTHERN PROTESTANT MINISTER from Alabama, J. Benton White might have seemed an unlikely ally in the war against institutional racism at SJSU. Yet in the fall of 1967, he became the nation's first college ombudsman, directed by President Robert Clark to do just that.

White had been the United Methodist campus minister since 1961. Harry Edwards had been leading protests of black student-athletes in the fall of 1967. Shortly before Clark arrived, White's Wesley Foundation students joined other activists in a study that demonstrated how black students were being denied access to apartments on the college's "approved housing" list. White's report to the dean of students got no satisfactory response, but Clark wanted details.

J. Benton White
...worked with
Harry Edwards

When Clark answered the student-athletes' complaints in a speech to the campus in the music auditorium, he said he would appoint a university ombudsman to address Edwards' concerns. When White later that day congratulated Clark on his speech, Clark responded, "I'm glad you liked it because I want you to be my ombudsman."

"I didn't know what an ombudsman was," White said, the Swedish concept having been suggested to Clark by professors Peter M. Buzanski and Theodore M. Norton of the Academic Senate Executive Committee. But White and Edwards set about changing things, starting with off-campus housing.

"We developed a fair housing seal that we asked all campus 'approved housing' units to display," White said. "By displaying that unit, they were affirming they would rent to anyone regardless of race. Students seeking housing would know they were welcomed if they saw the seal. The program was voluntary, but landlords would be added to the university 'approved housing' list only if they signed a non-discrimination pledge."

Next on the agenda were fraternities and sororities. "We gave them a deadline. End discrimination or cease being a recognized campus organization, they were told." This simple strategy caused a shake-up at the national level. Some groups were suspended from campus for a while, but within several years integration was happening throughout the Greek system.

White and Edwards had been meeting almost daily during that first crucial year. They continued to tackle issues including admissions policies and the treatment of student-athletes. According to White, "Harry Edwards was the catalyst for change. And it was an honor to work for a man as wise as Robert D. Clark." White served as ombudsman through September 1968, continuing as associate ombudsman with Ralph Poblano the next year and as assistant to Acting President Hobert Burns in 1969-70. In fall 1970, Burns asked him to establish the Religious Studies Program, which he coordinated and taught until retiring in 1992. Successive ombudsmen included: Mike Honda, Jo Ella Hannah, Charlie Whitcomb, St. Saffold, Beverly Miles and Savander Parker.

tion, became the responsibility of department chairs and their school deans, both guided by faculty initiation, consultation, and review.

No longer were departments to be run by department heads appointed by the president and serving indefinitely at the president's pleasure. Through the cooperation of Clark and the Academic Council, faculty nominated their chairs and reviewed their performance every four years. The new policy's implementation after 1964 coincided with the voluntary resignations of close to one-half of the previously secure Wahlquist-appointed department heads.

The teacher-scholar model, which Clark embodied as president, percolated its popular way through the organization with some interesting results. Those few faculty members who enjoyed an occasional turn at helping to run the college had to be very careful in aspiring to department chair or to higher administrative positions. Most faculty members simply distrusted any colleague who appeared enthusiastic for such advancement. As a common result, anyone who obviously wanted to be chair became virtually ineligible. Those who wanted administrative advancements and required the votes of their colleagues were wise simply to let be known their willingness to serve. Lobbying was unwise, but strangely enough so was too evident disdain for administrative position, particularly if expressed from a position of alleged superiority. Being regularly published or significantly recognized as a contributor to a field of academic or artistic specialization became accepted among faculty as a proper reason for administrative advancement. Under shared governance, faculty preferred those who understood the educational mission from the bottom up.

What had accompanied Clark's presidency was a relatively quiet, but extensive, internal revolution. From the vantage of the outside observer, readers of the *San Jose Mercury News* and viewers of local television, not much seemed to be happening besides the venting of former Dean Gilbaugh. But inside the college, the adjustments over which Clark and the Academic Council presided were profound.

During Clark's years the number of campus organizations expanded greatly. The membership-seeking groups ranged from the well-established American Association of University Professors (professional and academic standards) to the American Federation of Teachers (terms of employment and salary issues). Members of the emerging Academic Council, the official faculty body within shared governance, frequently distributed themselves across multiple organizations.

Much talk of labor organization emanated from late-afternoon cocktail parties at the campus neighborhood home of union activist John G. Sperling, who taught economics and history at San José State and subsequently founded the University of Phoenix. During Clark's years, the faculty consensus was definitely left of center. But until a defining crisis arrived, all points of view competed for attention. That defining crisis arrived during the winter of 1968-69 in the form of a faculty strike.

Throughout the late 1960s, turmoil had convulsed sister-college San Francisco State, and impact on San José State appeared to be inevitable. San Francisco State was radicalized, unionized and, for a while, shut down. Militant students presented their lists of non-negotiable demands to unprepared, imperiled San Francisco State presidents who came and went, becoming known as revolving door presidents.

Clark had faced the problem of institutional and community racism earlier when Sociology Lecturer Harry Edwards forcefully brought it to his official attention and to public attention as well. Clark attempted to improve minority conditions and to advance positive actions while maintaining respectful and open dialogue. Also, Clark himself advanced the democratization of the college through shared governance. So, of the two basic issues that convulsed San Francisco State — race and centralized governance — San José was applying a good faith effort toward one and had resolved the other. Clark's varying degrees of success in both areas reflected his own sphere of influence. African American and other opponents of racism accepted and welcomed Clark's positive role.

The overall left-of-center faculty consensus included campus activists who strongly sympathized with San Francisco's cause. Many sympathized with the demands of the Black Student Union at San Francisco State and were deeply shocked by the police-state mentality, which characterized the big city's campus and its extended Tactical Squad presence. The minority of the San José faculty who actually were union members discussed a sympathy strike for their colleagues in San Francisco who were already striking. Even though both San Francisco State and San José State had become sister colleges within the same state college system, their actual situations were not similar. The greatest difference was that the San Francisco State faculty was not significantly involved in basic policy formulation, as was the case in San José with Clark.

Critics who opposed strike action at San José State did not think sympathy for those suffering elsewhere was sufficient cause, and they doubted that a San José strike would help San Francisco State. Further, against whom was the strike to be directed? The San José State students, those most likely to suffer, were hardly perpetrators of apparent wrongs in San Francisco. Likewise, the San José administration was blameless for San Francisco State's misfortunes.

Clark attempted to reason with the union leadership and to dissuade them from taking a strike vote, arguing that the governance issues were resolved at San José State. Rather than striking and thereby forfeiting their own incomes, unionized faculty might consider diverting part of their salaries toward supporting those who were out on strike in San Francisco.

Sustaining those who ran the university
...Psychology Professors Robert Fox, Robert Hicks, and Kevin Jordan gathered $51 million to San José State in research grants, 1966-2000

A close vote favored the strike, and the clash of strong opinions split the union. Some members resigned. Others harbored serious reservations. A few who argued for the strike changed their minds and crossed the picket line. The fully committed union core ceased holding their classes on campus, established the picket line, and traded more than pointed remarks with clueless faculty and those who crossed the line in their own form of protest against the union. San José State was not a union shop, and union members were in a small minority.

The results of what was destined to be a failed strike were far more significant than the strike itself. The defining event shattered the left-of-center consensus among the faculty and disrupted friendships. Also, the union role, thereafter diminished, was often limited to defending individuals who alleged injustice or lack of due process as the cause of disciplinary action, or some denial of rights or advancements by the administration. In the 1982 collective bargaining election that took place at all state college campuses, the California Faculty Association emerged as the official representative of the system's faculty.

Progressives and activists who engaged campus issues did so by lavishing their attention upon both the Academic Council (Academic Senate after 1974) and the union. David H. Elliott (communication studies), Jack H. Kurzweil (electrical engineering), Wiggsy Sivertsen (counseling), George M. Sicular (civil engineering), Selma R. Burkom and John A. Galm (English), and David McNeil (history) were but a few. Others focused their service on one, either the senate or the union: Ruth I. Yaffe (chemistry), Peter M. Buzanski and George E. Moore (history), Terry Christensen, Theodore M. Norton and Roy E. Young (political science).

Perhaps the most notable development of the last years of the twentieth century was the leadership potential of women: Jo Bell Whitlatch (library), Wiggsy Sivertsen (counseling), Bethany Shifflett (human performance), Pamela C. Stacks (chemistry), Bobbye Gorenberg and Mary Jo Gorney-Moreno (nursing), Kay Schwartz (occupational therapy), and Irene Miura (education). Each rose to leadership (Whitlatch in the union and the others in the Academic Senate) in previously male-managed university organizations. Professor Ruth I. Yaffe was a forerunner of this trend.

By the end of the twentieth century women predominated within two major governance domains. For a while they were accompanied by Gail P. Fullerton in the presidency and Arlene N. Okerlund as academic vice president. Other women administrators included Linda Bain as provost and vice president for academic affairs; Monica Roscoe as vice president for student affairs; Mary L. Sidney as chief operating officer of the SJSU Foundation; and Sybil B. Weir, Lela A. Llorens, and Serena E. Stanford as associate vice presidents. Among the deans who managed the colleges of the university were: Sylvia Rodriguez Andrew (social work), Dolores A. Escobar (education), Lela Garner Noble (social sciences), and Rose Tseng (applied sciences and arts).

Governor Ronald Reagan and many of the California State College trustees of the sixties had not accepted the reality — not to mention the legitimacy — of campus politicization. That campus protests should be directed at authority remained befuddling as well as unacceptable. Governor Reagan and the trustees held traditional views on the state's role as well as the student's role.

Robert Clark's accounting for his San José State stewardship was ongoing, and his unlucky companion at what became a shared moment of truth was S.I. Hayakawa, the flamboyant, final revolving door president at San Francisco State. The California State College Board of Trustees requested that the two presidents appear before them and explain their campus problems.

Governor Reagan was in full command. In his multiple capacities as governor, ex officio member of the California State College Board of Trustees, and the board's president, he directed the questioning while the other trustees acquiesced to his dominance and his point of view. Clark recalled a single exception, Louis H. Heilbron, a senior member of the board and a San Francisco attorney. Heilbron was a holdover appointee from the liberal Democratic administration of Governor Edmund G. "Pat" Brown. His liberal influence among board colleagues was limited, but what remained he lent to Clark under fire.

Governor Reagan leveled his first barrage at Hayakawa, the session's first victim. Clark became so disturbed by the treatment Reagan gave to a professional colleague caught beyond his depth that Clark became testy himself. When his turn came to respond, he chose to answer each of the governor's pointed questions with as few words as possible. He gave facts, not commentary, and limited himself to statistics whenever he could. Heilbron helped Clark solidify his favorable position by asking questions that allowed Clark to highlight his campus successes.

Reagan had been a public critic of San José State and of President Clark following the 1968 Summer Olympics held in Mexico City. Superintendent of Public Instruction Max Rafferty and State Senator Clark Bradley of San José joined in the governor's criticism. Fortunately, Clark's terse representation detached Governor Reagan, at least on the issue of San José State, from his own right-of-center appointees and unfriendly politicians.

Gov. Ronald Reagan
...questioned campus presidents on student unrest

Reagan shared his satisfaction with Clark's leadership with his Republican Caucus, a confidence that Clark later learned from Assemblyman George Milias of Santa Clara County. A friend and a college supporter, the legislator told Clark that Reagan told the Party Caucus: "Now for San José...leave San José and Clark alone, Clark knows what he is doing." The hands-off policy remained through the faculty strike, anti-war protest, the students' Dow Chemical riots, and anti-Nixon demonstrations.

Trustee Dudley Swim, an early Reagan appointee, seemed far more aggressive than the governor in his relationship with the institutions he was appointed to oversee. Swim became publicly identified with popular annoyance about college students and the alleged permissiveness of their professors. Swim took it upon himself to bring before the board a series of unfocused complaints, many forwarded to him by critics of ungrateful and unruly students. Such complaints reflected the political polarization of the period. In less contentious times they would have been forwarded without comment to the relevant campus for whatever action, or non-action, a president chose. The sixties, however, were too contentious for such a sanguine operating procedure.

Clark found Ronald Reagan's role in politicizing California higher education unsettling. What bothered him most, far more than Swim's unfocused negativism, was the theater-like representation Reagan presented to the mass citizenry. Within the trustee meetings themselves, Reagan could be positive and responsible. His charm appeared to be as real as Clark's. When he stepped outside to meet the reporters and their TV cameras, however, the governor of California invariably assumed an aggressive posture toward the colleges. That image, of course, was in harmony with the anti-student perspective of the California electorate. Before the public he exercised his own form of political opportunism; he looked into the camera, and he played the part. In privately addressing the set agenda of educational business, however, the governor rose above the impulses that motivated Swim.

Clark disliked all duplicity. In this case, he feared that the governor's public truculence would continue moving Chancellor Glenn S. Dumke to the political right and with him his large and growing system's staff of vice chancellors. Dumke had already intervened deeply into the campus affairs of San Francisco State, the chancellor's own former campus.

The most bothersome board behavior was its tendency to involve itself in management matters within the system and its campuses. Rather than setting policy and letting the chancellor and the presidents implement the established policy, board influence dipped occasionally into individual campuses via the chancellor. Such was the case at San José State when Dumke pursued the firing of associate professor of psychology and union activist Dr. Eldred E. Rutherford. By having withheld their services for a sufficient number of days, Rutherford and his fellow strikers caused their state employment automatically to lapse. Other strikers went through minimal motions, which allowed their rehiring. Rutherford, as a point of honor or of defiance, refused any statement that could be interpreted as obeisance. Rather, he relinquished his academic career altogether and departed for a more tranquil life.

Through the 1960s and 1970s the Chancellor's Office grew in size and influence. San José State's long-term academic vice president and occasional acting president Hobert W. Burns found the Chancellor's Office simply overbearing and said so. Pressed and short of funds to advance San José State's academic mission, Burns responded to bureaucratic requests from Long Beach with short temper. Even requests for data, and data in a hurry, irked him to the point of telling one vice chancellor to "stick it in his ear." This encounter represents the skirmishing that took place around the edges of the system's bureaucratic power bases.

Burns' second president, John H. Bunzel, appointed in 1970 after Burns' initial interim presidency, felt more comfortable with the trustees and with the chancellor. For better and for worse, his personal ease rested on a distinct sense of his own intellectual, and perhaps social, superiority, which he occasionally displayed. He also had an advantage in that, as the 1970s advanced, campus political activity had declined. Bunzel felt that the trustees and Chancellor Dumke tried to give the campus presidents greater operational latitude. His defense of his sociology department in the face of trustee disapproval sustained his observation, and it also illustrated the interplay within shared governance.

During this period of greater campus autonomy, San José State's sociologists demonstrated the freedom of action available to a department. They did so by inviting the popular and controversial writer and social critic Jessica Mitford to accept a part-time, one-semester appointment as a department lecturer. Unlike more intense and aggressive colleagues, the sociologists knew how to have fun amid shared governance. They were serious, but with a smile.

Mitford was an arch critic of American icons during the decades when the Soviet menace prompted conformity and a need to sustain everything believed to be American. Mitford was rumored even to have been (maybe still was?) a member of the Communist Party. She published her autobiography in 1960 and her scathing indictment of the funeral industry in 1963, *The American Way of Death*. Her next best seller appeared in 1973 as an indictment of the American penal system, *Kind and Usual Punishment: The Prison Business*. These social and cultural criticisms made otherwise comfortable readers quite uncomfortable. Mitford gloried in celebrity status and greatly enjoyed media attention.

Many faculty members, including some sociologists, objected to Mitford's impending appointment. They cited her lack of academic qualifications — degrees and teaching experience. Mitford had been an established writer for over a decade, but a close review of her publications could not establish a command of a classified body of thought or extensive knowledge of a discipline.

Jessica Mitford
...refused to sign
California loyalty
oath

Trustees phoned President Bunzel and inquired if he thought this appointment was wise. "What is your feeling, Jack?" Bunzel remembered them asking. "How do you believe this issue is likely to develop?" Bunzel's own presidential appointment sprang in part from the trustees' image of him as a no-nonsense administrator. Bunzel did not mind talking to the trustees, particularly on an issue like Mitford's controversial appointment. Even though the sociology faculty had manipulated him into their defense, Bunzel did not allow himself to appear as if he were the middleman squeezed between his faculty and the trustees. Years later he reminisced: "It is a false notion that the trustees would call and say, 'Look! You can't do that! We won't let you...and if you do, we're going to give you hell!'" The trustees never behaved that way toward Bunzel. They liked Bunzel's aplomb, which he used effectively to keep the Mitford matter under control.

A master publicist of herself and her books, Mitford grandly and immediately refused to sign the California loyalty oath. For that salvo at the system she drew faculty support, at least from those who remained interested in such issues. Later she recanted, signed, and created a new sensation. She refused to be fingerprinted, another state employment requirement of the day. That she would not be paid until she submitted to the required identification process hardly bothered her. The successful writer was not at San José State for the salary, so she taught her over-subscribed class anyway. And on this issue she did not relent; rather, she challenged the fingerprinting requirement in the courts. Long after her grades were filed, appointment concluded, the judge settled the case by instructing San José State and the California State College system to "just pay the lady."

Mitford, at San José State, was an academic put-on. One department staged a happening for its own larger educational value as well as for amusement of themselves and their students. Put-ons, though not often like this one, are common enough on college campuses. Nevertheless, not really appreciating this, the trustees, with the chancellor, accepted the limits of power.

Academic closure to the Mitford affair came during a non-prayer "prayer breakfast" at the Faculty Club where professors had the opportunity to hear Mitford. She expounded on the excesses of the funeral industry and the dark and unpleasant aspects of the criminal justice systems — particularly state and federal prisons.

Expecting wisdom, or at least well-considered thought in response to his question, Ted Hinckley (history) asked what Mitford would do, "If you had absolute and total power over the prisons of California." Hinckley, whose field included nineteenth century American history, understood the horrors of the system which made scant distinctions among petty criminals, the mildly disturbed, the hardened criminals, and physically and mentally diseased psychopaths. Historian Hinckley first flushed slightly, then hyperventilated, when Mitford replied, "I'd throw open the prison gates and send them all home to their loved ones."

The sociology faculty demonstrated how, within shared governance, one department might define, even extend, its area of freedom and bend the president to do its bidding before outside and superior authority. However, not all tests of strength within shared governance were amusing or pleasantly concluded. Two departments served as less positive models: philosophy and economics.

Both academic departments had shared fully in the college-wide growth in students, expansion and upgrading of faculty, and the development of a more extensive curriculum. A strong majority of the faculty in the department of philosophy decided to alter the terms of their employment with the State of California without the union and without the Academic Senate. They decided that they would no longer teach the mandated 12 units; instead, they would teach only three courses — nine units. The philosophers reduced their own assignments during the interim year between Clark's departure for the University of Oregon presidency and the arrival of President Bunzel at San José State. Their decision would test the resolve of Acting President Hobert W. Burns and Acting Dean Burton R. Brazil.

All agreed that a 12-unit load was at the very top end of the national norm, well above the University of California System and most private colleges. Yet if one department were able to reduce its work assignment by a quarter, no logic could prevent college-wide application. What, then, would be the action of the chancellor and the trustees in dealing with San José State as the one defiant campus? Supplemental funding would not be forthcoming from the legislature, and semester course offerings could be reduced by twenty-five percent.

Brazil began sitting in on philosophy department meetings. He empathized with the chair, Dr. Lucius R. Eastman, who was not yet a full professor and conscious of his junior status. Before Clark and before shared governance emerged, this crisis simply would not have occurred. No faculty would have announced to the president their new terms of employment. With shared governance, however, the acting dean of humanities and the arts felt obliged to listen through the meetings. Under the new model, the chair was elected by the department and was to represent the department's considered views. Brazil was an insightful political scientist who also had served as mayor of the city of Saratoga. He appreciated Eastman's delicate situation. Brazil himself fully approved the faculty's participatory role in governance. He thought that a nine-unit teaching load would enhance the quality of the college. Brazil even lived the teacher-on-loan model through a successful thirty-six-year teaching-administrative career. He could call things the way he saw them as an administrator, and if his unvarnished opinion was unacceptable, he was pleased to return to the classroom, as he did on several occasions during his career.

As he put it in his oral history, Brazil did not like that the young Eastman had to be "the spokesman for that bunch of nuts." At the time, though, Brazil listened, kept his strong opinions to himself, and told the philosophers that what they were intent upon doing simply was illegal. Failing to dissuade them, he adopted stronger tactics.

Burton R. Brazil
...dealt with a
'bunch of nuts'

Brazil pointed out to the junior chair that, as the one who would be signing the department payroll, Eastman would be attesting to its accuracy and authorizing its disbursement. By doing so, of course, Chairman Eastman also would be stating that the full assignments were being taught. Next, Brazil told the philosophy faculty that if they were intent upon their action, teaching nine and not 12 units, he simply would put them on three-quarters pay. The result was the collapse of faculty insurgency over a college-wide issue.

The economics department displayed a far more complicated form of activism, which illustrated the limitations of administrative power and even presidential authority. This case of the economics department was the best example at San José State of Murphy's law in action within shared governance and faculty empowerment.

By 1974, a decade after Wahlquist's retirement and mid-way through the eight-year presidency of John H. Bunzel, the academic departments had become accustomed to holding internal elections for their chairmen. After counting the votes in secret ballots, they habitually forwarded the winner's name to the president via their dean and the academic vice president. While departments did not officially elect chairs, the election process had become routine, and some faculty forgot that their selectee was merely their recommendation to the president. The better-managed and more tranquil departments voted and then moved the selectee forward by unanimous consent. The larger departments had informal apprenticeships during which colleagues with suitable interpersonal skills and willingness to serve the department were tried out and offered appropriate experience. This heir-apparent method allowed the faculty a preview of their probable next chairman, and elections often were uncontested, with the full faculty in agreement.

The economics department definitely did not fit the stability-consensus model. The faculty members were highly contentious over matters extending from philosophies of education and their own subject matter to basic office perks and personal likes and dislikes. A small minority of the department considered themselves "radical economists," a beyond-left term that implied acceptance of Marxism and distaste for capitalism. Because there was as yet insufficient published work emanating from "radical economists" across America, the chairman, James F. Willis, admitted that he was unsure exactly what the term meant. With his own degrees from the University of Texas and Southern Methodist University, Willis was an economic historian. The department became hopelessly divided, which imperiled the academic mission. Further, the regional accrediting agency, the Western Association of Schools and Colleges (WASC), noted this as a serious problem for the college.

Because most of the "radicals" were teaching in the economics department on temporary-appointment contracts, Willis identified for permanency the one whose career already was well developed and most promising, Dr. Douglas F. Dowd, former department chair at Cornell University. Dowd disliked the prospect of becoming the single house radical. When an appointment at the University of California, Santa Cruz, became a serious possibility for Dowd, Willis sought a tenure-track position for him from the school dean, James M. Sawrey. All this compounded the department controversy.

When the not-too-secret ballots for chair were counted, Associate Professor Martin L. Primack emerged as the winner by a narrow margin. Primack's specialization was nineteenth century agricultural economics. He had earned his doctorate from the University of North Carolina in that field, and though he was a very forceful personality, he was no "radical" economic thinker. In this instance President Bunzel chose to disregard the department's faculty recommendation. Instead, he appointed Willis, which offended those within the department who favored their official selectee, Primack. It also offended those outside the department whose refined concept of shared governance extended to limiting presidents to accepting all department decisions for chair. President Bunzel's action converted a difficult, but contained, departmental issue into a difficult and no-longer contained university issue.

Faculty Senate shapes student rights, general education

SAN JOSÉ STATE'S FACULTY COUNCIL, formed in 1952, was the first of its kind among the state college campuses. "It was to be the official channel for bringing faculty opinion to the attention of the administration — when and if the administration wanted such information," according to Professor Theodore M. Norton (political science).

Its role in policy making became official after the formation of the California State College system, which asked each campus to form a faculty council. Among early policies that helped shape San José State was a comprehensive policy on student rights and responsibilities in 1968 that replaced the tradition of *in loco parentis*. Another milestone was the implementation of an innovative general education program with an emphasis on liberal education that foreshadowed the development of statewide standards.

The council, which changed its name to Academic Senate in 1974, continued to express opinions in a variety of "sense of the senate" resolutions. These advisory measures gave voice to faculty concerns — and often made newspaper headlines — on issues such as athletics funding and ROTC programs, to name a few.

In the mid-1990s, President Robert Caret involved the senate in the university's first program review, used to help prioritize finite budget resources and reduce curricular redundancy. He also looked to the senate to develop a library policy for joint operation of the new university/city library with the city of San José.

Personnel turmoil within the department complicated this volatile matter even further. Five radical economists' contracts were not renewed, and an assistant professor was denied tenure. In the case of tenure aspirant Dr. Sue Van Atta, she and the university had the misfortune of her vote in favor of Primack being publicly disclosed.

Van Atta earned her PhD degree from UC Berkeley, and her command of economics had little or nothing to do with the as yet unclear implications of radical theories. Union members rallied to her cause, but the tenure denial prevailed. All this took time, and most who felt improperly treated advanced their cases publicly and with gusto throughout the year.

As the problems escalated and compounded, President Bunzel found himself devoting more and more of his attention to the economics department. The problem, in fact, quickly became the campus's prime conversation topic. Next, press coverage spilled over from detailed *Spartan Daily* stories to articles and interviews in the *San Jose Mercury News*.

Following an investigation by an independent faculty committee and armed with their report, Bunzel planned vigorous, decisive action. He consulted with the Executive Committee of the Academic Senate, but he erred seriously by not specifically seeking senate authorization or approval for his own intended action. The president thus left himself vulnerable if his proposed solution did not work. The Executive Committee listened carefully and later declined responsibility in the president's action. From President Bunzel's perspective, his proposed action could have been seriously questioned or modified if he had genuinely sought their input. As it was, he took strong action, and he had to take all the responsibility when his plan did not work.

Bunzel disfranchised the department of economics by depriving the faculty of their rights to manage their department. According to President Bunzel, the faculty was to teach and pursue scholarship and nothing more. In place of the internal committee system, which sprang from shared governance, Bunzel appointed a receivership committee of outside professors who ran the department without regard to the wishes of the economists. Bunzel retained Willis to chair the committee. Critics pointed out that Bunzel had made Willis the most powerful chair on campus.

In the history of San José State, the academic year 1974-75 became the year of the "Economics Department Problem." The *Spartan Daily* carried numerous opinion pieces and stories about the impact on the students, grievances filed, court actions, and the president's escape to his hideaway apartment on Fifth Street when angry students picketed his Tower Hall offices. The *Spartan Daily* was an award-winning college paper sustained by a strong journalism department. The *San Jose Mercury News* picked up on the story and gave the problem substantial coverage, relating San José State actions to anti-radical crackdowns at other universities across America. The president, never one to shrink from controversy or verbal engagement, defended his actions because of what he diplomatically called the department's "severe internal disorders."

A veteran of the Academic Senate and an experienced union leader, George Sicular, delivered a rebuttal. Guided by his own faculty-unionist perspective of shared governance, he characterized the president's action as "a precedent for silencing faculty members who disagree with administrators." Sicular then concluded that faculty should oppose Bunzel's disfranchising the economics department for that reason alone.

The Academic Senate then requested that the receivership committee be disbanded and that the rights of economics department faculty be reinstituted. Bunzel declined. From his perspective, this was a case of a department unable to manage itself and had therefore compelled his actions. He escalated the rhetoric during an interview with *San Jose Mercury News* writer Dale Rodenbaugh. Bunzel felt that the faculty was "no longer content with academic affairs. They want a voice in the budget, public relations, and how to deal with the community, trustees and the legislature." Further, faculty behavior was depriving his office of the time needed for the exercise of educational leadership. The presidency, Bunzel maintained, was forced to assume a greatly reduced role in running the university. It was becoming an "administrative, caretaker role dealing with such parochial issues as collective bargaining, declining enrollment, job security and funding of projects.... Now, collegiality and trust have eroded and so we talk in terms of power instead of persuasion." All he said about shared governance was: "This new structure requires time and complicated deliberations."

By the spring of 1975 the Academic Senate concluded its own deliberations. The senate censured the university president for what the faculty body termed his lack of collegiality. The censure resolution was co-sponsored by numerous senators: David H. Elliott (speech-communication), Charles M. Larsen (mathematics), David K. Newman (counseling services), George M. Sicular (civil engineering). The resolution also criticized Bunzel for virtual withdrawal from participation within shared governance.

Academic Senates do not remove presidents, however, even under shared governance. But San José State's senate acted because of its firm convictions that Bunzel was wrong and that his wrong-headedness needed to be restrained. Five years of his eight-year presidency had concluded in 1975; the three years that followed censure were not easy ones for the president or other campus elements within shared governance.

Through these years, San José State's relationships with the state legislature, the governors, the state's education and finance bureaucracies, and the expanding staffs within the Chancellor's Office in Long Beach became an elaborate, steady routine. The resources provided to the university became highly structured, conditional forms of support. Outside guidance and control reached into the university to a depth unheard of by Wahlquist or Clark.

State and federal financial support arrived with extensive guidelines, which extended across California's new fiscal, legal, political, cultural, and social environments. State formulas authorized the number of square feet a professor might have for an office, and the office could not be carpeted because of the state's set formula for custodians. The tortured logic was that campuses received a larger entitlement of maintenance personnel when floors required daily sweeping and an end-of-semester scrubbing and waxing; thus, vacuuming was not allowed because vacuum cleaners were not authorized. Slightly higher on the scheme of things, faculty and staff committees conferred with campus experts to decide matters such as what color the tiles should be for new rest rooms.

Within the mature California State University system, the expenditures of all state funds had to follow a line-item budget, which the campus received annually from the

California Legislature via the Chancellor's Office. The Chancellor's Office conveyed the university's portion of the system's operating budget in its own *Orange Book*, a dense and extensive document that became a well-studied compilation of formula restrictions for presidents and their campus financial officers. The *Orange Book* determined how, on what, and under what circumstances, conditions, standards, and by whom university allocations of state funds were to be used in the operation of the campus and in support of the educational mission. The additional requirements of campus budgeting, bookkeeping, coordination, and management supervision became increasingly substantial, adding a business infrastructure to the university, which expanded and became burdensome and expensive.

The dictates of the *Orange Book* became so restrictive that presidents and upper echelon managers resorted to "bootlegging" positions. Occasional reviews by the state Department of Finance seized upon this "irregularity" and came down hard on the Chancellor's Office and the campus administrators. Such periodic audits uncovered no squandering, theft, or even mismanagement of state funds, but rather the use of such funds outside state and system guidelines. Lacking discoveries of malfeasance

Faculty diversity gets a jumpstart

WHILE THE STUDENT POPULATION became rapidly more diverse in the decades following the turbulent '60s, faculty diversity was slow to follow. By 1985-86, just 8 percent of the new faculty hired that year were minorities, 37 percent were women.

Pressure to increase faculty diversity grew both internally and externally, from the Western Association of Schools and Colleges accreditation team, from the U.S. Equal Employment Opportunity Commission, from the campus affirmative action officer, and from student activists. "In the hiring process, minority candidates somehow never got hired, despite the fact that they were in the pool," said Arlene Okerlund, who became academic vice president in 1986. "We were under enormous pressure."

Arlene N. Okerlund
...under pressure to diversify faculty

The "Off the Top" faculty hiring program Okerlund developed in response was controversial in itself, possibly violating affirmative action guidelines. She held back 10 new faculty positions for women and candidates of color. A department that identified a qualified faculty member could receive special funding for three years, with the position folding into the department budget as the faculty member moved toward tenure. Not all the new hires stayed at San José State, but most – including George Vasquez (history), Elizabeth Van Beek (history), and Tommy Lott (philosophy) – raised the level of teaching and scholarship in their departments.

"In teaching, we all have biases and perspectives which we foist onto students," Okerlund said. "There has to be balance. Increasing faculty diversity was not just a moral imperative. It was an academic imperative. It had to be done to break through." Okerlund also began early efforts at faculty development and diversity awareness through the Institute for Teaching and Learning. By 1991-92 an overall hiring shift had settled in, with 41 percent of the new faculty hires minorities, 51 percent women.

or even ineptness, state auditors noted that campus managers occasionally did what they found necessary to keep the university's infrastructure sound, not what extensive guidelines mandated. When discovered, "bootlegging" had to be corrected. Administrators at the vice presidential level usually balanced the risk of discovery and possible career retardation against the need to keep the university running.

The rigidity of the system, combined with the shrinkage of funding relative to the number of students, caused formula-driven control to collapse of its own age and weight. At the end of J. Handel Evans's acting presidency in 1994, and upon the arrival of Robert L. Caret in early 1995, after years of difficult budgets, the CSU system abandoned *Orange Book* formula management. San José State administrators welcomed the new flexibility.

Robert Caret began his presidency with symbolic, high-impact improvements, stating all the while that San José, as the oldest campus in the system, needed more capital repairs than other campuses. He hired an outside contractor to wash unknown numbers of campus windowpanes. Plumbing repairs and additional millions of dollars in long-deferred maintenance projects became his next targets. Caret utilized San José State's share of the CSU's standard distribution of funds and then lobbied the chancellor and his staff. In tandem, he parlayed his honeymoon status into more resources. Repairs and systematic upgrading followed, and satisfaction increased among staff, students, and faculty. After the honeymoon was well over, major buildings were repainted and a multi-million dollar infrastructure project commenced, which rewired and replumbed the campus for the electronics age of the twenty-first century.

The financial side of the California State University system had simply become too large and too complicated for micro-management from the Long Beach Office of the Chancellor. But as financial management by remote control gave way to local decision making, the modern lawsuit emerged as a new constricting force.

The life of the university had become guided and constrained by the growing body of state and federal laws which related to health and safety, the environment, labor relations, the disabled, and a host of equity areas as well as all those policies formulated by the Academic Senate and approved by the presidents. The total created an often-changing and ever-expanding web of relationships. The university chose to enter freely into many of the agreements and discovered others by surprise, sometimes in the form of a subpoena.

At the time of President Gail Fullerton's administration, beginning in 1978, none but the most innocent or timid faculty or staff employee would silently accept seriously negative personnel actions from the university. The arbitrary days of MacQuarrie and the authoritative days of Wahlquist were gone. Counter representation, protest, grievance, and litigation against the university originated from a wide variety of sources. Among them were fired coaches, victims of alleged inequity and discrimination, un-retained teachers, campus visitors, even a neighborhood stroller who tripped on a tree root when taking a shortcut across the lawn. Occasionally, the university initiated action against its own personnel. Simple firings no longer held, even in the most egregious circumstance; due process became an industry.

Administrative hearings and arbitration consumed great amounts of time and required expanded staffs. Disputes that could not be resolved at this level advanced into the courts, such that President Fullerton often joked that her husband regularly introduced her as his spouse, the "permanent defendant." She advised new deans and administrators to review their personal liability insurance and to abide by the rules of due process. The Attorney General's Office was officially bound to defend state educators sued in line of their duty performance. But some sought private counsel at their personal expense when the issue and the judgments could become grave.

To complicate things further, the character of legal advice provided to the university changed. System attorneys in the Chancellor's Office during the Fullerton and Evans administrations stated what the law said, offered editorial asides on how its application would be received within the contemporary political scene, and even speculated on how various degrees of the law's application might be received on campus. The result was extensive discussion within the university administration before sensitive alternatives were chosen. It became apparent that settling disputes before or during court actions often was less costly and less immediately injurious to the university than defending and even prevailing in court.

In Fullerton's day when the university lost or settled a legal action, the money came from the university's annual budget. There was no contingency fund during those lean budget years. The magnitude of the judgment or settlement determined how many fewer teachers would appear in the classroom.

Robert Caret's presidency coincided with two critical developments. First, he participated in the creation of a system-wide risk pooling self-insurance program. San José State paid a premium according to its previous history of adverse financial judgments, and its costs were relatively modest in comparison to other campuses. The fund's existence slightly emboldened the campuses in resisting at least those cases they considered frivolous and winnable.

The second development was a change in the power relationship between San José State and the Office of the Chancellor, when the system's attorneys ceased offering extended legal advice. Instead, house attorneys stated and explained the law to university officers who were free to choose a course of action. Caret welcomed these changes. Combined with the safety net insurance plan, it resulted in substantial relief. President Caret became less distracted than his predecessors by the legal demands upon his and the university's energy, time, and resources. Where President Bunzel had complained that shared governance gone awry was denying him his leadership role, President Caret's harmony with shared governance and the prospects of fewer nonsense lawsuits allowed him to fashion his vision of San José State University as a metropolitan university.

At the end of the century, most agreed that shared governance accommodated everyone who wanted to have a say — a critical feature in the life of a university. Even with all its requirements and aggravations, shared governance made all participants responsible for improving the present and the future, their own and their university's.

Modern presidencies

President	Years
John T. Wahlquist 1952–64	
Robert D. Clark 1964–69	
Hobert W. Burns acting, 1969-70	
John H. Bunzel 1970–78	
Gail J. Fullerton 1978–91	
J. Handel Evans acting, 1991–94	
Robert L. Caret 1994–	

| Years | 1 | 2 | 3 | 4 | 5 | 6 | 7 | 8 | 9 | 10 | 11 | 12 | 13 | 14 | 15 |

Chapter Two

Fifty Years and Seven Presidents

The Evolution of the Metropolitan University

GARRET W. McENERNEY, an accomplished and respected early-century attorney, devoted 41 years, 1901–1942, of voluntary service as a University of California Regent. During his extended years of institutional power, his hand weighed heavy in the appointment and removal of the presidents whom he and his colleagues charged with developing the early California system of higher education. Regent McEnerney had a very clear idea of what it took to be a president. His standard became California's standard and persisted even after the 1960 Donahoe Higher Education Act provided for the organization of the current California State University, creating its system-wide governing board of trustees.

According to the McEnerney criteria for presidential appointment, a successful candidate needed to be at the cutting edge of an academic discipline; the chosen one should have sufficient administrative experience so that the step up to a presidency would be comfortable and not too great a reach; career interests and educational contributions had to be in the future, not the past. Finally and decisively, once having made all possible contributions to the advancement of the university, a president was to be respectfully set aside with as much honor and grace as circumstances allowed. If the president did not know when the time to depart had arrived, the governing body would so inform the president.

Appointing and dispatching college presidents is a historic responsibility of official governing boards. In this respect, the California State University trustees did well by San José State. While competing with private universities and other state systems for presidential talent, they chose candidates from available pools who provided university management and leadership into the twenty-first century. Among the presidents, there were differences in styles, interests, and preparations as well as a diversity of talents, personalities, and perspectives; yet all advanced the well-being of San José State through distinct periods, under unequal conditions, and with fluctuating resources.

John T. Wahlquist
1952–1964

D R. JOHN T. WAHLQUISt was San José State's transitional president, the last to have been selected by the California State Board of Education. His 1952 appointment predated the Donahoe Act of 1960 and, therefore, preceded the organization of the California State Colleges system and its governing board of trustees. His 1964 resignation took place during this newly created board empowerment.

In 1952 Wahlquist replaced a retiring senior California educator, 73-year-old Dr. Thomas W. MacQuarrie, whose record presidential tenure had begun 25 years earlier in 1927. San José Rotarians, prominent community leaders in 1951, identified Wahlquist and secured his presidential appointment by successfully lobbying State Superintendent of Public Instruction Roy E. Simpson. The Rotarians had been impressed by the Utah educator's anti-Communist speech, delivered at their December 1951 meeting. They liked the way Wahlquist spoke, how he appeared, and the way

John T. Wahlquist
...identified by
San José Rotarians

he conducted himself. Wahlquist, unaware of their initiative, was approaching a career turning point at the University of Utah. State Superintendent Simpson responded favorably when these community men appealed on behalf of Wahlquist. He sought out Wahlquist and introduced him to the members of the State Board of Education. Appointment followed, not after a national search, but after the state superintendent and

JAMES D. HOUSTON is a prize-winning novelist, biographer, essayist, screenwriter, and Emmy nominee. He authored seven novels, including *Continental Drift, Love Life*, and *The Last Paradise*. His nonfiction works include *Californians; In the Ring of Fire: A Pacific Basin Journey*; and *Farewell to Manzanar*, which he co-authored with his wife, fellow San José State student Jeanne Wakatsuki Houston.

Connected not only to the Pacific Coast but also to SJSU, Houston often reflected on how important his relationship was with Robert Gut, founder of SJSU's radio and television department. Gut conveyed to his young student a passion to bring poetry and drama to life, making literature live in everyday moments. The true story for which Houston is perhaps most famous, *Farewell to Manzanar* (1973), was based on Jeanne's description of her early years in an internment camp in Owens Valley and the injustices inflicted on Americans of Japanese ancestry during World War II. Their film script, which was based on the book, was nominated for an Emmy and won the prestigious Humanitas Prize. "Writing has allowed me to stay on a path of personal and spiritual evolution. By its very nature, writing requires you to go both outward and inward. And as the years go by, that's something I've come to appreciate more and more."

On Campus: Met his wife, Jeanne, and played string bass.

board members met and were satisfied that his wife, Grace Dorius Wahlquist, understood the role of wife of the president.

Wahlquist served the college for 12 years. During his presidency he constructed a modern campus and gathered a modern faculty.

Over the decades following his 1964 retirement, San José and its university evolved into a new and far different world. The city and its surrounding Santa Clara County became the capital of a world information and communications epicenter known internationally as Silicon Valley. University presidents were no longer proposed at Rotary. In time a sixteen-person committee came to manage the highly formalized presidential search process.

Robert D. Clark
1964–1969

DR. ROBERT D. CLARK, appointed in 1964, became the first San José State president appointed by the California State Colleges Board of Trustees. The board was the governing body for the California State Colleges and was created by the 1960 Donahoe Higher Education Act.

The recruitment process itself was streamlined, still feeling its way within the recently organized system. Dr. C. Mansel Keene, assistant chancellor to Glenn S. Dumke, managed faculty and staff affairs. As official headhunter, he kept multiple presidential searches on track as the system's seventeen campuses required. With the establishment of the state college system, he assumed the old role of Roy Simpson of the State Board of Education.

Robert D. Clark
...presided over a 'golden era'

Robert Clark entered the area of consideration by having occupied all of the significant positions short of the presidency at the University of Oregon. Clark was active in regional and national associations that dealt with university education. His admirable reputation as an educator and administrator extended far beyond his Oregon campus. He was published, though not excessively so. He was exceedingly well spoken, refined, and thoughtful and was used to faculty participation in the formulation of university policy. Further, he was convinced that professors should do more than just classroom teaching. Even beyond research, professors should contribute to the educational decisions and the policy formulation of their institutions. His views sat well with the San José State faculty committee that served as the first recommending step within the selection process.

Clark had previously declined the initiatives of Keene to be considered for the presidency of Los Angeles State. Clark felt that he was not yet ready to leave Oregon. When Clark did feel ready, Keene was still recruiting for the expanding California State system. In fact, both San José State and Fresno State needed new presidents for the fall of 1964. Following his positive meeting with the San José faculty committee, Clark met with trustees. He was so well received that he might have had either appointment. While he greatly admired the community support that Fresno lavished upon its college, he preferred San José. His visit to the South Bay campus and his reading of the student publications, particularly the *Spartan Daily* and *Reed*, the literary and arts magazine, convinced him that San José offered his sort of intellectual activities, the "argument and criticism, the kind of ferment that...characterizes a university that is alive. I didn't find that at Fresno...."

Clark chose San José State, the faculty committee recommended him, and the trustees appointed him. His subsequent performance, under the most trying conditions in the history of the university, was thought by some senior insiders to have been a golden era of energy, excitement and presidential leadership.

The astute chronicler of San José State's recent history, H. Brett Melendy, interviewed President Emeritus Clark in 1983, at which time Clark observed that trustees regularly selected presidents to address the problems of the past. Only accidentally, by the uneven abilities of appointees to grow in office, did emerging new problems become resolved. Aside from Clark's consultative approach to leadership and his positive disposition toward faculty and their need to participate in policy formation, little else suggested how his talents might be engaged. No one in 1964, Clark included, expected the campus unrest over which the new president was successfully to preside.

The trustees felt that Clark needed to remove some holdover members of Wahlquist's upper management and thereby assure harmony on what was becoming a rather progressive campus. The reassignment of Wahlquist's central functionary, Dean of the Faculty John W. Gilbaugh, was highly symbolic and easy to accomplish. Clark did not intend to separate the veteran educator from his livelihood; rather, he would remove him from the administration and return him to the classroom, where he was tenured as a professor of education. Polite and genteel, Clark bided his time and allowed the younger faculty to make a first move. As expected, a faculty deputation appeared promptly.

Clark agreed to meet the unofficial group of faculty in his Tower Hall conference room. Gerald E. Wheeler, a young bright light in the history department, was seated at the far end of the long conference table. Wheeler had not been on the faculty screening committee that had interviewed Clark, but Clark had made it his business to become acquainted with him and most other faculty as well. Wheeler's background was right for the task of spokesperson, even though he had not been chosen for the role or anticipated it. He had written his PhD dissertation in diplomatic history at Berkeley and returned to California from the U.S. Naval Academy faculty where he had witnessed top-down, military-style management of higher education. Preferring the far more consultative shared governance model, Wheeler respectfully and effectively explained why, in the opinion of his faculty colleagues, Gilbaugh had to go.

Clark played it cool, his usual approach, saying that he would look into the matter. He thanked them for their courtesy, their concern for the college, and he promised to respond.

The Chancellor's Office already had authorized a new position, a second vice president based upon the growth of the student body. So Clark decided that instead of removing Gilbaugh he would reorganize his top staff and merely lose Gilbaugh en

California State College system established in 1960

THE DONAHOE HIGHER EDUCATION ACT of 1960 gathered California's "state colleges" into the California State College system, with a Board of Trustees and a chancellor. More importantly, it effectively transformed the state colleges from their founding as teachers' colleges to their current function as comprehensive universities.

The act followed the recommendations of *A Master Plan for Higher Education in California*, assigning different functions to the University of California, the California State Colleges and the California Community Colleges to ensure access to educational opportunities for the state's growing population.

State colleges were given the role of undergraduate and graduate instruction in the liberal arts and sciences as well as in applied, occupational and professional fields. Systemwide coordination of campus master plans for expanding both buildings and curriculum was quickly put in place.

"This is the most significant step California has ever taken in planning for the education of our youth."
—Governor Edmund G. Brown, as quoted in the *San Francisco Chronicle,* April 27, 1960, upon signing the act

route. Unanticipated as it was, this move also brought to the college Dr. Hobert W. Burns as the first academic vice president. With Burns came modern academic management and curricular reform.

Clark and Burns shared the same views on who correctly ran universities: the president was legally responsible via the trustees at whose pleasure he served. In actual fact, San José State was in a transition phase, which Clark facilitated. Through his subordinate administrators, he was responsible for daily operations, which were to be conducted under policies jointly arrived at by the president and the faculty. The actual focal point within this transition was the growing collegiality between president and faculty. In time the faculty side of the relationship would become institutionalized as the Academic Senate.

Transition from Wahlquist's top-down institutional management to the new model of consultation, cooperation, and shared policy formation became relatively easy. This was Clark's model, and Burns was in full agreement. However, according to Clark's recollections, the more adversarial faculty members were seeking a cause. Soon they would gather together in a faculty union, but their impact upon San José State in the late 1960s was preceded by a student militancy that first claimed Clark's attention.

An obscure but ambitious African American student-athlete from East St. Louis had made his way up the California Coast following his high school graduation. Coaches at the University of Southern California had encouraged Harry Edwards to join their athletic program. Their set recruitment process included the grand tour of the USC sports facilities with special attention paid to their banners and trophies. No one bothered to listen when Edwards said he was interested in sociology and wanted to find out about it. Highly intelligent, motivated and resourceful, the six-foot-eight-inch-tall discus, basketball, and football player was seeking a different life for himself. When he stopped at San José State, he chanced to encounter a very interesting facilitator — Professor Milton B. Rendahl.

Rendahl had arrived at San José State in the 1930s with modest degree preparation, intelligence, and a winning manner. Under Wahlquist's seniority system, Rendahl headed the joint department of sociology and anthropology. He also chaired the Faculty Council, forerunner to the Academic Senate. Quite approachable, he had time for everyone, particularly students.

When Edwards introduced himself, the easy-going professor responded cheerfully, happy to explain what he knew about sociology to the young aspirant. In later years Rendahl stated that Edwards was the smartest student he had ever encountered. By the time Edwards brought himself to the attention of Clark and Burns, he had completed his BA at San José State (1965), his MA at Cornell (1966), and had accepted a temporary teaching appointment back at San José State. His

Harry Edwards
...challenged racial climate as student and instructor, shown here, center, accepting an award from the NAACP

academic rank was Instructor in Sociology. By 1966 the PhD degree was required for appointment to tenure-track positions in the social sciences, and newly recruited faculty either possessed that degree or were completing final requirements. Edwards possessed only the Master of Arts at this early stage of his academic career and would acquire the doctorate later, following his teaching stint at San José State.

Edwards met with Clark and told the president face-to-face that racism permeated the athletic department, the campus, and the community. African American student-athletes were suffering discrimination in violation of basic rights and even in violation of university regulations and state laws, he said. Specifically, African American athletes had to continue to live in a motel because campus-approved community housing denied them equal access. In a college community geared to student rentals, black men were denied accommodations. Local "vacancy" signs disappeared, only to reappear when white students inquired.

Edwards' accusations against the athletic department were point blank. In recruiting athletes, white prospects enjoyed the hospitality of the then booming fraternities and sororities, while African American recruits were shown "a good time" on fifty

Campus housing provides room for change

THE STUDENTS WERE COMING. And there was no room at the inn. The fraternity and sorority houses and campus-approved boarding houses that had satisfied generations of San José State students were no match for the students of the '60s.

Robert L. Baron, San José State's first housing director, took inventory of his new domain in 1960, telling colleagues at the Western Association of College and University Housing Officers annual conference: "61 percent of the head residents in women's halls are widows; 65 percent are over age 60; 35 percent had no college training. Their median salary is $230 a month with room and board." Housing coordinator Izetta Pritchard had chosen off-campus facilities and house mothers with care.

The six red brick residence halls San José State built in 1960 — among the first in the new California State College system — were the start of change. "We didn't have enough housing, and more kids were coming," said Donald Ryan, hired as assistant dean of students, the position Baron had just left. Student financial aid programs further swelled the housing need, and "there was all of a sudden this influx of people who wanted to live on campus." They also wanted the rules to change. "We (administrators) live forward but understand backward. Students are imaginative, and they are not immobilized by tradition, rank, authority, and custom," Robert L. Baron told his colleagues at the 1965-66 conference.

"Women students favor lockout rules; the pressure to abolish them comes from men students," Baron reported in 1961. By 1965, planning had begun for yet more housing — this time a 12-story co-ed high-rise to be named after Joe West. When it opened in 1968, campus housing capacity topped 2,000. In 1968, the concept of *in loco parentis* ended with the Faculty Council's development of a comprehensive policy delineating students' rights and responsibilities for their own behavior.

Valerie Coleman Morris

BA, JOURNALISM, 1968

VALERIE COLEMAN, CNN Financial News anchor, speaker, talk show host and mother of two, got her start in broadcast journalism at SJSU. Returning to the Bay Area in 1969 after earning a master's degree from the Columbia University School of Journalism, she launched her career with KRON-TV as a researcher, general assignment reporter and, ultimately, anchor. Moving fluidly from television to radio in the 1980s, she created her own radio show in 1989 with KCBS called *With the Family in Mind*, a family-oriented national radio commentary where she served as host for 10 years. Morris left her position with New York's WPIX-TV as weekend anchor and host of *Best Talk* to join CNN Financial News (CNNfn) in 1996. Due to her stellar performance, she also hosted *Family Values*, leading CNNfn's primetime schedule. Morris received numerous awards for outstanding contributions to broadcasting. In addition, she was named SJSU's 1999 Evelyn T. Robinson Outstanding African American Alumna Award winner for her career achievements. Returning to SJSU as commencement speaker in the mid-1990s, she spoke of her start in journalism: "I tell young students there are many places to get an education, but if you're going to be in the broadcasting industry, then you need to start very early on broadcasting. SJSU gave me that."

**Valerie Coleman
...wanted to join a
sorority**

On Campus: Honed her burgeoning broadcast skills as anchor for SJSU Reports, which was taped on campus and also aired on KNTV-Ch 11.

dollars supplied by the athletic department. They could do what they pleased. Edwards also cited the gross insensitivity of the language some of the coaches used with young black men. Edwards informed President Clark that Valerie Coleman, journalism major, had been denied sorority membership because of her race. Coleman's case expanded the focus from male athletes to include the plight of a female scholar who participated in the best of campus life — when allowed.

Clark accepted the validity of the charges and fully acknowledged the racist realities. Edwards made them public and enlisted increasingly militant student backing. Anti-racism became the leading student issue on campus.

As Clark's progressive leadership charted San José State's course through this era of turmoil and change, he determined that there would be no confrontation between student militants and a reactionary administration. Rather, Clark accepted the problem and sought the best solution. There was no official denial stage, no subsequent student guerrilla warfare, and no reactionary call for armed counter-measures as took place elsewhere. Clark respected Edwards because the young teacher, in following his convictions, seemed to be risking whatever career he aspired to in higher education. He accepted Edwards' confrontational style, even his apparent anger, because those

Black athletes played the game

St. Saffold
...stayed at San José State to help others

ON THE SURFACE it looked the same: parties, star athletes, huge crowds at football and basketball games. Only the white players went home at night to fraternity houses, a world not generally welcoming to the black players.

Basketball got St. Saffold's foot in the door at San José State in 1962 and introduced him to Harry Edwards, a varsity basketball player. Harry taught St. how to play the game. "He was using his scholarship to get his degree, and that's what we needed to be about." Edwards told St., "When I play my last game here, I will never touch another basketball." Edwards graduated in 1964 with a degree in sociology and went to Cornell for his master's (and later his doctorate), returning to San José in 1966 to teach. He remained both friend and mentor to a tightly knit group of black student-athletes.

In some ways, their college experience was typical. "Socially, there were, at least at the beginning of each semester, still a lot of parties," Saffold recalled. "Often, black students came from San José City College to party along with us. However, by about the fourth week of classes, the number of black students would settle in at about 30, others having partied in and partied (dropped) out. ...We had some great times, but the good old days (to white students) were not the good old days to us, at least not in the same way that white students experienced them."

The star status awarded to black athletes ended at the classroom door. "The physical qualities that it took to be an athlete were somehow less than the quality it took to be an excellent student. In other words, while our physical/athletic prowess was generally accepted, we were still considered as, by nature, having less intellectual ability than our white counterparts." Yet under Edwards' mentoring, they played the game. "As undergraduates, we often felt perceived as 'good boys,' a credit to our race, as long as we did not cross the (racial) line."

When Edwards returned in the summer of 1966, it was to rewrite the rules of the game. One of the coaches asked him to talk to a class about his master's thesis, "Black American Muslim Family Life." Everything was OK, "until he started talking about Abraham Lincoln. Harry told about the real Abraham Lincoln. He didn't care about slaves; he cared about keeping the Union together. It was a new persona for Harry. It kind of marked the beginning of Harry talking about the needs of black folk in a kind of new way that people were not used to, both in a general sense and in a Harry sense. He could articulate the kind of quiet struggles that were going on," Saffold said. Like having to "talk white" on the phone when inquiring about renting an apartment. Like being isolated in "our own little Spartandom." Like having no black employee mentors on campus.

Unlike Edwards, Saffold did not put the ball down when he graduated with his BA in physical education and history minor in 1967. He had qualified for a fifth-year scholarship in football and played for the San Diego Chargers in 1967 and the Cincinnati Bengals in 1968, but he kept coming back to San José State. In 1969 he met his wife, Jacqueline Gray. She earned her BA in social sciences in 1971 and her elementary teaching credential in 1972 and teaches in the Milpitas Unified School District. St. added his master's degree in counselor education in 1978.

Four decades after he came to San José State as a freshman basketball player, Saffold was still there, helping many students as university ombudsman, then as associate vice president for campus life. He still played basketball, during his lunch hour.

were guaranteed under the First Amendment. Also, he saw that Edwards clearly opposed violence as a violation of constitutional guarantees.

Edwards echoed his original theme three decades later when he addressed San José State's graduating African American students. Justified anger was appropriate when victims faced injustice; violence was not. In the fall of 1967, however, neither Edwards nor Clark remained in full control of events.

Clark assigned his experienced and sensitive Administrative Vice President William J. Dusel to the volatile issue. Dusel held open hearings and established the facts. An agreed-upon action plan was to be next. Fast moving events, however, overtook Clark's plans as well as Edwards' actions. Daily incidents were captivating public attention, and the participants were receiving liberal press and television coverage. Harry Edwards became as notable as the college president.

The San José Police Department passed along to President Clark the generic threats to the college they had received. He took seriously the police accounts of threatened violence, which included torching fraternity and sorority row just east of the campus and north of Clark's home in Naglee Park, a residential neighborhood adjacent to campus. No sooner had Clark shared this intelligence with Edwards than Clark received other ominous threats — disruption and violence at the upcoming football game at Spartan Stadium against the University of Texas, El Paso.

As game day approached, the San José Police Department became worried about its ability to protect Greek row and Spartan Stadium simultaneously. The dean of women encouraged sorority members to take an extended weekend away from campus. Likely fraternity reactions to possible violence were unknown. In Clark's mind, Edwards had brought into being, for just cause, a situation that even together they could not control. Clark consulted broadly and acted decisively, but in a way that remained controversial. He canceled the football game for security reasons. This was the only time in the college history that a president canceled a sporting event. Criticism ensued immediately. Other than the reactions of the University of Texas, El Paso, the strongest criticism emanated from political sources such as Governor Ronald Reagan and Superintendent of Public Instruction Max Rafferty.

Having chosen San José State because he anticipated the clash of ideas and commitments, Clark got what he asked for. He spent more than full time on campus addressing the new problems for which the trustees had not selected him and for which his experience had not prepared him. And mostly, he slept well. The exceptions included those nights when irate, anonymous callers awakened him to lament that he had canceled the Saturday afternoon football game. Characteristically, the former speech professor listened, even said thank you, and returned to restful slumber.

Signed correspondence received by Clark documents a frequently genteel form of racism. Edwards was not privy to Clark's incoming mail, but it bore out the young sociologist's characterization of racism California-style. It stood behind a smile. The calls and the letters lent dramatic credibility to Edward's claims of racism.

While Clark was concentrating on the San José State athletic department, student services, Greek life, and his own administration, the future arrived at a gallop. Berkeley's activist students had challenged the old order in 1964, the year Clark came to San José State. Their free speech movement expanded into challenges to American racism and into the portentous anti-Vietnam War protest. By the time Clark had advanced shared governance on the San José State campus, violence, tactical squads, helicopters, strikes, and close-downs were convulsing not just Berkeley, but also San Francisco State. At San José State, Vice President Burns felt that the threats, violence, and property damage the campus experienced were exceptions, and minor at that. Superintendent of Public Instruction Rafferty disagreed, believing that students should not be indulged; administrators should enforce the laws — and demand respect besides. Obviously, California higher education was politicized.

College males were exempt from the draft and, therefore, from the escalating carnage of war in Vietnam. Yet instead of being quiet evaders, many Bay Area students were in the vanguard of war protest. During Clark's absence from campus, while he was returning from a required inspection of a college-sponsored project in the Dominican Republic, protest overwhelmed San José State. A large number of students gathered in front of Academic Vice President Burns' office. Their intent was to protest

Professor ends up making history, along with teaching it

DAVID EAKINS was a student editor of "Studies on the Left" at the University of Wisconsin, but it was his Sunday school teaching experience that caught the eye of President Wahlquist during a faculty recruiting trip to Chicago. Eakins joined San José State's history faculty in 1962, poised to be part of the period he described as "one of the more deeper expressions of democracy in our recent history." By 1967 he was adviser to "Students for a Democratic Society," the most vocal group on campus. He was also active in "Professors Against the War," organizers of a summertime "Vietnam be-in."

Dr. David W. Eakins
...spoke out against the war, was arrested

When the confrontation over Dow Chemical job interviews came that fall, "our main concern was that somebody would burn a flag or throw a brick through the administration door." So the faculty lined up between student protestors and police officers. Students burned an effigy, and "some kid with a flag was hanging around there. We kind of steered him away. Things sort of cooled off.

"At that point the cops decided to try to charge through the line we'd set up. They just came charging through, smashed people about and banged me on the leg" with a nightstick. But the camera only caught the bearded professor ducking and his picket sign hitting a police officer.

"It was really a police riot. There was absolutely no reason for the cops to intervene. It was at that point that somebody did light a flag on fire and throw a chair through the door of the administration building." Another faculty member was the "hero" of the day, having been bloodied by the police. But Eakins was in the spotlight some days later when police came to his office to arrest him. Despite these distractions, Eakins finished his dissertation and eventually earned tenure in his eighth year. He retired from San José State in 1994.

and disrupt previously scheduled job interviews conducted by representatives of Dow Chemical, the company burned into the minds of students as the suppliers of napalm to the American war machine.

When the students threw a chair through the closed door of the Administration Building where the Dow Chemical interviews were scheduled, the San José Police Tactical Squad assumed physical control of the college and responsibility for security. Burns, viewing the protest from the second floor,

President Clark engaged students in dialogue about the war and avoided violent protests.

became both apprehensive and protective. San José State, like other colleges, ran on such a collegial basis that he was unsure who was in charge during the absence of the president — himself or Administrative Vice President William J. Dusel. Not really caring about the detail, Burns attempted to maintain the integrity of the campus.

Chief of Detectives Bart Collins called over his walkie-talkie and personally ordered the tactical squad from its ready position just to the north of San Fernando to cross over onto the campus and to disperse the students. This was the failed tactic so clearly associated with the disastrous and repressive practices at student demonstrations at San Francisco State. Burns objected, "You can't do that. I'm acting president and this is my campus. I'm telling you I don't want any cops on campus." To this Collins responded, "Kid, I'm running this university today." Burns' commitment to campus integrity and shared governance was brushed aside.

By their own standards, the San José police were restrained in their actions. They did disperse the yelling and chanting students, while Burns maintained they were not a mob. The police used tear gas and their own massed and armed presence, but no brutality. One injury resulted from someone being hit by a tear gas canister. And the police arrested one professor, Dr. David W. Eakins, a young historian who was to become a respected teacher and scholar. Eakins simply opposed the war, repeatedly said so, and in police eyes encouraged students to say so, too.

Rather than prepare a dismissal file for the president's action, as would undoubtedly have been the case under prior administrations, Burns considered bail for Eakins. But first, he attended that evening's American Federation of Teachers meeting, the local union to which the young professor belonged. The leadership told Burns that they were taking care of the bail problem and their member.

The students did not intend to go away permanently just because the police drove them off once. The campus was normally theirs, and for the police to assume physical control over the opposition of the vice president entailed considerable risk, expense, and aggravation for the city. When sufficiently motivated, the students could show up without risk and express their opinions, largely in any manner that they wished, individually or en masse.

Police presence and police efforts at control of the campus without and over the expressed wishes of the administration were and always remained regrettable to an overwhelming number of faculty and staff. To watch the police tear gas students was intolerable. In Burns' case he opposed the war and he opposed authoritarian behavior as much as Clark did. From the Burns-Clark point of view, the police were to respond to the college's needs as determined by authorized college authority. Clark was the leader to move into the impasse.

Later, when assistant professor Eakins was free, the aroma of tear gas lingered, and the students gathered again. The police, at the ready, awaited their call. Rather than looking to police support, however, Clark addressed the reconstituted crowd from atop a large planter in front of the Administration Building. He attempted to engage

'That day at San José State changed me'

VALERIE LEWIS walked out of class, hands full of art supplies, wondering what they'd paint in Professor Eric Oback's class. She crossed the street just as a cloud of tear gas wafted through the crowd. She and a male student retreated along Seventh Street, looked up and "saw a V-shaped clump of policemen with riot gear on. He pulled me out of the way, and they walked right through us."

The image of police wearing gas masks and marching lockstep burned in her mind, "inhuman from the inside and the outside. They'd been transformed into something that was very powerful and very violent. They didn't look like people, and from the inside I don't think they were thinking like that."

Valerie Lewis
...got caught up in
tear gas, protest

Lewis was in her senior year, an art major with a minor in English, her long dark hair in braids adorned with hand-spun naturally dyed woven fibers, but mostly apolitical. "I really cared, but I didn't have the nerve at that time in my life to stand up in front of a group. That day at San José State changed me."

She became more active in civil rights issues that fall of 1967. "People I had known as friends who happened to be black suddenly became African Americans who were radical and angry. Every direction you looked, there was something that had to be changed." People gathered in small groups around campus and in living rooms, talking about "what are we gonna do and how are we gonna stop this? We just really tuned in to be a part of the victimization that was going on." Lewis became active and wrote to her Congressmen, but she didn't drop out and into the drug culture. "I came from a very strong, tight family, and my father never would have put up with it."

Lewis, who graduated in 1967 with her art degree and English minor, opened Hicklebee's Children's Bookstore in Willow Glen in 1979. She published *Valerie and Walter's Best Books for Children, a Lively and Opinionated Guide* (Harpers, 1998), reviews children's books for the CBS morning show, and writes for *Creative Classroom Magazine*.

the ranting and jeering students in rational dialogue and, despite student turbulence, came close enough to defusing the situation. As a result, the police took no action.

In the end, it was San José State's faculty, not the students of the sixties, who provided the reason for Clark's eventual reconsideration of another presidential offer. Clark was a presidential success by any informed standard. He had addressed the original problem of the trustees — updating the college administration. Thereafter, he addressed the other real and volatile problems sparked by the protest generation, problems neither he nor the trustees had anticipated. When first queried about returning to the University of Oregon as its president, Clark declined. He liked San José State, as much for all the excitement and ferment as for the satisfaction associated with his obviously successful leadership.

By the fall of 1968 Clark had presided over the reasonably peaceful reordering of college management and governance structures. He responded to black militancy by guiding it into productive channels. He contained student anti-war violence and preserved the integrity of his institution while at the same time successfully negotiating with the pro-war Governor Ronald Reagan. And all the while, his students joined with the nation's students to make their political statement — one which grew until it captured the full attention and action of the national administration, ultimately contributing to Lyndon B. Johnson's decision not to seek a second full term as president of the United States. Amid all of this, it was no wonder that Clark felt comfortable in remaining at San José State. So confident was he of concluding his academic career at San José that he informed his potential successor, Burns, that he would remain despite the Oregon offer. Based on Clark's decision to stay, Burns stayed, too, foregoing his own professional opportunities elsewhere in California.

Then things changed, and Clark's mind changed, too. Oregon's new president died suddenly, and the university launched its second presidential search. Just before Christmas vacation in 1968, the faculty union at San José took a strike vote in sympathy with striking faculty at San Francisco State. Clark addressed the San José State union, the activist segment of the much larger and unorganized faculty of the college, and argued that the membership should not take their strike vote. The problems facing San Francisco State, Clark pointed out, had already been successfully addressed on the San José State campus. But the membership did vote, and the result was 123 for the strike and 44 opposed. Clark understood that the union membership was 300 or fewer among a faculty of over 1,500. In that context, the strike numbers were unimpressive. Obviously, the continued functioning of the college would not be in jeopardy even with a strike.

But strong convictions of strike leaders prompted a subsequently disputed action — a two-day sit-in at Clark's Tower Hall office. In his oral history memoirs, Clark registered a profound sense of disappointment that members of his own faculty would do this to him. He perceived himself as a leader in the shared-governance movement, perhaps even the chief spokesperson of faculty, and as a faculty member himself on temporary assignment to administration. To Clark, the office sit-in symbolized rejection of him and what he stood for — by those he otherwise respected most. The strikers, Clark later remarked, had within their scant numbers "some very good faculty...some of the exciting teachers on campus." He felt deeply wounded because those who turned on him, those who arbitrarily seized his office, were his colleagues in shared governance.

Faculty activists wanted dialogue with Clark. They felt the meeting in his office and their subsequent occupation of the premises were appropriate confrontations. They also felt it was appropriate retribution for his failure to join the strike himself! They maintained that Clark, the communicator, rebuffed their efforts at dialogue. So, when Oregon called the second time, Clark said yes.

In addition to convincing Clark to depart, the failed strike had even more unintended, long-term consequences. It destroyed the left-of-center campus consensus and disrupted numerous friendships and working relationships among the faculty.

Hobert W. Burns
ACTING PRESIDENT, 1969–1970

D R. HOBERT W. BURNS accepted appointment as acting president in 1969. He moved from his Administration Building office into the president's suite on the second floor of Tower Hall and appointed staff on an acting basis. In his own extended oral history memoir, Burns explained that he wanted to be a college president, but only at San José State. From his regular position as academic vice president and as acting president, he provided continuity and was a sustaining force through most of four administrations, including his own. His service extended from his arrival in San José in 1966 through a post-retirement, second interim presidency which concluded at Sonoma State in 1984, only to be followed by teaching at San José State until 1986. He was offered permanent appointment at Sonoma, but by then he concluded that his best contributions to university life had been rendered.

Hobert W. Burns
...gave his best to San José State

In their *History of San José State University*, Professors Benjamin F. Gilbert and Charles Burdick focused upon Burns amidst the student anti-war protest movement. During May 1970, sparked by U.S. troops entering Cambodia, the Academic Senate, with strong student presence, debated and resolved that because of America's continuing and expanding war in Vietnam, all teaching should cease. Final grades were to be assigned based upon the then current grade-book records, and what remained of the academic year was to be made available for teach-ins to focus on the evils of war and aggression. Acting President Burns listened to the debate knowing that he could not sign such a policy despite his anti-war views. His immediate frustration, however, was his inability to be recognized and heard by the senate during the debate. After the resolution passed, Burns promised to veto it on the grounds that the college's function was teaching subject matter, not engaging in social activism, despite its merits. Further, since he was convinced that no president could lead a college without the cooperation of the faculty, Burns informed the senate that he was withdrawing his application for the permanent presidency. He also requested Chancellor Glenn Dumke to replace him in his capacity of acting president and to appoint in his place Executive Vice President William J. Dusel. Prudence prevailed, though, and Burns fulfilled all the responsibilities of his acting appointment.

As the sustainer and developer of the educational enterprise through the bulk of four presidencies, Burns molded the basic academic program at San José State. As a result, general education ceased being a smorgasbord of courses from which a business, engineering, biology, French, or any other major might choose the least demanding or the most bizarre. Burns' plan advanced general literacy and became a model for the California State University system.

As Clark's first academic vice president, Burns had presided over faculty personnel matters, using tenure and promotions as the most incisive tools to mold the faculty. With the establishment of a multi-leveled committee review system, tenure and promotion were no longer based upon seniority, as had been the case under President Wahlquist, but instead upon teaching effectiveness, published scholarship, and service to the university. Perhaps because scholarship was the ingredient that could be most readily evaluated, faculty who researched and published often received tenure and promotion sooner and with greater ease. In time, the culture of evaluated teaching, publishing and service became the culture of the promotion process.

John H. Bunzel
1970–1978

D R. JOHN H. BUNZEL, on leave from his chairmanship of the San Francisco State political science department, had spent the year prior to his 1970 appointment as San José State president as a visiting scholar at the Center for Advanced Study in the Behavioral Sciences in Palo Alto. His earlier years at San Francisco State had included sustained campus unrest and violence. Bunzel's response to those experiences became the propellant of his lengthy career.

John H. Bunzel

Bunzel attracted national attention by his reasoned resistance to intimidation and his defense of academic freedom amidst campus uproar and attacks against his person and his property. *The New York Times* featured him on page one, "Liberal a Target of Militant Students," in March of 1969. Bunzel followed up on this advantageous exposure and firmly established his position as a committed liberal-in-the-middle. He penned an insightful article, "'War of the Flea' at San Francisco State," which *The New York Times Magazine* published on November 9, 1969.

His views attracted the approval of liberals fearful of the destruction of traditional campus values as well as conservatives intent on repression in reaction to such a threat. Conservatives could interpret Bunzel's position as anti-insurgent and pro-status quo — down with faculty and student radicals and up with law and order.

Simultaneously, liberals could interpret Bunzel as an advocate of traditional liberality — academic freedom, freedom of speech and association. This juxtaposition characterized San Francisco State in 1969 and Bunzel's scholarship and politics thereafter.

C. Mansel Keene was still headhunting for state college presidents when the faculty of Sonoma State College took it upon themselves to nominate Bunzel for their presidency. They were familiar with *The New York Times Magazine* article, and they liked what they believed it meant. Keene responded by sounding out Bunzel's interest, only to discover that it was nonexistent. Like so many academics, Bunzel had entered higher education with lofty expectations of teaching and writing, central responsibilities to be punctuated by the delivery of an occasional public lecture. In Bunzel's case, he enjoyed these intellectual activities and performed them well, but he also indulged himself by talking about the intellectual life. Bunzel told Keene and Chancellor Dumke that he was not interested in becoming president of Sonoma State. The college was new and located within the Northern California wine country. He considered himself an urbanite, and wanted to remain in or near a large metropolitan center. Dumke, on the spot, turned to his Vice Chancellor Harry E. Brakebill, and asked if any other presidencies were opening up. San Diego State was. So the chancellor turned and asked Bunzel, "How would you feel about San Diego State?" Bunzel was warming a bit when Dumke thought again and asked, "Harry, what is happening at San José State?"

The exploration had sunk to a verbal shopping trip through the state college campuses at a time when Bunzel did not know that he really wanted to leave teaching to become a college president. He did, however, agree to an interview at San José State with faculty representatives. Soon Chancellor Dumke wanted Bunzel to meet with a committee of trustees at the San Francisco airport, a short drive from Bunzel's home

---

Friday Flicks, hot coffee, thanks to Alpha Phi Omega

HOMECOMING 2000 kicked off, like many before it, at the campus BBQ pit. If there were a dedication sign on the pit, it might read, "Lead engineer: Phil Clark. Dump truck driver: Tony Vega. Diggers and bricklayers: Alpha Phi Omega fraternity brothers."

The pit was half demolished in the early '70s when Vega attended SJSU. His fraternity adviser told them, "There's a BBQ there now. There should be one when you guys are done, right?" Clark designed the project. Vega rented the truck and dumped a load of sand. The brothers finished the new pit in one weekend. Cost to the university was zero.

Alpha Phi Omega brothers didn't have a fraternity house, but their impact on campus was measurable.

Their motto: service to campus, community and country. Handy with both tools and fund-raising, the service fraternity built many projects – wooden stands holding maps of campus, benches, outdoor tables, etc. They also donated an audiometer for the speech department, a giant dictionary for the School of Business, whatever was needed.

Alumni of the pre-computer era might remember APO brothers as bearers of hot coffee and free donuts, an especially welcome sight for students, often hundreds deep, waiting in line overnight to register for classes. "That's how we met a lot of folks," said Vega, past president of APO. They also entertained the campus with Friday Flicks in Morris Dailey Auditorium, showing first-run movies for 50 cents. There was no extra charge the night frat brother "Psych" streaked across the stage.

APO projects also aided the community – senior citizen homes were repainted, the Boy Scout camp got a new jungle gym, and underprivileged kids went ice skating. Service to country, in Vega's era, was more complicated. He went home one weekend to find that he'd been drafted. He reported in, said he was in college, and waited. "I was a 1-A. It was a cloud over my head for my entire stint at State. They just never called." Vega came face-to-face with anti-war sentiment most closely in Europe. Studying at the Netherlands School of International Business, he and several other Americans jumped in the car one weekend for a road trip, only to find themselves amidst anti-American demonstrators on the streets of Paris. "The good thing was all of us had long hair at the time (to keep warm), so we looked like Europeans."

Vega graduated in 1974 with a degree in marketing and co-founded Luminous Networks, Inc. He served on the Alumni Association board, where he ran into another former APO president, Hal Riddle, class of '48, who'd helped build the original BBQ pit in 1947.

---

in Belmont. Unfortunately, those trustees were interviewing for the Sonoma presidency, which Bunzel had already rejected. Either Dumke had forgotten that conversation or some other coordination mix-up had occurred. Agitated greatly, Keene asked Bunzel to stay by the phone, and in the return call asked Bunzel, as a special favor to the chancellor, if he would meet with the Sonoma committee of trustees who were flying into the airport specifically to speak with him. Incredulous but still cooperative, Bunzel participated in the charade. Throughout the two-hour interview, no trustee asked him why he wanted to be president of Sonoma State College, which he did not.

Next, the grateful Keene, undoubtedly reflecting the relief of his superior Chancellor Dumke, phoned again. "You did very well," he said, and promptly arranged an interview with the correct trustees selection committee for San José State. On the day of Bunzel's meeting, the trustees were to choose and appoint three presidents — one each for Fresno State, Sonoma State, and San José State. There were multiple candidates as well as interested professors from the colleges and assorted supporters in Dumke's dining room, munching on club sandwiches.

Ushered into the conference room, Bunzel took his seat among the trustees. Governor Ronald Reagan was in charge, and the conservative Superintendent of Public Instruction Max Rafferty was prominent. Each elected official was held in low esteem by liberal college communities, yet both were riding high with California voters. The California Field Poll linked Reagan's tough stand on student unrest to his general popularity. Reagan and Rafferty thought they understood Bunzel, having selected the half of his analysis that harmonized with their views — enforcing the laws and reestablishing order on the campuses. Despite his other, quite liberal, convictions, the trustees had already decided, unbeknownst to Bunzel, to appoint him.

This disconnect (Bunzel thinking and doing "interview;" trustees thinking and doing "appointment") left such a deep, negative impression on Bunzel that he considered publishing the experience as a farce. The system and its leadership, from his view, were a joke.

Why the mostly conservative trustees chose Bunzel, a Democrat who cultivated his own liberal credentials, is a matter of some conjecture. His competition consisted of Dr. Hobert W. Burns, the very well respected and reliable acting president and permanent academic vice president. After Bunzel's appointment, Burns continued his best work at San José, through the reorganization of general education and improved faculty standards.

John H. Bunzel was a different experience for San José State. He talked the talk of academic excellence to the point that faculty tired of it. During Bunzel's leadership, many faculty members began arguing that his research and publishing requirements approached those of the University of California. This was a divergence from the California Master Plan for Higher Education, which assigned the research role to the University of California. Also, faculty stressed the fact that state college faculty carried a much heavier teaching load and had scant access to research grants and freed-up research time.

Bunzel's approach, of course, suited the newer research-oriented faculty. Because of their own rapid promotions, they had assumed influence within personnel committees and contributed to the perpetuation of the standards by which they advanced.

Unionized faculty and those held in rank complained bitterly about President Bunzel's alleged "publish or perish" requirements, while those who advanced under the system were less sensitive to the problem.

Throughout, Bunzel talked scholarship while Burns implemented the stronger promotions criteria passed by the Academic Senate. During Bunzel's administration, Burns, the deans and the department chairs knew the standard was high. Executive Vice President Burton R. Brazil, a political scientist, agreed that Bunzel's talk about scholarship and the intellectual life was important, but he also agreed with Burns that the president should work at developing the resources faculty needed in order to reach the desired goals. The talk, without tangible help, ultimately became counterproductive. In one campus survey, initiated by Roy E. Young of political science and Geoffrey H. Tootell of sociology, Bunzel came up on the unpopular side in most categories.

It was in this climate that Bunzel seized the opportunity to leave when it appeared. He opted for the solitude of his own intellectual life and accepted appointment as a senior research fellow at the Hoover Institution. Housed at Stanford, the Hoover allowed Bunzel to return to the campus that had remained close to his heart since his earliest days as a junior faculty member. In his oral history statement to historian Brett Melendy, President Bunzel, rather than listing his contributions to the university, concluded that he had learned a great deal at San José State.

Gail J. Fullerton
1978–1991

D R. GAIL J. FULLERTON is the only woman who has served as president of San José State, and her tenure of thirteen years, 1978-91, is the longest in the modern history of San José State. She was the first faculty member to be promoted to the presidency since the appointment of Morris E. Dailey in 1900. Patient, enduring, hardworking, positive, and very private, she served during the years of Jerry Brown's governorship when he instructed Californians to "lower their expectations." With close attention to the details of administration during years of dwindling resources, Fullerton kept the campus running on less.

Gail Fullerton
...tapped community for campus construction needs

Hobert Burns, who worked close to her as academic vice president, gave her the highest marks for hard work and long hours but was more critical when it came to delegation of authority and responsibilities. This was during an era of perpetual lawsuits, when the president was a perpetual defendant. Her practiced reserve, if an advantage in dealing with potentially contentious faculty, could leave others in the dark. Yet what Fullerton did not say could hardly be used against San José State.

Fullerton, a sociologist, enjoyed strong academic credentials and a rapid administrative ascent at San José State. Born in Lincoln, Neb., she secured her bachelor's and master's degrees at the University of Nebraska by 1950. Four years later she completed the PhD at the University of Oregon, where Robert Clark was then graduate dean. She and her then husband, Snell Putney, who likewise completed similar degrees at the same universities, came to San José in 1960 when Putney joined the department of sociology and anthropology. Restricted by the anti-nepotism rule of those years, she continued her research and writing, taught part-time when allowed, and cared for their two children. She and Putney co-authored a well-received book, *The Adjusted American: Normal Neuroses in the Individual and Society,* which Harper & Row published in 1964. The following year she received a tenure-track appointment in sociology. Remarried before the appearance of her second book, *Survival In Marriage: Introduction To Family Interaction, Conflicts, And Alternatives,* which Holt, Rinehart & Winston published in 1972, Fullerton focused her scholarly interests on the family. By the time Dryden Press brought out her second edition in 1977, she was administratively well placed as Bunzel's executive vice president. Her appointment had followed a very brief tenure as sociology department chair, followed by three years as dean of graduate studies and research.

When the trustees were required to select Bunzel's successor, conditions and timing were right for Fullerton. Just previously she had been a candidate for the presidency of San Diego State and had acquitted herself very well before the trustees who, at the moment of decision, nevertheless selected another candidate, Thomas B. Day. President Bunzel's prompt departure for the Hoover Institution in 1978 provided the opportunity for her follow-up and successful candidacy.

In her own oral history conducted by Sandra Varney MacMahon, Fullerton reflected upon the personal and psychological transformation she underwent by stepping out and up to a university presidency. Previously she had not envisioned herself in such a role and, therefore, had not assessed herself with presidential demands in mind.

Fullerton was fully aware of two immediate campus problems that undoubtedly had contributed to Bunzel's decision to join the Hoover. First, there were the near bankrupt relations between the president's office and the faculty's Academic Senate. Second, there was the highly publicized low morale experienced by some faculty.

As it happened, Fullerton's disposition suited her for improved relations with the Academic Senate. She was quite content to attend all meetings, listen attentively, respond when appropriate, and agree to be advised. In addition, Fullerton became more accommodating in the annual awards of tenure and promotions. Seasoned deans such as Lester H. Lange of science recognized the change and started writing more effusive faculty evaluations. Deans did not wish to be overturned from above and then have to spend an extended career managing tenured and pointedly discontented faculty. The old and presumably higher standards remained on the books, but their application wavered from what Bunzel had publicly required.

The faculty and the Academic Senate liked Fullerton because she was indeed likable and because she did all of the administrative work that needed to be done. Even on occasions of potential conflict, as when the Academic Senate resisted her use of academic resources in support of intercollegiate athletics, senators did not reject her leadership as they had her predecessor's.

Fullerton's real problem, not anticipated at Bunzel's departure, resulted from an extended enrollment decline. Because the university budget was directly tied to enrollment, the downturn resulted in insufficient resources needed to manage the campus at the previously understood standard. Associated with the general paucity of instructional funds were the growing needs of athletic programs.

Among all of San José State's presidents Gail Fullerton was the one who committed the greatest part of her time and energies to intercollegiate athletics. She served as a member of the NCAA President's Commission for almost six years. She developed the clearest profile of what athletics at San José State should be. And, without doubt, she was the most substantial supporter of athletics among modern presidents. Yet, ironically, Fullerton became the only president publicly attacked by members of the athletic boosters.

Fullerton felt that sports requiring a great amount of teamwork deserved higher priority in a university. The contrast was sports she thought relied more upon individual performance. Football in a university, therefore, was more worthy than track in a university. Her explanations for her preference were educational and training based. Teamwork was a skill that universities needed to teach, and team sports (as opposed to individual performance events) were an appropriate way to teach such cooperation. Only in part, however, was it this conviction that created estrangement and hostility between the university athletic boosters and the most interested and tangibly supportive president of all times. The basic education of the athletes, measured by graduation rates, was the initial and critical wedge of division.

Claude Gilbert was a competent and successful football coach who enjoyed widespread respect, including respect among the alumni boosters. His recruitment process included substantial reliance upon community college transfer players as a strategy to address San José State's competitive disadvantage relative to the Pacific Coast Conference and other national teams, which San José continued to schedule.

Recruiting successful community college players meant that every year, every two years at most, became a real adventure. Gilbert's calculated advantage was that he did not have to develop raw recruits. Transfer players were older, stronger, and more experienced. The few scholarships Gilbert had to offer could be filled more often with more fully developed players and with the greater likelihood of success on more Saturday afternoons. Gilbert's formula for victory worked.

Fullerton certainly understood the advantage of improved odds, but her continued participation in NCAA deliberations created a strong commitment to graduating San José State's athletes. She accepted and advanced the concept of the "student-athlete" with the student part of the formula first. Community college transfer players whose compelling interest had been football often arrived with poor or unfocused lower division course work. All too often, many of them used up their athletic eligibility well before they fulfilled San José State's degree requirements. Prior to direct NCAA intervention in this national problem, the end of a player's eligibility often meant the end of college attendance. Not being drafted into professional sports meant the end of the line, no degree and often little true education.

The president directed that the coach shift recruiting away from transfer students and focus on freshmen — in four years, or five if need be, they would graduate. When little changed, Fullerton acted decisively and concluded the popular football coach's appointment after the 1989 season. He responded by bringing legal action against the university. Simultaneously, Gilbert received the public support of boosters who took out large and pointed advertisements in the *San Jose Mercury News*. University administrators judged them to be highly negative in depicting not only the president's role, but also the university at-large. Rather mindless of the danger and potential consequences to their own long-term interests, the boosters persisted publicly in their support of the coach and criticism of the president. Over Spartan Stadium's 30,000 persons in attendance during Commencement 1990 exercises, a slowly circling bi-plane pulled a paid advertisement: "Fullerton — rehire the coach and fire yourself." The deans and distinguished members of the platform party winced as the president read on from a prepared annual script.

Fullerton endured the declining budget years, which fatigued Burns, who ultimately opted for retirement. Throughout, Fullerton worked the state funding system with admirable success. Among her advantages were her positive relations with two well-placed and well-disposed local legislators. During those years Alfred Alquist chaired the State Senate's Finance Committee and John Vasconcellos chaired the Assembly's Ways and Means Committee.

It was the Fullerton administration that clearly marked a turn to non-state funding for the physical development and renovation of the oldest university in the system. When President Emeritus Fullerton wrote her "Personal Commentary" for the 1997 issue of Biographies published by the Emeritus Faculty Association, she listed four development projects among her most satisfying achievements. They were the new engineering complex (with Dean Jay D. Pinson and the high tech community), the Event Center (with students), the expanded Spartan Stadium (with the community), and the groundwork for closing San Carlos Street (with the San José City Council). Each of these was arduous, but in different ways. What was similar was the limited-to-zero state funding. Through necessity, joint projects were becoming a required alternative to full state funding.

Unlike all her modern predecessors, Gail Fullerton departed the presidency in her own well-considered time and on her own terms. She would not be hurried, and she set her departure according to her own retirement planning. The one major public celebration which drew the former president back to San José from her tranquil northern retirement home was Dean Jay Pinson's 1994 retirement party, where she contributed the best laugh to the evening's long program. Fullerton advised the high profile dean of what awaited him in retirement. Only three years out of office herself, Fullerton recounted her recent phone call to San José State to accept Pinson's retirement party invitation. In doing so, the former president had to explain who she was to the new staff in her former office — twice! Turning with resignation to the distinguished honoree of the evening, Fullerton playfully added, "Jay, I hate to tell you this, but it's a short step from *Who's Who* to who's he!"

J. Handel Evans
Acting President, 1991–1994

THE ACTING PRESIDENCY of J. Handel Evans began when Evans accepted the appointment on a caretaker basis until the system could recruit and the trustees appoint a new permanent president. Rather than a single year, the Evans presidency extended from the fall of 1991 through the fall of 1994, three and one-half academic years. As Fullerton's long-term administrative vice president, he was familiar with the physical campus, administrators, and high-profile faculty. Trained in architecture, Evans was less familiar with the strictly academic management of San José State. Within the university bureaucracy, he utilized the staff, attended the Academic Senate, and ameliorated problems as they arose. His initiatives were directed more at the community and advancing the university's influence beyond its established relationships.

J. Handel Evans
...led development of Fort Ord campus

Experienced administrators continued to direct the day-to-day operations of student services, personnel, and curriculum delivery and review. The Council of Deans, on their own initiative, decided to cease applying budget reductions across-the-board to all academic programs. Having applied that organizationally timid approach too often over previous years, the deans lamented the inevitable trend — creeping mediocrity. Without permanent presidential leadership, the deans pooled start-up funds from their individually diminished budgets. Their objective was curricular improvements that the university and the community needed without regard to budget. Subsequently, the deans agreed upon subsidizing a multi-disciplinary advance in the field of environmental science, which drew together faculty, programs, and community service advocates from among engineering, science, and environmental studies.

The adequacy of temporary leadership and reliance upon mid-level managers and experienced staffs soon would be officially validated. During this extended period when interim leadership also extended beyond the presidency to each of the three vice presidencies, San José State underwent accreditation by the Western Association of Schools and Colleges. San José State's self-study, directed by Professor Nancie L. Fimbel of the College of Business, and the campus visitation by WASC officials met the accrediting body's standards.

All of this was fine enough until the required national search conducted under trustee direction failed to produce a new president. Evans was not a candidate, and none of those who emerged as finalists attracted a significant body of support. Equally damaging, however, was the appearance of a set-up. As the screening process advanced, campus observers wondered if candidates had been chosen on the basis of their race, gender, and sexual orientation rather than their leadership abilities. That appearance, plus the lack of strong support for any candidate, doomed the effort. Before the trustees moved to appoint, their likely choice simply withdrew her candidacy. The search had been a debacle, and Evans' year one was becoming year two.

Throughout the contention of the failed search, Evans had been acquitting himself quite well on campus, in the San José community, and in a new capacity at Fort Ord near Monterey Bay. Over the years San José State had provided off-campus instruction to the Fort Ord region. With the closure of Fort Ord as a military base and its conversion to civilian uses, San José State and Evans found themselves in the position of sponsors, under the direction of the Chancellor's Office, of the preliminary planning stages for what was to become a new system campus: California State University, Monterey Bay. At this, too, Evans appeared to move the tasks along smoothly and expeditiously. Quietly, he had also supported the efforts of intercollegiate athletics and the sports boosters who were working to create an expansive new league for their Division I-A teams.

Evans eventually opted to be a presidential candidate for the second national search. By taking this step Evans created what for San José State was a quite normal situation, the inside candidate vs. the outsider.

Standing at stoplight, waiting for street to close

WHEN WANDA HENDRIX-TALLEY attended San José State in the 1970s, waiting at stoplights on San Carlos Street between classes was a major irritation. "You would be going from one class to the next and have to stand at a stoplight," she recalled. When she came back for her master's degree in the 1990s, she found herself still dealing with San Carlos Street traffic.

Hendrix-Talley had transferred from UCLA in the mid-1970s to take advantage of small classes and be in a friendly environment at San José State. "You could actually have interaction with professors," she recalled, though add/drop paperwork and standing in line were a recurring frustration. Having earned her sociology degree with a minor in statistics in 1977, she took a position in criminal justice administration with Santa Clara County, eventually holding administrative posts with the cities of Palo Alto and Hayward as well as in the private sector. She earned her master's degree in public administration while working as Hayward's assistant city manager/budget manager, in preparation for her next post as principal management analyst at East Bay Municipal Utility District

Wanda Hendrix-Talley
...supported women's athletics

Her graduate student experience was both typical and atypical. Typical in that she found graduate student classes more directly applicable to her work, and she was able to meet other practitioners working in the public sector. Atypical in that she became more focused on campus involvement, especially athletics and alumni activities. Along with classmate Diana Hunter, who also earned her master's degree in 1993, Hendrix-Talley became a regular attendee of Spartan football, basketball and baseball games — and a key supporter of women's athletics. She sponsored numerous teams for the Women of Sparta Golf Tournament, a major fund-raiser that helped provide funding for San José State's gender equity plans and expand opportunities for female student-athletes.

She also became active in the SJSU Alumni Association, where she was able to witness San José State Acting President J. Handel Evans work with the San José City Council on permanent closure of San Carlos Street through campus.

Robert L. Caret
APPOINTED 1994

THE MEMBERSHIP of the second presidential search committee included professors and a staff representative from the campus, three trustees, executives from the Chancellor's Office, one student, one representative of the university community, and a college president. The selection committee makeup was decided by the trustees in response to dissatisfaction about the lack of faculty and staff participation in the first search. With heightened motivation, the second committee faced a considerably altered set of circumstances. Evans was a known quantity, generally liked and respected. By entering the race and becoming the in-house applicant, he assumed the burden and the advantages of virtual incumbency. Like other such candidates so positioned, Evans had to defend the record he had helped to create. On the other hand, outside candidates would enjoy greater freedom to recommend substantial changes in the organization and direction of the university.

Robert L. Caret
...brought vision
of metropolitan
university

Dr. Robert L. Caret's application and resume captured committee attention. Arriving from the other side of the nation, Towson State University in Maryland, his application noted that Caret had served at every level of university administration except president. He was well published as a chemist. In his mid-forties and with ideas, his best years were clearly before him. He definitely met the classic McEnerney criteria for presidential consideration — scholarship, experience, and promise. But a century had elapsed since California's model board member had created the state's presidential standard. By 1995 a fourth requirement had emerged. The successful candidate should not only be capable of intensive community involvement — the candidate should actually enjoy it and appear genuinely to thrive on it.

Caret interviewed very well at all levels of the recruitment process and gathered supporters from among those campus figures who were looking for change. He enjoyed a record of participation in a large number of professional organizations (public and private) and was acquainted with the individuals who administered their programs. As a result of his administrative experience and professional activities, he appeared exceedingly well informed and had no trouble fielding questions from all interested parties. Caret's fluency and his gregariousness impressed those who were looking for someone to fill the role of an external president, one who could bring the university into cooperative partnership with the community. To the progressive members within the selection process who envisioned San José State's future, all of this was promising. It suggested potential success at university outreach into a larger community of growing wealth and importance. Also, those who warmed to Caret tended to equate his obvious enthusiasm with the high energy they thought a future president would be required to have in order to advance the best interests of San José State. Those who noted his command of new educational technologies considered it an additional bonus.

The trustees, not the campus committee, determined the outcome. Evans and Caret were the obvious best choices among the four names that the committee advanced, via their trustee members, to the full governing board. The trustees' choice was Caret. And the propelling force was the commitment to change. The trustees felt that the university's curriculum and the programs it supported had become overgrown, perhaps stagnant. Even with so many years of budgetary retrenchment, no programs had disappeared. Everything seemed to remain the same — only thinner and perhaps less relevant. This was the same problem that the deans had addressed by pooling start-up resources rather than downsizing. The trustees, as a commitment to change, looked to an outsider, one completely free of old interests and old ways. The trustees saw in Caret what they wanted, including an outgoing and comfortably engaging person who could become the university's ambassador to the community at-large. Their decision redirected San José State's potential at the end of the century, the potential to evolve from a comprehensive institution into the metropolitan university of the Silicon Valley.

Mayor, president dream of new library

STUDENT PROTESTERS in the mid-1990s learned how to speak out from earlier generations. They carried signs and wore gas masks. They joined with faculty and staff to voice their concerns. But it was the mayor and the president who had the dream this time.

At issue was the idea of sharing a new library with the city of San José. For President Robert Caret and Mayor Susan Hammer, the idea they put forth early in 1997 was full of benefits — both needed expanded library facilities but neither had the funding to do it independently. For some students and faculty, putting research materials and popular bestsellers in the same building seemed flawed, especially when the resulting construction would mean the relocation of some student services staff to new offices on the first floor of the 10th Street Parking Garage.

Susan Hammer
...shared vision of metropolitan university

Associated Students President Heather (Cook) McGowan held a Town Hall meeting to listen to student protesters and gathered information on student needs for longer library hours, more study areas, and a laptop-friendly facility. Academic Senator Ken Peter led the development of a new library policy governing the co-existence of student researchers and browsing city residents. A city/university users' advisery group sought answers that helped turn a political process into an educational one.

"He looks opposition of an idea in the face ... and doesn't walk away from it," said McGowan of Caret. "He works to build consensus." When the Academic Senate voted in December 1998 — by voice vote — to approve the new library policy, McGowan remembered, "it sounded very close. We'll really never know what the exact vote (count) would have been."

Construction on the new library — the first such collaboration between a major city and university in the nation — began on Oct. 20, 2000.

CHAPTER THREE

Campus Life
COMPARING TWO DECADES
1960 AND 1990

CALIFORNIA'S population was well into its post-World War II growth in the 1960s and had more high school graduates than ever before. Affordable and available, San José State College was a traditional choice for the aspiring student. When President Robert D. Clark arrived in 1964, the student population had exceeded 20,000, a benchmark of institutional growth.

The 1960s

PARENTS WHO HAD THEMSELVES enjoyed higher education largely assumed that their children's college experiences would mirror their own. Those without college experience thought college would be challenging and beneficial for their children, and that campus life was ordered and refined. But the decade of the '60s and its immediate aftermath witnessed dramatic, invigorating, and sometimes dangerous changes to campus life. Activist students drew to their causes many others who had previously been uncommitted. Numerous students participated in one event and observed the next, selectively engaged in the transformation of campus life. To maintain that the activists set the public tone while the others sustained traditional campus life would be too facile. Activists and traditionalists were not mutually exclusive, even if contemporary critics thought so.

Many students simply found it difficult to figure out what was happening around them; a few were absolute in their certainty that they fully understood. Those who felt challenged by the normal requirements of personal and academic development had all they could do to stay alive academically and still participate in the larger changes sweeping the campus.

GAYLE SCHUBACK KLUDT and Paul Cheetham were among the many whose approaches to San José State were rather traditional. Gayle Schuback had been a bright and energetic student in nearby Fremont High in Sunnyvale. Her grades were good enough and her test scores were even more recommending. Full of enthusiasm, energy, and initiative, she shared coming of age with the same group of friends she had met at kindergarten. By high school she had been a cheerleader and understood sports and the student sports culture.

Gayle Schuback and Paul Cheetham never met at San José State even though their years overlapped. Typically, the vast majority of San José State undergraduates hardly became acquainted with one another. Cheetham majored in business administration, Schuback in social science. Schuback always knew that she wanted to be a teacher. But Cheetham was not sure for some while what he wanted to do with his life. Student Services counselors offered their help, and Career Planning and Placement staff gave him direction at graduation time.

Gayle Schuback Kludt
…joined a sorority, but lived at home

Cheetham's older brother had gone to San José State, and his parents, particularly his father, encouraged higher education for all four of their sons. Cheetham grew up in Marin County, just north of San Francisco's Golden Gate Bridge. His dad was a police officer looking forward to his approaching retirement. His son Paul loved the party life and kept up with his wealthier teen-age friends through part-time jobs. Working allowed him the cash to buy and maintain his own car, have a social life, and still run track. Classes took second place to these diversions. It was the threat of the draft during the Vietnam War and his boot camp experience in the U.S. Marine

Robert Graham

ART, 1961-63

ROBERT GRAHAM, sculptor, is one of the nation's premiere artists, exhibiting internationally as well as in some of the most prestigious galleries in the United States. His one-man shows have been staged at the San Francisco Museum of Modern Art, the Los Angeles County Museum of Art, the Robert Miller Gallery, and the ARCO Center for Visual Arts. His artwork also adorns several San José sites, including Quetzalcoatl in the Plaza de Cesar Chavez and a statue of two women in front of the Peckham Federal Building on South First Street.

Born in Mexico City in 1938, Graham moved to California in 1950 and studied art at San José State. His heritage is Scottish, English, and Inca. Graham was very young when his father died, and he was reared by his mother, grandmother, and aunt, whom he referred to as his "three mothers." Having been surrounded by women during his childhood created an interest in the female form and probably helps explain his "passion for and awe of women." Graham intuitively understands how the human body moves, as evidenced in his sculpture. Graham has been awarded many public commissions including the Duke Ellington Monument in New York, the Franklin Delano Roosevelt Memorial in Washington and the Olympic Gateway in Los Angeles.

On Campus: Prepared for his first one-man exhibit at the Lanyon Gallery in Palo Alto.

Corps Reserves that focused his attention on school. College did not teach Cheetham that he needed a draft deferment. Quite the reverse. The Marines taught him that he needed an education.

Schuback's motivation had solidified earlier, in high school, and she overcame her father's opposition to college enrollment. Hank Schuback's blue-collar perspective accepted traditional roles for women, roles that neither required nor encouraged college education. But her mother wanted the best for her only daughter, and to advance this goal, Jean Schuback took a job on a local motel housekeeping staff so that Schuback could attend San José State. Each fall Jean took her daughter shopping for new back-to-college clothes. She wanted her daughter to look and feel as if she belonged with the children of those who had always gone to college.

Schuback began college life by living at home and taking public transportation to downtown San José. Walking toward campus, pawnshops punctuated the first blocks, followed by desolate streets lined with deserted storefronts, the result of the downtown's economic decline due to the development of suburban shopping malls. Four years of these walks never bothered her. The college experience was positive and exciting; it was a new and wider world.

"School opened with a big dance at the Civic Auditorium," she fondly recalled a generation later. At dances and on campus she met all sorts of new and interesting people, all more or less her own age. College was liberation from the social cocoon populated by neighborhood kids she had always known. She had to focus on courses like anthropology, where Professor Joseph A. Hester actually expected students to know the names of the Native American tribes of California. She joined a sorority, but continued to live at home. She worked part-time as an electronics assembler. This experience, like Cheetham's boot camp, created the determination to complete her degree and to acquire a teaching credential.

Nevertheless, social life remained a swirl in which parties, dates, games, and studying constituted a happy and successful mix. Her social life, by and large, developed within a system that was about to collapse. While Schuback lived at home with a highly supportive mother, sororities and even private residences still had housemothers who managed many of the women's social events.

Paul Cheetham
...learned value of education at boot camp

The student body of the late '60s came of age during the decade of protest. Protest against institutional racism came first. Protests against the war in Vietnam followed. Schuback, who earned her BA in sociology in 1970, a teaching credential in 1971, and her master's in educational administration in 1981, recognized the critical nature of both protest movements. Amid these and all of the rest — educational striving, personal growth, and social awakening — she met her future husband and married. Her college years, like those of the other thousands of her colleagues, were vibrant, challenging, and quite positive. But the representative student profile she brought to San José — traditional background, social exuberance, and career focus — had already crested. What had been the majority student population became the minority during the last decades of the century.

The case of Paul Cheetham was complementary, but hardly identical. His Marin County youth included Catholic schooling through twelfth grade. A highly structured home life punctuated by an active social life and a few terms at the College of Marin made San José State very attractive. Cheetham was 21 years old when he enrolled, and he did not anticipate campus unrest. He certainly did not enroll for social activism or to oppose the war in Vietnam or racism in America.

Cheetham's parents paid his part of the monthly rent for an apartment near campus, and his part-time jobs (up to 20 hours a week) paid for books, clothes, food, and other expenses. He earned $20 for each weekend drill with the Marines, but he had to drive home to Marin County for each meeting.

Cheetham and his friends next rented a large home where they learned to entertain on a grander scale, particularly communal dinners and cookouts with coeds in the adjoining buildings. Happy hour at the Warehouse bar on South First Street also became a regular event. Beer was 10 cents, and when happy hour concluded, most of Cheetham's friends nursed a 50-cent non-happy hour beer for the rest of the night of talk, music, dancing and light shows.

Drugs entered their social mix late in their years at State, in 1969, the year Cheetham would graduate. Cheetham admitted being scared off. He considered drugs to be dangerous and uncontrollable. If others wanted to try them out, that was their business. Nevertheless, he came close to one arrest. It was at a roaring campus neighborhood party in somebody's third-floor apartment. Non-student neighbors, fed up with the noise and lateness of the hour, called the police who then confronted the celebrants at the apartment front door. Cheetham looked to the window for escape, but possible arrest was less threatening than a 30-foot fall. The officer looked through the marijuana smoke and told the college crowd just to "hold it down." Cheetham could not tell from his experience if the police did not enforce the laws on all students or just favored his suburban crowd.

Cheetham worked at Al's Market on the corner of South Tenth and William streets, a popular student shopping spot for junk food and beer. Al's had been held up more than once despite the managing presence of "Fat Jack," the owner's 300-pound son-in-law. Al's was a world apart from any of Paul's retail experience in Marin County. The San José decor featured a semi-automatic shotgun prominently hung on the wall over the cash register, later replaced with a pistol conveniently positioned on the shelf under the cash drawer.

Classes went well enough for Cheetham. He studied, liked the faculty and greatly appreciated the consideration of business department chairs. Although most faculty members continued to teach and to dress as they had before the arrival of the counter-culture, Cheetham got a kick out of faculty striving to be "with it," those who wore work shirts with neckties. He had completed most of his general education at the College of Marin, so he missed the displays of some of the younger social science and humanities faculty with beads, beards, sandals, and "challenge authority" buttons.

CHEETHAM NEVER MET STEVEN MILLNER, a contemporary and a junior college transfer student from Southern California. Although his economic background resembled Cheetham's, Millner's expectations of racial equality were a critical difference. Those views, which Millner shared with other young African American students who became activists for equality, would contribute to the emerging campus ferment.

Millner's parents had gone to Ohio State University and appreciated higher education. Millner's father had decided to move to California because of the state's educational opportunities. Charles Millner took a Post Office job in San Bernardino, and the children went to Los Angeles County public schools. Steven's older brother Charles, Jr. was a National Merit Finalist when he graduated from high school.

Steven Millner
...expected big
things to happen at
San José State

Millner was the all-American-boy, successful academically and athletically and active in the local branch of the National Association for the Advancement of Colored People. Although he won a Kiwanis Club scholarship to college, going away to San José State was not possible until after he had earned the AA degree.

Millner liked what he saw on his post-high school visit to San José State. Later he stated that for him it was "the spot," the place where he fully expected important things to take place, not just for him, but for African Americans and the rest of society, too. Yet his visit had preceded the turmoil and struggle of black students focused by Harry Edwards in protesting racism.

Luis Valdez

BA, ENGLISH, 1964, HONORARY DOCTORATE

PLAYWRIGHT, DIRECTOR, PRODUCER, filmmaker, actor and advocate, Luis Valdez is considered the father of Chicano theater. Author of such productions as *The Shrunken Head of Pancho Villa, Zoot Suit, La Bamba, The Cisco Kid, Tibercio Vasquez, Corridos, I Don't Have to Show You No Stinking Badges, Fight in the Fields*, and *The Mummified Deer*, Valdez depicts with humor, compassion and intelligence the state and promise of Chicano culture.

Friends with Cesar Chavez since he was just a boy of 6, Valdez is renowned for founding the internationally acclaimed El Teatro Campesino. With Chavez's support, Valdez began his Theater of the Farm Workers on flatbed trucks in picking fields a year after he graduated from SJSU. World recognition came with the success of *Zoot Suit* and, from there, his career as an advocate for Chicanos in the performing arts escalated to national attention. Winner of the George Peabody Award, an Obie, numerous Los Angeles Drama Critics Awards, and an Emmy, Valdez also received the California Governor's Award in 1990 and Mexico's prestigious Aguila Azteca Award in 1994.

Awarded honorary doctorates from San José State, the University of Santa Clara, Columbia College of Chicago and the California Institute of the Arts, he also is a council member of the National Endowment for the Arts. In addition, Valdez is a founding member of both the California Arts Council and the California State University at Monterey Bay. A warm, often funny and accessible artist, he has been the inspiration for a new generation of Latino actors, directors, producers, and writers. Valdez said his stories "reflect the culture, and the culture has no borders."

On Campus: Debuted his first play, *The Shrunken Head of Pancho Villa,* in 1964 at SJSU.

Years later, as a respected faculty member, Professor Millner admitted that he had never seen the face of racism until he tried to rent student accommodations near the San José State campus. He had always lived at home with his financially modest, protective family. Arriving weeks before the fall semester commenced, Millner noted scores of "for rent" signs along 9th, 10th, and 11th streets to the east and south of the campus. When he knocked or rang the doorbell, usually a face would appear at the window, but the door remained shut. Others, presumably caught unaware, opened the doors and either said the accommodations were just taken or handed out a form for Millner to complete. In all cases the result was the same. No rental, no place to stay. The landlords who turned away black students, however, were operating college-approved housing, and were registered with the student services office at San José State. They had agreed to abide by all pertinent laws and code requirements. This was the time when non-discrimination in housing was upheld by the California courts, and the discrimination Millner and other African Americans experienced was illegal.

Millner rented a room in a black fraternity house for $40 a month. At this same time, Harry Edwards was raising directly with President Clark the problem of housing discrimination on behalf of stranded black athletes. In Millner's case, his social education advanced even further when he made his next move, out of the rented room and into Allen Hall at South Tenth and San Carlos streets. He thought he would be safe and comfortable living on campus and in the company of four other African American young men. Instead, he recalled in 1998, it was "dangerous, exciting, challenging, and depressing." Thirty years later Millner the sociologist suggested that Allen Hall was worthy of a study in and of itself. He and his African American male friends shared accommodations on the top floor. Whenever they walked down the first-floor hall, "Through every third open door you could see in full view drugs and drug paraphernalia."

Within a student body that was approaching 25,000, the African American students numbered a hundred or more. Roughly half of them were greatly admired star athletes, though admired from a social distance by track enthusiasts like Cheetham and his friends. For their own part, black students felt unwelcome and unwanted. Courses were no problem for the very competent Millner. He could read, write, and think with the best. A regular admit, Millner was among the first recruits through the Black Educational Opportunity Program, receiving financial assistance that enabled him to attend college.

One of Millner's close associates, Emile Thompson, was deep into the drug culture, and Millner knew that he retained the effects of an abused childhood. Thompson's father had encountered his own set of problems as an officer on Oakland's otherwise white police force. Thompson, on his own in San José and filled with youthful independence, became caught up in drugs, militancy, and the rhetoric of the movement. At Black Student Union meetings he talked about what should be done with police "pigs." Thompson's commitment gradually became more than just rhetoric. Not long after midnight, on Thursday, August 6, 1970, armed with a handgun, he walked up to a San José police patrol car parked at North Eleventh and Empire. Inside, the officer was writing a traffic ticket. Thompson reached through the open passenger window and shot officer Richard Huerta in the head. Confronted with a first-degree murder charge, Thompson's attorney offered an insanity defense. The defendant received a life sentence for taking the life of Huerta, a Latino officer whom he did not know. The jury declined to invoke the death penalty. No matter what the interpretation of the psychological-social context, the outcome was tragedy.

One of Millner's young sociology professors, Dr. Robert Gliner, recognized his ability and encouraged his scholarship as he completed his bachelor's degree in sociology in 1970. This included applying to the University of California, Berkeley, where he earned his sociology PhD and launched his academic career. Millner had survived far closer to the epicenter of danger than had Cheetham or Schuback and, like them, he obtained what most parents sent their children to San José State to acquire — an education and a future.

Millner, Schuback, and Cheetham — three undergraduates who could have met, but never did. If they had, the most likely place would have been old Spartan Stadium, and the most likely event would have been the rock concert featuring an as yet unrecognized group, Ike & Tina Turner. As a member of the Black Student Union, Millner was busy organizing the event, which was jointly sponsored with the College Union Program Board.

Governor Ronald Reagan had closed California's public universities during the preceding Thursday and Friday as a precautionary measure after President Richard Nixon's announced incursion from the Vietnam War into neighboring Cambodia. Rather than rioting, many students took advantage of the unexpected four-day weekend and went home. The resulting concert turnout was disappointing for the organizers but quite the reverse for the select spectators. Some who attended fondly recalled being among a crowd of about 10,000 students and fans. Dr. Leonard Jeffries of the black studies department complained that only 7,000 appeared. An article in the *San Jose Mercury News* reduced the attendance estimate to a low of 3,000. Spartan Stadium's amateur organizers had not hired professional security, nor had they requested the presence of city police. What security there was became young Millner's assignment as a member of the Black Student Union. The event was to be a benefit concert for the Educational Opportunity Program.

Not knowing quite what to expect, Millner watched while many early arrivals promptly got high on marijuana and wine. He had thought that 35 male students would be sufficient to direct the crowd and address whatever else might unfold. His distinct under-planning and his student volunteers' non-training quickly became all too apparent. Sporadic fights punctuated the afternoon and, finally, toward dusk, the big one erupted. From Millner's vantage point, about 50 Hell's Angels started the melee. Like many other spectators, the motorcycle club members were drunk and unruly, and they were disrespectful of the black and Chicano men who were supposed to be in charge. When 12 Angels refused to back off from the crush of humanity at the rock stage, words followed, then blows. Hell's Angels went to the hospital, but not before declaring war on the black students.

At a previous concert the year before, Paul Cheetham recalled seeing an intoxicated spectator hit a Hell's Angel over the head with a half-filled jug of wine. That assault drew a brutal retaliation, which left the initial assailant beaten and seriously injured. At the Turner Concert, a riot ensued between the Hell's Angels and the "security force," yet Ike and Tina Turner rocked on.

The newspaper-reading public (parents, politicians, and taxpayers in general) could easily conclude that the students ran the colleges during the '60s. Where were the administrators, where was the staff, and where was the faculty? Were they collaborators with the students, allowing students to do as they wished? In fact, Robert Clark's administration had its hands full with swelling enrollments, an expanded new faculty, new student recruitment, the impact of shared governance, racism on and off campus, the growth of anti-war and anti-draft opinion, student protests, riotous disorders, and a faculty strike.

The Academic Council committee under leadership of Professor Harold J. DeBey, provost of New College, and assisted by Professor Theodore M. Norton of political science, who also was a lawyer, recognized the new order and developed a statement of student rights and responsibilities. DeBey and Norton had the wisdom to include

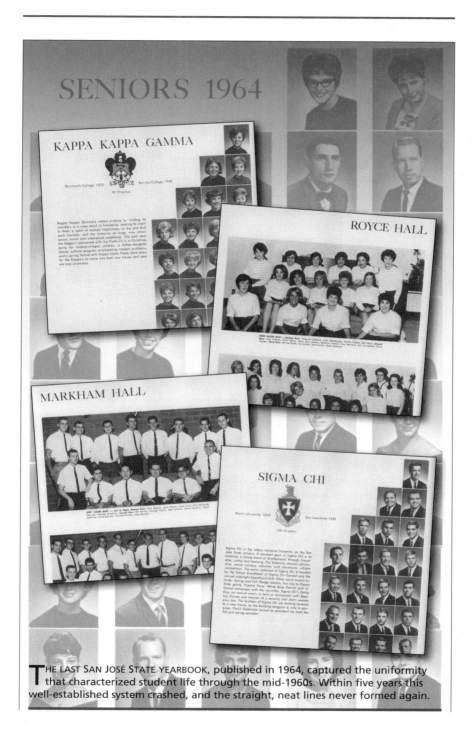

THE LAST SAN JOSÉ STATE YEARBOOK, published in 1964, captured the uniformity that characterized student life through the mid-1960s. Within five years this well-established system crashed, and the straight, neat lines never formed again.

students in their committee membership and to draw upon their insights. Attentive faculty felt that if the students were going to demand their rights, they might as well be faced with clear and official responsibilities, too. The historic doctrine that the college rightly acted *in loco parentis* officially ended in 1968 and with it the entire basis on which the approved housing system depended for validation. The single most critical ingredient that created such dramatic change was the assault on the system's racism, which student Millner experienced and which instructor Edwards publicized. The decline of the Greek system at San José State and its near extinction followed. Anti-racism, black militancy and then Mexican American militancy were the most clearly identifiable forces for change. Men and women in student services offices, as well as academic department secretaries, remained the first line of service and response, just as in quieter times.

Wiggsy Sivertsen, who earned her undergraduate sociology degree from San José State in 1962, returned to a changed campus after earning her master's in social work at Tulane University, accepting a counseling position at San José State in 1967. Federal Bureau of Investigation agents hung out at the student counseling offices, presumably to identify draft evaders or anti-war protest organizers. Personal counseling had expanded its domain beyond the usual post-adolescent, young-adult problems of new relationships, self-discovery, and career goals. For a growing number of students, such traditional matters became subordinated to problems stemming from drugs, free love, and facing up to or evading the central question of the war in Vietnam. Not only did affected students suffer their personal agonies, but their and their parents' worlds had become so very different that students suffered estrangement from their families.

Many, however, were able to figure out their part of this new world on their own. In Cheetham's case, he addressed the war by joining the Reserves. He read the *Independent Journal* when he went home on drill weekends and knew that the young attorneys who were officers of the weekend units maintained a strong lobby against activation. He kept his hair cut short for the mandatory Reserve meetings, so he always looked right to his parents. Most students just let their hair grow, much to the detriment of the Varsity Barber Shop on South Fourth Street.

Wiggsy Sivertsen
...counseled students in era of drugs, 'free love'

New College — born and died with changing times

BEGUN IN 1968 by faculty members Harold DeBey, Jack Pierce, and Jack Douglas, with the blessing of Academic Vice President Hobert Burns, New College was a revolution in keeping with the times, tearing down the walls between disciplines and recreating a closer teacher-student relationship. It took the ideas of interdisciplinary teaching and honors tutorials and created a new type of study for general students.

The New College program was a self-contained, four-year liberal arts interdisciplinary program that was part of the regular undergraduate curriculum at San José State from 1968-1981. The faculty included tenured professors as well as temporary teaching faculty, including: DeBey (chemistry), Pierce (anthropology), Fanny Rinn (political science), John Galm (English), Bob Gliner (sociology), Cindy Margolin (psychology), Lois Helmbold, Todd Gitlin and Douglas (library), Lou Lewandowski (English), Terry Christensen (political science), Lela Noble (political Science), and Robin Brooks (history).

A student's first two years consisted of team-taught lectures and seminars in the sciences, social sciences and humanities, equating with the university's general education skills and breadth requirements. The team-teaching approach, with a strong emphasis on cultural pluralism, focused on the theme of developing students intellectually, emotionally and physically as individual and social beings. The second two years of study were spent on an individualized major. Students used a combination of independent study contracts, small group seminars, and a senior project or thesis for their 30 units of upper division coursework. Students completing designated courses also satisfied requirements for entry into the credential teaching program.

By 1981, the freewheeling program found itself out-of-step with the times but a fantastic experience for students and faculty who participated in it. "We were a pain to the administration for our rather outlandish activities, and we didn't hire enough tenured faculty," Margolin said. Rinn and Sybil Weir wanted to tend the program, but President John Bunzel brought in a new provost from outside the program, and the descent began. "It ran its course and faded with the times," Margolin added.

As to "free love," the sense of liberation brought about by the advent of the birth control pill, Millner recalled that it was rampant. And the initiative roles were not limited by gender or race. Yet those like Millner, who were in committed relationships or had none at all, still constituted the majority. Even President Clark noted the strength of "the revolution" when he welcomed the faculty back in the fall. Commenting on the range of changes within student culture, the dignified but engaging Clark wondered if the faculty generation had merely missed the boat by having been born too soon, before the "new morality." For most faculty and staff, this provoked an innocent or heedless laugh.

Campus counseling services offered group therapy and individual counseling on the draft, the war, drugs, and relationships. All drew willing participants who, with the staff, sought an understanding and an exit from the destructive aspects of the '60s youth culture. Cheetham took advantage of group counseling in order to set a career goal. On his own he negotiated the draft and rejected drugs. He never did discover any girls devoted to free love, and his beer consumption hit the college norm. Millner's personal judgments, his family stability, and the faculty encouragement he found at San José State allowed him to actualize his potential. Teacher credential advising helped Schuback focus on her career goal while her lifestyle and family deflected the obvious threats of the times.

According to Sivertsen, matters of sexual orientation simply had not risen to the level of becoming an issue during the '60s. The gay community had not yet emerged. The percentage of gay people in the general population presumably paralleled that of the campus community, but being in the closet would remain a standard tactic for years to come. No counseling on this subject was made available. The very term "gay" was not yet in use and would take some while before it prevailed.

San José State in the '60s reflected diverse life-styles and offered numerous career options, yet a good number of students chose none of them. In fact, dropping out of school was statistically, if not emotionally, a popular enough alternative to everything. You did not even have to be in any at-risk category to opt out.

GABRIEL REYES AND MICHAEL HONDA, two undergraduate science majors, opted out. Both had come from agricultural laboring families who settled down in San José. When Reyes' mother, tired of moving with the crops, convinced her husband to take steady work, they settled into a home just southwest of the campus. The Honda family spent much of World War II in internment camps, despite the fact that Michael's father provided Japanese language instruction to military intelligence officers. Later the family earned a living laboring in fields that surrounded the historic Hayes mansion in south San José.

Reyes and Honda came to San José State with reverse influences. Reyes'

Gabriel Reyes
...took time out to serve in Vietnam

Michael Honda
...took time out to serve in Peace Corps

father first thought that a high school education was sufficient and that his son's responsibility was to the family. He should work. Reyes qualified for admission, but went to San José City College with his friends. First, he had to convince his father that two more years would be good for him. He was next to the last born, and the employment of his older brothers and sisters had eased the financial strain.

Honda's situation was quite different. In Japanese American culture, it was merely assumed that he would go on to college. Years later, as a state assemblyman with bachelor's degrees in biological sciences and Spanish and a master's degree in edu-

Marches, boycotts and watchdogs help Hispanic causes

HISPANIC STUDENT LEADERS hoped their march would force the issue of continued funding for the Educational Opportunity Program with then-Governor Ronald Reagan. Three hundred San José State students set out on foot, headed from San José to Sacramento during spring break in March 1971. The students knew that the EOP services were vital to recruiting and retaining more minority students.

"We marched all the way," recalled Pete Michel. "It took us almost a week. We slept outdoors and had our meals on the road." Vietnam veterans such as Gabe Reyes, used to long marches, helped the others prepare for the trek, giving advice on boots and nutrition. The outcome of the march was positive, EOP funding continued, and the blisters were worth it, Michel said.

San José State's Hispanic students had other community issues to unite around, including farm workers' plight and police harassment. Various groups formed, including Hispanic, Mexican American and the more radical Chicano organizations. A unifying organization, known as MASC (Mexican American Student Confederation), was formed to address problems at San José State. Working with the United Farm Workers, students set up a grape boycott of the Lucky's grocery on Santa Clara Street near campus, which eventually decided to remove the grapes from its shelves. A group of students and community members organized the Community Alert Patrol, "which would watchdog the police department" until the city hired Joseph McNamara and police attitudes and practices began to change.

In 1968 a small group of Chicano graduates protested the lack of Chicano students at San José State by walking out of the commencement exercises at Spartan Stadium. In 1969, the students again decided to protest, but this time on the field. "We were promptly escorted by the police to the outside of Spartan Stadium," Michel recalled. In 1970, student Mauro Chavez suggested an "alternative" commencement, and the first "Chicano Commencement" at Our Lady of Guadalupe Church honored 15 graduates. "Graduating students were encouraged to wear native attire and the program was in both English and Spanish," Michel said. Chicano Commencement became an annual event, though it has grown in size.

Michel helped chronicle Hispanic issues in a *Spartan Daily* column called Mano y Mano. One week he submitted his column half in English, half in Spanish, and the *Daily* initially refused to print it. Ombudsman Mike Honda helped resolve the issue. Michel, who earned his bachelor's degree in political science in 1973 and his master's in urban and regional planning in 1980, went on to a career helping others in San José State's EOP. He retired in 1999 and started a 3½ acre habitat for monarch butterflies in Aromas, 50 miles southwest of San José.

Comparing two decades

1960s 1990s

cation, he recalled that his father and mother never reviewed his grades or his test scores. They were equally inattentive to admissions requirements or major selections. His cousins were attending college; therefore, he would, too. Both Honda and Reyes studied hard once they arrived at State, but felt rather isolated within the then Greek-led student body. Both opted to drop out in non-traditional ways. Reyes left San José State for Vietnam. Honda opted for the Peace Corps. Both survived, but with vastly different experiences.

Reyes quickly concluded that "the war was a mess" over there. His Latino community, somewhat divided, possessed its own anti-war activists as well as its numerous volunteers and cooperative conscripts. Honda's hiatus from State was less disillusioning and far less dangerous. Yet both young men returned, themselves changed, to a changed college. Reyes earned his bachelor's in political science in 1972 and his master's in Mexican American studies in 1976. He added his EdD from the University of Southern California in 1997.

The new campus atmosphere, still in the throes of black and Chicano militancy, the rise of the Women's Movement, and Asian awareness, had settled into the pattern of attacking barriers. Before Reyes and Honda stepped out, being a member of a minority group had been a clear disadvantage. After they returned, minority status, fashionable or not, was positive and exciting. Diversity, a California reality, had become a fact of campus life at San José State, as well.

The 1990s

B Y THE LAST DECADE of the twentieth century, campus life and the economic environment in which the university existed had been transformed. With the end of the Cold War and the eclipse of the defense industry, electronics and the information-communication age promptly filled the void with high tech, progenitor of the new world economy. The entire infrastructure of the region served by San José State strained under new growth driven by new technologies, higher employment, more demanding qualifications, larger population, more traffic, a high cost of living, and enhanced financial opportunities. In 1999, the California State University system was providing the higher education that helped sustain the unprecedented boom that had its start at San José State's doorstep: Silicon Valley. San José State's business and engineering colleges advanced the regional economy as well as the economy's national and international extensions by educating a new work force and providing technical and financial leadership.

San José State in the 1990s found itself a facilitator of the unprecedented changes outside its doors as well as a recipient of the results of those vast changes. The former teacher training school that matured into a comprehensive university was now the metropolitan university directly linked with Silicon Valley, which it served, and from which it drew new sustenance. En route, San José State's focus changed from the social sciences and the humanities to primarily business and engineering, as well as science and the applied fields.

Under the leadership of Dean Marshall J. Burak, the College of Business revised and upgraded its curriculum and augmented its faculty. The College of Business moved into Silicon Valley by offering on-site MBA programs to older, more established students who were seeking to re-educate themselves and to remain personally competitive in the fast-changing high tech economy.

Engineering's major boost came under the leadership of Dean Jay D. Pinson. From the time of his appointment as dean in 1979, Pinson recognized the physical and technical limitations of the college's buildings and equipment. The accelerating advancements in electronics and information age technologies merely dramatized the growing gap between what Pinson considered his students needed and what the physical, curricular, and personnel limitations allowed his faculty to teach. When the

Gays and lesbians gain protection, seek acceptance

WHEN WIGGSY SIVERTSEN was offered a fulltime position in San Jose State's Counseling Center in 1970, she insisted that President John Bunzel first know that she was an "out" lesbian. "The president said, 'Great, just as long as she does the job.' At the time, I was the only out gay or lesbian person on the campus," said Sivertsen, who had been fired from a local service center that discovered that she was a lesbian.

An early support group, the Gay People's Union, was not designed for "out" people at that time. But in 1976, California legislator John Briggs decided to put an initiative on the ballot to keep gays and lesbians from teaching. "That really ignited the gay community into statewide political action," Sivertsen said. Following the successful campaign to defeat Briggs, efforts began to press the university to include sexual orientation in its non-discrimination policy. Many universities nationwide began to include sexual orientation in their statements, and California Governor Jerry Brown issued an Executive Order including the category, but it remained absent from federal non-discrimination guidelines.

Protection against discrimination "opened the door to students and employees to come out and feel safer," Sivertsen said. The battle to solve issues locally when federal guidelines were found wanting soon moved to the issue of campus Army and Air Force ROTC programs. Sivertsen asked the Academic Senate to invite the Reserve Officers' Training Corp to leave campus because of the military's policy of excluding gays and lesbians from commissioning. In 1984, the senate did vote to force ROTC to comply with the university's non-discrimination policy. But President Gail Fullerton was unwilling to make the university an agent for political change, instead making minor program changes and leaving the larger issue to the military and the courts.

But Sivertsen kept at the issue for more than 16 years, through President Clinton's military policy of "don't ask, don't tell." In the mid-1990s, Congress attached a rider on a military budget bill that said any school refusing to allow ROTC on campus would lose its federal funding. The threat of losing federal grant and scholarship funding effectively ended the debate. President Robert Caret talked to Sivertsen, who said later, "I thought that SJSU and most of the colleges across the country took a pretty non-courageous stand on this issue."

The campus has changed since she was an undergraduate student, said Sivertsen, who eventually became director of Counseling Services. "But students still struggle to find acceptance in this culture and still need to have role models."

state of California failed to commit itself to the construction and equipping of a new engineering facility, he took matters into his own hands. With support from major corporations and their CEOs, Pinson put together a public-private funding and construction plan that allowed San José State to create its own state-of-the-art engineering facility. Pinson's strongest selling point in acquiring financial support from among the Silicon Valley corporate leaders was the trained workers and managers San José State was already producing for their firms. Pinson's question to them was simple and direct. Why not improve both the quality and the quantity of your work force?

Pinson's dramatic upgrading of San José State's engineering capabilities and Burak's quieter, but no less successful, stabilization and modernization of business instruction reflected changes in campus life beyond their own colleges. Both made the university more professionally interactive with the community at large. And those sectors, engineering and business, were growing and becoming more dominant. Simultaneously, during the decades of the '70s and '80s, elementary and secondary education within the valley was in serious decline. Many public schools closed their doors, and the need for San José State to produce more teachers all but ended. Likewise, career opportunities for those graduating in the so-called "softer" disciplines within the humanities, arts, and social sciences went into eclipse.

Though quiet and orderly, the transformation from the '60s and "revolution" to the '90s and "innovation," was profound, and it centered upon the students' professional orientations. Business, engineering, mathematics, science, and other applied fields kept growing while social science and the humanities scaled back. During these years, Career Planning and Placement, later named The Career Center, hosted larger and larger Career Days. Each year the record rose for the new number of corporations and other employers sending representatives and headhunters to arrange interviews and hire upcoming graduates. The Career Center staff dedicated itself to maximizing opportunities for "all majors," but it was an up-hill struggle. Engineering and business were in command.

Over these years the nature and goals, even the appearance, of the student body adjusted to the new realities. In reviewing scholarship applications, for example, faculty selection committee members soon noted an entirely changed student profile. Veteran faculty had all but forgotten the days when most applicants submitted resumes heavy in Greek life, suburban backgrounds, and advanced placement curricula. Often the award applicants of the '90s had been the dropouts of the '60s. The '90s group also included a substantial representation of women who had put off higher education opportunities for marriage, family, and their husbands' careers. It became commonplace for the *San Jose Mercury News* to feature a photograph of a mother and daughter graduating at the same commencement. Father and son combinations rarely appeared because San José State, again, was enrolling more women than men. Infrequently commented upon, the grade point averages of the re-enrolled women often exceeded those of their children.

Another major shift that senior faculty recognized was the enhanced achievement levels of students who, in the '60s, would have been termed *minority* students. Many in this group, which included recent immigrants and their children, were highly competitive. Scholarship seekers for the most part, they met the basic application requirements, possessed high grade point averages, had strong letters of recommendations and sound resumes. What had changed by the '90s was the content of the graduates' resumes. Service to the university had generally faltered, and service to the community also had become a distinct casualty. Pressure to excel — in classes, laboratories, internships, and GPA — had become the chief motivation. Student life by the '90s had become the reverse of the '60s.

Women make early push for studies, resource center

THE WOMEN'S MOVEMENT establishd its foothold at San Jose State in the 1970s — in a basement office for the Women's Resource Center and with the first formal class about women.

"More than 100 students came to those early classes, hungry for new ideas, challenging themselves and their teachers to see the world differently," explained Lois Helmbold, who taught the first women's studies course in the fall of 1970. "An inspired offspring of the Civil Rights Movement, feminism was sweeping the country. Optimism about social change was in the air we breathed. I read voraciously, trying to keep ahead of the students, and combined my activism in the Women's Liberation Movement, as we called it then, with the intellectual content we were rediscovering and inventing."

Meanwhile, the Women's Resource Center opened in a basement in an auxiliary building that filled with water when it rained. Director David Newman soon gave the center shelter under the umbrella of Counseling Services. Wiggsy Sivertsen, a counselor named faculty adviser of the center, said the program has been run by students for three decades, with a focus on service and education, and sometimes political action. A series of sexual assaults in the 1970s led the students to agitate for more police walking beats around campus, more education for students about how to stay safe, and a change in cultural stereotypes about rape victims.

The students also joined in the push for more women faculty and administrators, as did professors Fanny Rinn and Sybil Weir, early coordinators of the women's studies program in addition to their other teaching duties. "A small group of the first students decided that they needed graduate work," Helmbold said, "and with dedication they helped create a master's focus in women's studies through the social science master's program, one of the first in the country." Twenty-five years after the program's beginning, Helmbold wrote, "SJSU, once a pioneer in women's studies, regrettably lags behind many women's studies programs" at other universities, with only two tenure-track faculty and without its own major or master's degree.

Sivertsen, who has remained adviser to the Women's Resource Center, said students still struggle with "how to maintain a sense of energy to address those issues which continue to negatively affect women in our society," particularly domestic abuse and sexual abuse. "We need to educate those women who somehow or other believe that everything is fine now. Women need to be more assertive about being at the table."

Large numbers of incoming freshmen were required, at century's end, to register for remedial courses in English and mathematics. The standard lament over the quality of public preparatory education persisted. On top of that, however, were far more specific causes. The '90s student population came to a greater degree from homes in which English was not the primary language. Also, in homes where families appreciated the need and value of higher education for careers in Silicon Valley, the families often lacked a tradition of higher education.

In the 1950s, during the early years of John Wahlquist's presidency, admission standards rose largely because Wahlquist could not provide enough new buildings in which to educate all who qualified for admission. He and his faculty, therefore, did not deal significantly in remedial education. The same rule of supply and demand remained true in the '90s, but the weight of the factors had reversed themselves. San José State, despite substantial growth, did not meet the greatly accelerated enrollment targets set by the California State University system. Greater and more open opportunities for higher education had, by the '90s, become a California commitment, with a focus on recruiting the area's underrepresented populations. The general budget drove most other forces, and enrollments continued to drive the budget. San José State's problem was that enrollments remained soft and, therefore, never drove the budget high enough.

Statistical studies of class, gender, and race aside, the faculty encountered case after case of young immigrants or the children of recent immigrants who did thrive, who by high school graduation at 18 had not only mastered English but also math and computer skills. Some new immigrants even attained the honor of high school valedictorian, and they maintained the same focus and concentration at San José State, often with the community college as a steppingstone. Case histories contained in award applications also revealed the personal costs, the absence of a robust social life or of time for community service. For the students of the '90s, time had become as valuable as money, and its budgeting was all the more careful. After all, many of the new students worked 30 hours per week, often in a struggling small business operated by family members. For the overwhelming number of students without a family tradition of college attendance, campus life meant preparation for careers, the striving for first-time entry into professional status. And to that extent, the university hardly seemed the fun place of traditional alumni memories. But while the campus ceased to be fun, it also ceased to be militant.

In the '90s no one replicated the undergraduate experiences of a Paul Cheetham, Gayle Schuback, Steven Millner, Mike Honda, Gabriel Reyes or the thousands of degree recipients among their cohort. Both student generations impacted and responded to the problems, opportunities and demands of their times. Likewise, both shaped and became shaped by the institution.

GAYLE SCHUBACK'S ENTHUSIASM and intelligence were apparent in students of the '90s such as Lisa Derby, whose focus and religious commitment became paramount. Derby represented the best academically prepared students the university was attracting in the '90s. Besides grade point average and Scholastic Aptitude Test scores, her record included advanced placement, satisfaction of the math requirement, and eligibility to waive the otherwise required upper division writing requirement. Grades from Valley Christian High School were universally "A" marks, but for one A- blemish in driver's education. Four years at San José State University resulted in an all-A transcript, including a semester abroad. The *Summa Cum Laude* graduate (BA Communications '95) worked throughout, gave her time and talent in church-related undertakings, and benefited by extensive travel. Both Derby and Schuback identified teaching as their career objectives. What differed were their respective approaches to campus life, '60s vs. '90s. For Schuback, San José State was an immersion experience guided and restrained by family and traditional values. For Derby, family and religious values prevailed to the point that San José State was not an immersion, but rather an exercise in careful selectivity. Both women attained their goals; Derby departed San José State for three years of sponsored and prestigious PhD work in Dublin, Ireland.

THE STORIES OF ALFONSO DE ALBA and Ruth Estrella also reflect the larger picture of '90s students. De Alba, born in Los Angeles and brought up in Mexico, made his own way to San José at age 16. He found employment at a Round Table Pizza parlor by convincing the management that he was older. For a while he did not have to deal with unwelcome inquiries because he couldn't speak English. His life was an adventure, though not always a happy one. He moved from abode to abode, sometimes with families, sometimes in unsettled and dangerous circumstances. As his English improved, he took it upon himself to start attending high school in Eastside San José. Next, he had himself declared legally independent — an emancipated minor. His savvy friends at Round Table had suggested this and told him how to do it.

Enrolling at San José State was a complete accident. Well after high school graduation, DeAlba went one afternoon to the Silver Creek High School campus to meet a friend. At the open door of an office, a professional woman asked him if he was so-and-so. He was not and said so, to which the woman responded with pretended anger. She had made a special trip there from her community college to help the no-show enroll. At this point De Alba simply asked if he could take the other fellow's place. Thus began the steps leading to successful community college education, matriculation to San José State, a student career in campus politics and Associated Student Government, and graduation in 1996 with a BA in political science and public administration. Thereafter, De Alba conducted payback sessions with his community college mentor, Minerva Santiago. Together they met with at-risk youngsters at the Five Wounds Catholic Church and explained, in Spanish and English, what more education can do for the students and their families, and how to get it.

De Alba had been a student activist in Mexico. In fact, his youthful activism is what exiled him to life in the United States. At San José State he wanted to join fully in Mexican American student activities. But it was not quite so easy.

The Mexican American student movement at San José State got its start in the late '60s, and the students fully controlled and directed the movement. They met and negotiated with President Clark, and they advanced their cause. The Mexican American students correctly pointed out to the college administration that their group was the largest minority in Santa Clara Valley and that a contemporary film on race relations being produced by the college was blind to this reality. By the time of De Alba's arrival on campus in the '90s, the student revolution had institutionalized itself. Chicano faculty, administrators, staff, and curriculum were in greater evidence. But Chicano students no longer commanded the power of earlier decades. Direct action and prompt results gave way to frequent internal discussions of philosophical differences. The talk was punctuated annually by allocations from the Associated Students budget, which determined the extent of their group's cultural program for the year. The Mexican American student organization became a competitor among other groups for official funding.

De Alba found it difficult to appreciate arguments over what to be called: Chicano, Hispanic, Mexican American, Latino, or La Raza. He noted that some '90s students doing the most ardent arguing did so in English; it appeared to him as if their families no longer spoke Spanish. As an elected member of the Associated Student Government, De Alba operated on the standard democratic assumption that government should be positive, and positive for everyone, particularly those most in need. The Associated Students' budget drew its income from fees paid by each enrolled student. Back when enrollment was advancing from 20,000 to 25,000 and then approached 30,000 students, the budget distributions encouraged innovation within student groups. The standard committee process was to review the recent historical record and to continue funding what seemed to be working well enough, and to put new funds behind innovations from new student clubs and other *bona fide* campus groups. Enrollment decline and diminished budgets played a role in reviving ethnic militancy and ending the period of student political tranquility. This time, however, the renewed activism was contained within the university institutions. The student movement of the '60s had become institutionalized, and by the '90s it was less visible to the general public and attracted less media attention.

De Alba chaired the Associated Students budget committee when Jerome Martin headed the Black Student Union. Committee procedure was to hold public hearings during which applicants made their best case and accepted decisions. Harmony prevailed during years of rising budgets. The downturn years resulted in general cuts and denials, particularly to the newer student clubs. The Black Student Union believed that its reduced allocation was inequitable and that reduced funding seemed disproportionately directed at African American organizations, which constituted racism. De Alba disagreed, and, as the chair of the critical committee in student government, immediately found himself caught in the middle.

Jerome Martin
...demanded more funding for Black Student Union

Martin had grown up as an "Army brat," the oldest child in a stable family that had enjoyed foreign travel and opportunities within the regimented system of the U.S. military. He had part-time work experience at a military hospital, and he had earned good grades and scored high on the Scholastic Aptitude Test. He could not agree more with his supportive parents that college was the best route up in life. San José State, he concluded in 1998, was "…one of the greatest things in my life."

Martin and each of his BSU friends and associates decided to wear prominent lapel badges fashioned from torn matchbooks to the budget hearings. The symbolism was as clear as it was threatening and intimidating to De Alba and the Associate Students budget committee members, whose own diversity was no shield against charges of racism. Obviously, the advent of diversity within campus life did not eliminate racial tensions. But one change was absolute by the '90s; it was the total absence of any majority whatever.

The match-decorated lapels were a throwback, a symbol of the tactics of black anger and frustration of decades past. Older black community leaders, who understood the symbolism, had suggested the boutonnieres to the new campus generation. Black campus leaders of the '60s had been more on their own, but in the '90s the new generation of African American student leaders received highly spirited advice from their older advocates.

The focus of student social life continued to shift away from the campus as the demands and opportunities of Silicon Valley's economy left less and less time for campus-related social life. When militancy reawakened, it did so because of individual behaviors rather than institutionalized racism. In such cases, counseling became the administration's first intervention of choice. Reassignment or departure occasionally followed.

By the late '90s, when Ruth Estrella, her two sisters and her brother received the Hispanic community's La Familia Award for educational achievement, Estrella credited San José State with providing the four of them with five degrees and multiple credentials. However, their lives were family and community-oriented, not campus-centered. The university provided the means for them to improve their individual lives, meet the expectation of striving and loving parents, and reinvest their talents in the community that had sustained them.

DEMETRIA TITUS REPRESENTED a complicated student type of the waning century. As an African American woman, she never felt discriminated against at San José State and simply advanced with all the opportunities she encountered. A loving family, high GPA, and Catholic prep school helped. Her outreach volunteerism took the form of hosting Halloween and Easter parties for children of low-income families of the campus community with her Delta Sigma Theta sorority. She worked as a resident assistant for three years in the campus dorms, appeared in *Who's Who Among College Students*, graduated with honors, and received the prestigious Evelyn T. Robinson Memorial Scholarship as the outstanding African American alumna of 1998. She also received scholarship assistance to Duke University Law School beginning in the 1998-99 academic year. Like Fernando Torres-Gil, student militant of the '60s and United States cabinet member of the '90s, Titus was drawn to causes, made her contributions, but

Demetria Titus
…took advantage of campus life

also remained focused upon her best career opportunities.

Heather Cook, daughter of parents with a long and happy relationship with the university, was the last president of the Associated Students to serve out her term within the twentieth century. When she moved into her office atop the Student Union, basic student needs were already well addressed. But the construction of the Student Union and the Event Center had obscured early student recognition of the need for childcare on campus. During Cook's student presidency, in the winter 1998-99, ground breaking for a new student-financed childcare facility took place. Cook, who earned her bachelor's degree in political science in 2000, looked forward to progress for childcare because so many of the metropolitan university's students needed the services. However, as a product of traditionalism, President Cook also intended to advance into the new century what she considered the best among the old values of student life. The central ingredients of her revival formula included intercollegiate athletics, residence life, and Greek life. But the powerful new realities of the diverse student body, the demands of Silicon Valley's economy and the exciting opportunities it offered to the young and the talented, meant that preparing for those opportunities had become more time consuming than ever before.

Student life had changed more from Cook's parents' years on campus to her own than in any other single generation of students since the institution's founding in 1857. Nostalgia was attractive, but change was irrevocable. Returning campus life to patterns of the '60s — even the best ones — could not compete against the enticing promises and the powerful grasp of Silicon Valley.

CHAPTER FOUR

The Challenge of Athletics
DEFINING ITS ROLE

BEFORE PRESIDENT Robert D. Clark's arrival in San José in 1964, the largely suburban and small-town students who swelled the rather homogeneous ranks of the student body enjoyed considerable leisure time. Their lives clustered near or on the campus. Spartan Stadium was a vigorous ten-minute walk south, and the downtown San José Civic Auditorium was even closer to campus. Sports ranked among the popular and affordable college amusements. Old Spartan Stadium, a New Deal (WPA) project of 1935-36, was small and friendly. Filling it was easy then, and the fans conveyed a sense of excitement and spirit. Basketball at the Civic was even more intimate. Balcony ticket holders were close enough to enjoy good moves and exciting play. In the spring, baseball attendance usually was lighter, but the sport had its loyal followers. So, too, did soccer, boxing, fencing, gymnastics, and all the other gymnasium sports.

But the sweeping cultural and demographic changes that began during Clark's leadership would reshape not only the university and its surrounding community, but also the role athletics played within the academic institution. By the century's end, many of the changes in college sports mirrored the evolving American culture, most of which dramatically rearranged interests and priorities within the athletic program. One change — a multicultural student body rapidly refocusing on work and family priorities — became so profound that its impact questioned athletics' claim to the attention of its former mass base of devotees. The second change — the need to expand athletic opportunities for women — created a new and energizing dimension to the old mix of interests. Throughout, a persistent lack of resources remained a festering issue.

From a faculty perspective, the role of athletics became more and more separated from the academic side of the institution. Back in the '50s when the physical education faculty coached the teams on a part-time basis, Friday faculty meetings ended with reminders from the president about the upcoming game. Certainly, by the time of Clark's

Post-season play produces alumni pride

IT WASN'T MONEY BUT PRIDE that Ed Mosher wagered on his alma mater early in the spring of 1996. The Spartan basketball team was 4-15 in February when Mosher told some friends that the Spartans were about to go on a winning streak, would win the Big West Conference Tournament, and would play a team in the final four of the NCAA tournament.

The Spartans went on to win nine of their next 10 games, including a one-point overtime victory in the Big West tournament, made possible by a three-point shot from the team's most unlikely outside shooter. Rich Taylor's second three-point shot of the season took the team from relative obscurity into the media spotlight as the Cinderella team of the 1996 NCAA tournament.

Moments after winning the Big West championship, Coach Stan Morrison's Spartans learned their draw in the NCAA tournament — the No. 2 ranked Kentucky Wildcats. Four days later, as Spartan fans waved yellow signs in the stands, the Spartans took on the Wildcats, Mosher's pride on the line.

"For 16 minutes, they were national champtions. For 16 minutes, the Spartans of San José State could claim that title as much as anyone," wrote Mark Purdy in the *San Jose Mercury News*. "Why not? They were beating Kentucky. They were outrebounding the Wildcats, outshooting them. The public address announcer at half-filled Reunion Arena was uttering incredible words."

Kentucky came out in the second half and turned the tables on the Spartans, taking the game 110-72. But Mosher was proud. His prediction, he said, was not that the Spartans would play in the final four, but that they would play a team in the final four. Kentucky not only filled that bill, but went on to defeat Syracuse for the national title.

arrival in 1964 this had become impossible. Thereafter, it was preposterous.

Higher competitive performance meant that coaching became fulltime — fulltime coaching, fulltime recruiting, fulltime community relations, and then even fulltime record keeping behind the enormous growth of regulations, bureaucracy, and compliance required by the courts and by the National Collegiate Athletic Association (NCAA), the governing body of college sports. In time the coach even became responsible for the athlete's academic progress. Among the significant side effects, coaches ceased teaching physical education courses, even during their off-season. Compartmentalizing the athletic coaches altered the academic environment and extended the distance between athletics and the remainder of the college.

Academic growth and subject matter specialization caused general faculty meetings to be replaced by department-level gatherings. At the department meetings, curriculum, personnel, and research requirements crowded the agendas. For new faculty recruited after 1952 by President Wahlquist, sports became an afterthought. Faculty interest in athletics followed well after their concerns for better teaching, shared governance, research and publishing.

In time, demographic changes within the student body also began to affect athletics. Students tended to be older and self-supporting, and their personal responsibilities were more extensive. They had families and part-time or even fulltime employment. Coursework competed with careers. Commuting and many other non-college challenges impacted their time and their freedom of movement. Rather than living on campus or in the immediate community, they drove in, and they drove away. Some, even, were fulltime employees, part-time students. Their efforts to balance child care, employment, freeways, high-rise parking, and classes marginalized college sports.

The closer the university moved toward the new century, more and more non-sports-minded, career-oriented students became alumni. During these years, the largely unrecognized disconnect between the metropolitan university and the athletic tradition became apparent. What tradition preferred to ignore, attendance and gate receipts refused to conceal.

A Focus on Football

FOOTBALL — WIN AND LOSE — remained the dreadnought of university athletics. The football tradition always claimed press coverage and the enthusiasm and support of core alumni and other boosters. Stalwarts Pat and Arm Hanzad, reminiscing in 1998 after years of personal support of both men's and women's athletics, thought that perhaps their best memory was the 1980 Spartan victory over ninth-ranked Baylor on the Texas university's own gridiron in Waco. Pat recalled that some of the Baylor fans thought that San José was in Mexico.

For San José State sport fans, and some professors with Berkeley and Stanford degrees, beating the flagship universities was quite satisfying. These outstanding teams maximized attendance and elevated ticket sales. But they never did so high enough or long enough to ease the permanent and growing financial stress in the athletics program. Even successful back-to-back seasons with spectacular games failed to produce a much-needed revenue stream from gate receipts.

San Jose Mercury sports writer Mark Purdy, trying to understand the 1986 San José State victory over 19th-ranked Fresno State, suggested that the subject required a doctoral thesis. In college football at its wildest, quarterback Mike Perez brought the Spartans back to win, 45-41, by passing for two touchdowns in the final 16 seconds. All the advanced indicators had suggested that the contest would be the game of the decade. San José State had destroyed Cal the weekend before, beating the Bears in Berkeley by three touchdowns, 35-14. Fresno was nationally ranked. The rivalry was a tradition. And the game was the Spartan's homecoming. Even though 6,000 Fresno fans helped boost attendance by busing in for this pivotal game, about 2,000 seats nevertheless remained empty in the 30,000-seat stadium.

Purdy pointed the finger at the alumni: "Shame on those who didn't come. But at least they will serve their penance. They must live the rest of their lives knowing what they missed." What they missed caused San José State to miss out. The university failed to transform significant winning seasons with spectacular victories into an energized fan base and predictable revenue stream that big-time intercollegiate athletics came to require for success on all those other Saturdays, ordinary days when the variables did not align themselves so miraculously. Intercollegiate athletics was to remain a financial struggle that would exact its own costs.

Bronzan builds Spartan football legends

BOB BRONZAN spent 34.5 years, to be exact, in San José State's athletics department. Bronzan was a Spartan football lineman in the 1930s, San José State's head football coach from 1950 to 1956, and athletics director from 1960 to 1972. He then spent eight more years as a San José State professor before becoming an international sports facilities consultant, planner and designer.

"It's a great life," said Bronzan, now retired and living in Lincoln, near Auburn. "I had chances to leave San José State...but we had a wonderful cadre of coaches who loved to coach and teach. It was almost like a fraternity. I could hardly wait to go to work."

Bob Bronzan
...coached NFL legends
Walsh and Vermeil

Some of football's best and brightest are in Bronzan's "fraternity." Two NFL coaches with Super Bowl rings — Bill Walsh and Dick Vermeil, played for Coach Bronzan in the 1950s. In addition, Bronzan coached five assistant NFL coaches, 18 university coaches, 42 community college coaches, and 151 high school coaches. Bronzan played for the Spartans' 1939 team that was the only undefeated team and the highest scoring team in the nation. He was in the Air Force during World War II and developed the physical training program for the Air Corps. He earned his master's and doctorate from Stanford. When he took over as Spartan head coach in 1950 at age 31, he was the nation's youngest major college coach. Under his leadership, San José State took a strong stand in recruiting African American football student-athletes.

Bronzan was inducted into the San José State Sports Hall of Fame as a player and an administrator. He was awarded San José State's Tower Award in 1987.

Professor Thomas A. Tutko, a member of the psychology department and an international authority on sports psychology, used a bracket theory to explain athletic success and failure. In the elementary sense, the theory could apply to individual or to team performance. A contestant at any sport performs within a bracket bounded by both the best and the worst performance he or she is capable of reaching. On a given day, the athlete performs within such a personal bracket. The opponent possesses a bracket, too. The bracket of professional basketball star Michael Jordan at his prime, for example, was so elevated that no lesser player, even performing at peak accomplishment, could have the higher edge of his bracket approach the lower edge of Jordan's. Therefore, and without introducing other variables, Jordan would win every time — easily. The same is true for teams, only the variables are greater and more interesting.

Tutko's conceptualization, when applied to football teams such as San José State and Stanford, explained why Stanford won most often and why San José State pulled off satisfying victories, but only occasionally. Overlap took place at the top of the Spartan's brackets and the bottom of Stanford's.

Occasionally the variables of coaching, recruiting, talent and fate gathered simultaneously. Then San José State's bracket elevated, and winning seasons materialized. Avid fans could then assume that victory and success were the norm. Most fans never studied the bracket theory and allowed their hopes to rise when the team had several or even one good season.

Spartan Football Generates High-profile Alumni

MODERN SPARTAN FOOTBALL COACHES such as Darryl Rogers, Lynn Stiles, Jack Elway, Claude Gilbert, and Terry Shea compounded two decades of winning records through the 1970s and 1980s. High profile player Steve DeBerg spent two decades in the National Football League quarterbacking Kansas City, Denver, Tampa Bay, San Francisco, and Miami. He even set the endurance record by stepping from retirement and a coaching career back into action for the injury-ridden Atlanta Falcons in 1998.

Other Spartans, though less enduring over the decades, became the champions who helped to advance their professional teams to success in Super Bowls: David Diaz-Infante (Denver '98), Greg Cox (San Francisco '89 and New York '90), Sam Kennedy (San Francisco '88), and Dwayne O'Steen (Oakland '80). Players, such as Bill Walsh and Dick Vermeil, made their professional contributions as successful coaches.

Periodic victories over Stanford and Cal salved a multitude of losses in some years. In 1981, Coach Jack Elway's Spartans defeated both Stanford and Cal before capturing the Pacific Coast Athletic Association championship during a 9-win and 3-loss season. In the Stanford game, Spartan pass rushers distinguished themselves by repeatedly sacking Stanford's young quarterback, John Elway (San José State's coach's son and future Denver Broncos repeat Super Bowl champion and 1999 MVP) and by forcing five interceptions. They did this at Stanford before 67,888 fans, mostly Stanford season-ticket holders, and went home with a 28-6 victory. The following year, San José State's victory over Stanford and Elway's heralded son was closer and far more exciting.

Spartan fans cherished those memories until San José State went 10-2 in 1986, won the league and the California Bowl over Miami of Ohio. That season and the next, also 10-2, fixed the team's profile as an offensive powerhouse. Defeating Stanford and California in 1987 was just one highlight of a much larger story. Wild and blitzing defense was still a State hallmark, but Coach Claude Gilbert enjoyed better talent than his well-respected predecessor, Jack Elway. Quarterback and serious Heisman Trophy candidate Mike Perez was so good and became so strong that he roughed pass rushers who occasionally penetrated his protective pocket.

At season's end, San José State set a record of 12 players taken in the National Football League draft, arena football, and the Canadian league. Quarterback Mike Perez ended the season as the nation's leading offensive player with 3,225 passing yards. He also became the NCAA's leading offensive player with an average of 309.1 yards per game. Helpers, besides Coach Gilbert, included a constellation of receivers, runners, tacklers and blockers: Guy Liggins, Johnny Johnson, Kenny Jackson, James Saxon, Lafo Malauulu, and Greg Cox. Sergio Olivarez, smallest of the Spartans at 5-foot-8, was always there to add the extra points.

West Coast Offense brings excitement to NFL

THE MOST NOTED OF ALL San José State players to impact the sporting world was Bill Walsh. He did so as football coach and architect of victory for the San Francisco 49ers, taking over a losing team in 1979 and engineering six NFC West division championships and three Super Bowl championships (1981, 1984 and 1988) in just 10 years. He retired from coaching in 1988, the first coach in team history to reach the 100-game plateau. He was twice named NFL Coach of the Year (1981 and 1984) and earned the designation of NFL Coach of the Decade for the 1980s.

During his coaching tenure at the 49ers, Walsh also assumed management responsibilities, was named general manager in 1982 and president in 1985, helping to lay the foundation for the team's future

Bill Walsh
...led 49ers to three
Super Bowl titles

success. After stints in broadcasting and college coaching, he returned to the 49ers as vice president/general manager in 1999 to tackle salary cap problems and search for new talent. Walsh was instrumental in bringing San José State quarterback Jeff Garcia to the 49ers. In his own career with the Spartans, Walsh was an end on Coach Bob Bronzan's teams in the 1950s and was a member of the junior varsity boxing team.

Walsh's stature was unique among those San José State graduates who claimed sport as their profession. His victory record aside, Walsh's creation of the "West Coast Offense" injected a major new component into how the game of football was played. He is one of only 14 coaches elected to the NFL Hall of Fame. He also was instrumental in establishing the World League of American Football, now known as NFL Europe. A member of the San José State Sports Hall of Fame, Walsh earned his bachelor's in education in 1955 and his master's in education in 1959.

Athletics Funding Becomes a Concern

GAIL FULLERTON was the one SJSU president who devoted the greatest amount of time and energy to intercollegiate athletics, yet she was also the president who garnered the greatest public criticism related to SJSU athletics. This was due in part to her termination of Claude Gilbert, the popular football coach, after the 1989 season. Gilbert had neglected her directive to recruit freshmen as a first priority and to shift from the practice of recruiting transfer students, who were more seasoned as players but less likely to complete their education and graduate.

The few faculty who were interested and sufficiently observant watched campus discord ripen into public controversy. Coach Gilbert's attorneys subpoenaed financial records relative to football as a preparation for court action against the president and the university.

Though unknown to the general faculty who presumed themselves to be the major part of shared governance, university funds had been redirected for years from academic programs in order to top off athletics. It started when President John H. Bunzel directed Academic Vice President Hobert W. Burns to convert $25,000 from the instructional budget to the needs of football Coach Darryl Rogers. As Burns put it years later in his oral history: "That was the beginning...of what can be called creaming off money from the top of the instructional operating budget to support athletics." Thereafter, the quiet subsidy from the classrooms to the athletic fields grew regularly. Each year, the athletic program, unlike the other departments of the university (including women's

Baseball team makes College World Series debut

ACADEMIC SENATE RESOLUTION, SEPTEMBER 25, 2000:

Whereas: The SJSU Men's Baseball team, overwhelming many obstacles, finished in a first-place tie for the Western Athletic Conference, then earned an at-large berth in the 64-team NCAA playoffs in Waco, Texas; and

Whereas: The SJSU Men's Baseball Team then overpowered both Southwest Texas State and Florida in the NCAA's regionals to advance. Next, the Spartans played a best-of-three series against host Houston, with the winner advancing to the College World Series. The Spartans performed so well in this competition that they received a standing ovation from the University of Houston fans, after the Spartan's Super Regional victory over the fifth-ranked Cougars, and earning a place in the College World Series; and

Whereas: The first-ever Spartan team to play in a college world-series game fought hard against both Clemson and Louisiana-Lafayette at Rosenblatt Stadium, Omaha, cheered by a crowd estimated at 17,000 for their opening games. The team had some challenges early on which cost them the games, but settled in nicely after the third inning and showed their stuff; and

Whereas: Great credit for these achievements is due the members of the team for their skill and spirit and also to Coach Sam Piraro for his knowledgeable, sincere, and effective leadership; now therefore be it

Resolved: That the Academic Senate of SJSU, on behalf of the academic community, commends the team and Coach Piraro for their outstanding achievements in the 1999-2000 season.

sports), overspent its budget. With equal predictability, the booster organization would proclaim fundraising success. The compounding result was that the rest of the university was left suffering the deficit. The administratively awkward part was that the rest of the university was largely unaware of the matter, and successive presidents found themselves in the delicate position of living without transparency. By the time Burns was considering retirement in 1983, that original athletic department top-off of $25,000 had grown to $400,000 a year and required debits from the general university budget.

Knowingly or not, Gilbert and his attorneys, abetted by the boosters, had threatened the most supportive administration in university history. At the same time, of course, they jeopardized the academic subsidy system on which their interests were based. Creaming was not illegal or in any way fraudulent. Presidents did retain considerable authority over the internal budget. The relative secrecy within the dynamics of shared governance was the problem, and it could become serious if the faculty discovered it and the Academic Senate chose to make it a problem.

No explosion took place and an uneasy tranquility, of sorts, returned. The courts dismissed Coach Gilbert's case, and he advanced his career in professional football abroad.

Fastball defines Langston's early career

MARK LANGSTON'S BASEBALL CAREER started as quickly as his fastball. In his rookie year with the Seattle Mariners, he vied with teammate Alvin Davis for the 1984 Rookie of the Year Award, led the league in strikeouts, and set a Mariners' record with 17 wins.

Langston began honing his fastball at San José State, where he recorded 111 strikeouts in 101 innings pitched in 1980 and was named an all-conference pitcher, with a 6-2 record and a 2.49 ERA. He culminated his Spartan career in 1981 being named by the *Sporting News* as a second-team All-American.

Mark Langston
…pitched for 16
MLB seasons

The southpaw pitcher continued to mow down batters in the 1980s, leading the league in strikeouts again in 1986 and 1987. In 1987 he also set Mariners' records with 19 wins, the team's first Gold Glove, and team records in innings pitched, complete games, strikeouts and shutouts. In a now-infamous trade, the Mariners sent sure-thing Langston to the Montreal Expos in exchange for a pitcher having control problems, Randy Johnson, and two other players. The Expos didn't have Langston for long as he winged his way to the California Angels in 1990, the first of his eight seasons in Anaheim.

In addition to his fastball, Langston added a repertoire of pitches during his 16 seasons in the majors and earned seven Gold Gloves for his fielding ability. Langston was known as a workhorse, averaging 247 innings pitched in the middle of his career and remaining relatively injury-free until the latter part of his career. Langston joined the San Diego Padres for his first post-season appearance in 1998, then went to the Cleveland Indians, where he battled injuries till his retirement in 2000. In Cleveland, Langston also hosted Tribe Jam, an annual rock-n-roll fund-raiser for charity, in 1999 and 2000. The guitar-playing baseball star doubled as rock star during the Jam. Langston went on to do commentary for Fox Sports Net and manage the varsity baseball team for Lutheran High School in Orange County.

Also, the Academic Senate came to what it thought was a solution to the problem of the athletic department's habitual overspending. Representatives of the boosters, the administration, and the Academic Senate worked out a plan for the increase of booster funding and the gradual and formulated reduction of university funding for athletics to a set level.

The most substantial infusion of resources came from Alan and Phyllis Simpkins, mainstays of the university, who initiated funding and built an athletic facility adjacent to Spartan Stadium. They topped it off with the donation of expansive athletic offices immediately to the west of the stadium. Years earlier they had donated the International House and made other non-athletic gifts to the university. The Spartan Foundation, of which the Simpkins were a driving force, and its members, individually and as an organization, helped the university immeasurably over the years. Many members did so at substantial personal expense. Yet the sports enterprise continued to grow in its seemingly insatiable appetite for funds. All of these contributions considered, there simply never was enough money to run the programs.

President Robert Caret discovered this less-public side to sports history upon his arrival on campus. He responded to questions of *Spartan Daily* reporters by noting that the 1998 athletic shortfall was still approaching $400,000. Almost at the same time, alumni boosters announced that they had fully met the fundraising goals for the upcoming year.

Caminiti becomes baseball's tough man

A DOMINANT FIGURE out of Spartan baseball is Ken Caminiti, a local boy from Leigh High School in San José who arrived at San José State in 1983. Coach Gene Menges fondly recalled Caminiti's home runs, particularly two against Stanford — one from each side of the plate — a switch-hitting feat he would repeat as he built his slugging reputation in the majors.

After graduating in 1984, Caminiti played for the Houston Astros before joining the San Diego Padres. Throughout his professional career, he was a consistently strong switch hitter and a superb fielder, earning three gold gloves. But he was plagued with injuries. He became known for his toughness and his ability to play through pain, including a series of strains, tears, chronic back

Ken Caminiti
...earned baseball's 1996 MVP award

pain and even reconstructive surgery. But that pain took a high toll on Caminiti, who behind the public persona battled substance abuse in addition to the physical pain.

For Caminiti, 1996 was his hallmark year. He was named the National League's Most Valuable Player and helped the Padres to an NL West title. Despite injuring his rotator cuff in April, Caminiti came on fire after the All-Star break. That year, at age 33, he chalked up 40 homers, 130 runs batted in, and a batting average of .326. He also received two ESPY awards, one for Baseball Player of the Year and one for Baseball Play of the Year, a spectacular grab of a drive down the third base line and an unbelievable throw to first base for the out.

Caminiti led the Padres to another division title in 1998, then as a free agent returned to the Astros. He ended his career with short stints for the Texas Rangers and the Atlanta Braves before injuries finally forced his retirement.

Title IX — Women Athletes
Attack Gender Discrimination

PROGRESS DID OVERCOME TRADITION in the field of women's athletics. Bunzel and Burns removed men's and women's athletics from the physical education department and in 1971 appointed Joyce Malone to direct the women's program. Malone was a San José State graduate who taught physical education at Edison Senior High in Stockton and at Rio Vista High during the 1950s, when Sacramento River Delta towns regularly sent their graduates to San José State. She had a talent for organization and a reputation for getting on well with students and colleagues.

Malone's job, as envisioned by Burns, was "to move out of the blue bloomer stage into competitive athletics." So charged, and amid all the general financial problems confronting athletics, Malone advanced the program from genteel exercise for ladies to competitive athletics for women. Among the examples of her superior judgment was the hiring of Mark Gale as women's golf coach. Malone also understood power and was not above leveraging Burns and the university. While women's athletics were not fairly treated financially, Burns and Malone nevertheless cooperated in advancing the program within the then-assumed general welfare of the university. Throughout, Malone operated the women's program within its annual budget. More rapid change from beyond the university made this gradualist approach by Malone and Burns obsolete.

An explosive event got its start at San José State and ended with a formal consent decree of the California Superior Court between the California National Organization for Women and the entire California State University system. Just as the initiative of Harry Edwards against racism in athletics began at San José State, so did women's attack against gender discrimination. The activism took the route of litigation, however, not direct public confrontation. The ultimate resolution contained no admissions of wrongdoing by the CSU. It established a timetable and a set of equity standards for the participation levels of women athletes, facilities, funding, and contracts of coaches.

After the passage of Title IX in 1972, very little really happened in the nation's intercollegiate athletics programs that significantly changed the rate of women's participation in sports — until the 1990s. Confronted by shrinking budgets, booster tension, and rising costs at San José State, Fullerton gave her personal attention and public support to women's sports. The key to revolutionary change within university athletics, however, began with reorganization.

Mary Zimmerman was named head of the woman's program after Malone, but she did not make the finals for the combined program's athletic director's position during either of two searches in the early 1990s. Throughout, progress on gender equity was all but overwhelmed by the costs of sustaining the Division I-A football team, a problem common to universities with football and its large number of student-athletes, and by inertia. Certainly, gender equity progress did not meet the expectations of increasing athletic opportunities for women that Title IX addressed, the expectations of women for whom Zimmerman spoke.

During that period, Zimmerman's own position changed from director of women's athletics, to associate director of the combined athletic program, to unemployed. Throughout the reorganization, consolidation, budget cuts, and downsizing, the unbalanced funding for women and men student-athletes continued.

From the perspective of interested outsiders, this obvious tension came to a climax

San José State expands women's athletic opportunities

IN 1992 SAN JOSÉ STATE was randomly selected for review on gender equity in athletics by the U.S. Office of Civil Rights. As with most institutions fielding a football team, with its large squad size, San José State had more male athletes than female athletes. Unlike many institutions that addressed this issue by reducing men's sports, SJSU entered into a ground-breaking consent decree with the OCR in which it agreed to significantly expand women's opportunities.

Putting the plan into place required not just adding more women's sports, but raising more funds for women's scholarships and renovating facilities. The Spartan Foundation and many alumni helped the university raise additional program and scholarship funds as the university moved from 70 percent male participation to a proportional level of opportunities for both men and women.

Title IX of the Educational Amendments of 1972 sought to ban sex discrimination in educational programs. Its language was simple: "No person in the United States shall, on the basis of sex, be excluded from participation in, be denied the benefits of, or be subjected to discrimination under any education program or activity receiving Federal financial assistance."

Its effect was much more complex. No sooner was the law signed by President Nixon than its applicability to athletics came under scrutiny. Legislative attempts to exclude athletics failed, and in 1975 the Department of Health, Education and Welfare issued regulations, signed by President Ford, prohibiting sex discrimination in athletics. Discussion of how to apply Title IX to athletics abounded, and in 1979 HEW issued what is now called the three-prong test. But another decade would pass before the Office of Civil Rights, under the Department of Education, published its Title IX investigation manual and began examining compliance, looking for 1) athletic opportunities proportionate to the percentage of men and women in the student body, 2) program expansion to address underrepresentation, and 3) a study of whether the interests and abilities of women are being accommodated.

Soccer, a new women's sport

As San José State sought to increase opportunities for female athletes as part of its commitment to gender equity in the 1990s, new women's sports made their debut, including women's soccer, diving, cross country and water polo. It did not take long for women Spartans to make their mark in the nation's sports annals.

Just six years after the first Spartan women's soccer team competed in 1995, Spartan soccer players found themselves in the role of spoiler in the 2000 Western Athletic Conference tournament, defeating Tulsa in the championship match. After a scoreless first half, the Spartans put in three quick goals to mark their first championship and a new chapter in Spartan sports history. After semifinal losses in 1996, 1997 and 1998 and a 1999 loss in the finals, the Spartans had earned their first WAC championship in women's soccer. The Spartans lost to Stanford in the first round of the NCAA tournament but set new goals for future teams.

when the new athletic director, Dr. Thomas Brennan, tried humor to diffuse difficult moments during staff meetings. Not only did the women not laugh, they sued Brennan and Acting President J. Handel Evans via CAL-NOW for gender discrimination.

Actually, Zimmerman was off the job by then. The state's National Organization for Women took the initiative and invited Zimmerman to join them in their broader legal action against the CSU, including San José State.

The resulting out-of-court settlement with CAL-NOW and with Zimmerman included a consent decree that established San José State and the CSU at the vanguard of gender equity changes in the nation. Many thought 21 years after the establishment of Title IX as law was too long to have waited for implementation, and then at the cost of additional legal action. Women's water polo team member Suzanne Hughes researched the modern story, wrote it up for her class ("Rhetoric of San José") and published it on the web. Hughes maintained that the national collegiate record for gender equity was so pitiful that by being sued into compliance (and with subsequent goodwill) San José State captured leadership in the equity movement. During a five-year period of court-induced readjustments, San José State moved from a 70/30 ratio of men to women in sports to a 48/52 ratio that was proportional to the ratio of men and women in San José State's student body. That increase in women's opportunities put the university in full compliance with the court order.

At the end of the century, women constituted the new energy in athletics, much as they did in the Academic Senate and in the classrooms and the labs. Yet overall in athletics, one missing ingredient remained, a sufficient spectator base and the financial support that it would generate. Simultaneously, and as a tempting hope, women's games were emerging in their spectator appeal. Spartan Stadium, for example, hosted the NCAA women's soccer finals in December 1999, at which the national attendance record was established at 14,410. The two-day total was 28,416.

Women's Golf Takes NCAA by Storm

WOMEN'S GOLF was among the most successful sports at San José State. Only the women's golf teams won multiple NCAA championships. Women's golf was not a team sport at San José State until 1974 with the appointment of Betty Hicks as the first head coach. A San José State alumna in journalism and aviation, Hicks was an amateur golf champion and Associated Press Woman Athlete of the Year in 1941. By the third year of its organization, the women's team concluded its conference play undefeated. Then entered Mark Gale, the coach who elevated the quality of play by successfully recruiting nationally and abroad and then developing a remarkable ensemble of golfing talent. An extraordinary string of championships followed.

Gale was a colonel in the U.S. Air Force assigned to the university to head the Air ROTC Program. From that career he stepped over into coaching, much to the satisfaction of the university. Gale was a low-profile gentleman, strict, with a refined sense of humor. He was very proper, always direct and clear, and simply devoid of nonsense and trendy indulgences. From the start he radiated trust, trust that success validated.

During Gale's lengthy tenure as head women's golf coach, his San José State teams captured the NCAA national championship three times (1987, 1989, 1992), the first university to do so. The women's team tied twice in regulation play for the national championship (1991 and 1996) and also was runner-up twice (1995 and 1997). In 1995 the team established the Stanford University course record. Throughout the remarkable run, honors and awards abounded. Gale himself achieved National Collegiate Golf Association Hall of Fame status in 1993.

Speed City Puts SJSU on the Map

SPEED CITY located San José State track and field at the very pinnacle of college track programs — nationally and even internationally. Under the heading "San José: Speed City," for the March 1968 issue of *Track and Field News*, sportswriter Dick Drake listed 20 sprinters, all record holders, who trained in San José. Drake

Women's golf program shoots to the top

WOMEN'S GOLF was among the most successful sports San José State sponsored at any single time during the late twentieth century, winning three NCAA national championships (1987, 1989, and 1992). The Spartans also tied for the national championship in 1991 and 1996 and were runners-up in 1995 and 1997.

Many Spartan golfers have gone on to the Ladies Professional Golf Association tour. The most well-known may be Julie Inkster, who in 1999 completed her Grand Slam of the four major women's tournaments: Dinah Shore (victories from 1984-1989), LPGA Championship (1999), U.S. Open (1999), and DeMaurier Classic (1984).

Julie Inkster
...won LPGA Grand Slam in 1999

Spartan standouts include:

Diane Ammaccapane* (1989-90) one-time All-American

Dana Lofland Dormann* (BS 1988, Business Administration) three-time All-American

Tracy Hanson* (BS 1993, Human Performance) four-time All-American, Spartan Sports Hall of Fame

Pat Hurst* (1988-91) two-time All-American, Spartan Sports Hall of Fame

Julie Inkster* (1979-82) three-time All-American, Spartan Sports Hall of Fame

Nicole Materne* (BA 1996, Behavioral Science)

Janice Moodie* (BA 1997, Psychology) four-time All-American

Patty Sheehan* (1980) LPGA Hall of Fame, All-American, Spartan Sports Hall of Fame

Pernilla "Ninni" Sterner (1990-93) three-time All-American

Vibeke Stensrud (1993-96) four-time All-American

Lisa Walton (1992-94) three-time All-American

* On LPGA Tour

even suggested that the best competition that Speed City runners could encounter in 1969 would be a San José State "A" Team running against a San José State "B" Team for NCAA 440-yard relays.

Speed City became synonymous with San José State track during the 1960s and extended its aura over Santa Clara Valley. Ideal for training, San José drew the very best amateur athletes who together prepared themselves to become world champions and, after that, national collegiate champions. Many sprinters came to San José State from feeder schools, including San José City College and San José High, during the peak years surrounding the spectacular and controversial Mexico City Olympics of 1968. From those premier international games, the San José State champions brought home five track Olympic medals, more than athletes associated with any other university. That, too, was an Olympic record.

Those rarefied summer days provided Lee Evans, Tommie Smith, Ronnie Ray Smith, and John Carlos (and with them San José State) the most glorious and most controversial exposure to the sporting world. The triumphs of these young men created a vivid page in sports history, one with which San José State remained fatefully connected. Accompanying the international visibility came a profound and lingering backlash that moved the athletic achievements of Tommie Smith and John Carlos into an extended eclipse. Their action on the victory stand was what rocked the world. The San José men, American champions and the gold and bronze medalists in the world record (19.83) 200-meter dash, offered a black-gloved salute during the playing of the Star-Spangled Banner. Radio, television, press and news magazine coverage was immense and worldwide. The results were two-fold, political and athletic.

The San José State medalists had asked themselves what their contribution to the progress of the black protest movement should properly be. Most had experienced their own political awakening in San José under Robert Clark's presidency and Harry Edwards' initiative. Blessed as they were in their youth and their strength, they actually anticipated Olympic victory. They understood that their moment of victory would be their moment of power. As the Olympic Games drew closer their single uncertainty was how they should apply that moment to advance their strongest beliefs.

The San José State contingent to the Mexican Olympics had discussed and rejected Edwards' plan for a boycott of the games. That option would have wasted their great personal opportunity, African America's special opportunity, and an American opportunity as well. Their intent became the capturing and focusing of national and world attention on the plight of ordinary African Americans in their life struggles. The dramatic and provocative actions of Tommie Smith and John Carlos evolved from that decision.

San José State track and field Coach Lloyd C. "Bud" Winter watched the unwelcome demonstration from the stands in Mexico City. President Robert Clark listened to Howard Cosell's broadcast of the events. Clark felt pride in his students for accomplishing an unprecedented athletic feat. Years later, still like a protecting father, he blamed Cosell for the backlash against San José's Olympic champions. Clark felt that the sportscaster made more of the black-gloved incident than it merited. And again, like an indulgent parent, Clark fully accepted the Smith-Carlos explanations of the uplifted black glove at victory's salute. It was pro-American, not anti-American.

But the black-gloved salute from the champions' platform was immediately and immensely unpopular. President Clark did his best to ignore this reality throughout the controversy and to focus upon his students' athletic prowess. In this he remained resolute, no matter what interpretations the media attached to the champions' clearly political statement. He did his best to rise above the racial backlash that swept America and San José.

Moment in history was an affirmation for human rights

THE IMAGE OF TOMMIE SMITH AND JOHN CARLOS, gloved fists raised at the 1968 Mexico City Olympics, is an indelible moment in the nation's history. Their record-breaking performances on the track were quickly overshadowed by their social statement on the medal stand. Against the background of the Star-Spangled Banner, Smith's raised right fist represented black power in America. Carlos's gloved left fist stood for unity in black America. Together, Smith told the media, they represented an arch of unity and power. Smith also wore a black scarf around his neck representing black pride. The two wore black socks, without shoes, to represent black poverty.

Widely misperceived as a hateful act of Black Panthers, their silent statement met immediate resistance. They were suspended from the national team and banned from Olympic Village. But for Smith and Carlos, they had accomplished what they came for. San José State lecturer Harry Edwards and the Olympic Project for Human Rights had wanted black athletes to boycott the Olympics, but the athletes chose to use the 1968 Olympics as center stage. San José State's "Speed City" student-athletes earned

SJS students Tommie Smith and John Carlos took gold and bronze, with Australian Peter Norman taking the silver in the 200 meter. All three wore green buttons from the "Olympic Project for Human Rights."

multiple medals in Mexico City. And all eyes were on Smith, receiving the gold in the 200-meter dash, and Carlos, who took third, as they took advantage of the positions they had earned on the medal stand. "I stood up for the rights of all people," Smith said.

As Smith and Carlos awaited their climb to the podium, Australian Peter Norman, the silver medalist, discussed the issue of racism with Carlos and donned his own green Olympic Project for Human Rights button. Smith was praying. "I was praying underneath the bleachers. I was praying on the walk up to the victory stand and the entire time I was up there." In HBO's "Fists of Freedom" special in 1999, Smith said, "We were not antichrists. We were just human beings who saw a need to be recognized. I don't like the idea of people looking at it as negative. There was nothing but a raised fist in the air and a bowed head, acknowledging the American flag — not symbolizing a hatred for it."

President Clark's news release for the *San Jose Mercury* read in part:

I hope their gesture will be interpreted properly. They do not return home in disgrace, but as the honorable young men they are, dedicated to the cause of justice for the black people in our society.... We at San José State College are proud of the achievements of Smith and Carlos in the Olympic games.

Persisting, Clark attempted to organize a recognition banquet for the returning medal winners and the other college Olympians. He failed. The community rejected his effort to confer upon the San José champions the status of hero that victory before the gods of Olympus historically conveyed. At this point in the controversy, Clark judged the weight of backlash and decided that the best he could do was simply to be true to himself. He and his wife, Opal, attended a tribute dinner offered by the local African American community to its own sons, the Olympic champions. In his oral history years later, Clark recalled that only one other white couple attended.

Out of this fire, Speed City came of age. Coaching was already well in place with Bud Winter. Over his previous 26 years at San José State, he had developed numerous All-Americans as well as previous Olympians. What had eluded him was the NCAA championship, but his new season would be different. The Olympic medal winners and the new aspirants they attracted gathered yet again at San José State, only with greater expectations. Lee Evans, winner of two Olympic gold medals (400 meters and the 400 meter relay), captained that 1969 San José State team. Headliners included John Carlos, the bronze medalist, and Ronnie Ray Smith, who won his Olympic gold

Mexico City 1968 Spartan Olympians

John Carlos, USA, bronze medal, 200-meter dash

Lee Evans, USA, gold medal, 40- meter dash

Lee Evans, USA, gold medal, 4x400-meter relay

Ronnie Ray Smith, USA, gold medal, 4x100-meter relay

Tommie Smith, USA, gold medal, 200-meter dash

Lynn Vidali, USA, silver medal, 400-meter women's individual swim medley

Spartans who competed and coached in the 1968 Olympics:

Bert Bonanno, Mexico, men's track and field head coach

Ed Burke, USA, men's track and field (hammer thrower)

Tom Dooley, USA, men's track and field (race walker)

Tom Haine, USA, men's volleyball

George Haines, USA, men's swimming head coach

Art Lambert, USA, men's water polo head coach

Neville Myton, Jamaica, men's track and field (middle distance runner)

Chris Popanicolaou, Greece, men's track and field (pole vaulter)

medal in the same relay with Evans. The only San José State Olympic champion missing was Tommie Smith, who had completed his college eligibility.

Backing up the high-profile runners was a constellation of other outstanding competitors, particularly in the field events, which also had to produce Spartan points in order to ensure victories. Winter, in fact, had a knack for developing unnoticed potential for the more stolid field events. He had introduced football player Ed Burke, for example, to the hammer and told him in the fall that if he could throw it 160 feet

'I hardly ever thought about how fast I was going'

TOMMIE SMITH HAD TO BE FAST. In high school, "my daddy told me, 'You can compete, but if you take second place, then next Saturday you'll be out in the field picking cotton.'" Even at San José State, he said, "I hardly ever thought about how fast I was going, only that I was coming in first place."

At six-feet-five-inches tall, Smith took many honors, but none as well known as his 19.83-second world-record in the 200-meter dash at the 1968 Olympics in Mexico City. For Smith, his raised, gloved fist on the victory stand was a simple statement. "I stood up for the rights of all people."

Tommie Smith
...world records include seven individual records and five relay team records

James Richard Smith, Sr. raised a church-going family of 12 children, working in the fields in Lemoore, Calif. Not the type of father to hug his children, "he looked at me really funny when I came back from the games. He said, 'A lot of people said you did a bad thing. I don't know what you did, but you're my son, so it must have been good.'"

Smith was 23, finished with his degree in social science (and minors in military science and physical education) but needing one more semester for his teaching credential. He said in later years that he didn't realize how President Robert Clark had tried to shield him from public criticism. He did know he was scared. Smith graduated in 1969, then followed in roommate St. Saffold's footsteps — playing wide receiver for the Cincinnati Bengals for three years.

But education was his passion. As a student teacher at Central Union Elementary School in Lemoore, "some of the teachers thought I had returned to help my father scrub the floors." Smith returned to the Bay Area and taught in East Palo Alto and Milpitas before returning to San José State as a graduate student.

Smith spent six years at Oberlin College coaching basketball, track and football, teaching sports sociology and physical education, and serving as athletic director. But the notoriety of the 1968 Olympics followed him. "People viewed me as a black militant who got up on the victory stand and embarrassed America."

He returned to California, Santa Monica College, to teach sociology, health and physical education and coach the SMC Corsairs — men's track and field and cross country — for 25 years.

By the end of the century, Smith said, students hadn't heard of Tommie Smith, even though he was the only man ever to hold 11 simultaneous world and Olympic records. An HBO special, "Fists of Freedom: The Story of the 1968 Summer Games," aired in August 1999. Smith was inducted into the USA Track & Field Hall of Fame in 1978, the Bay Area Sports Hall of Fame in 1999, and the San José State Sports Hall of Fame in 1999.

by the spring, he would take him to the Mount San Antonio Relays. A Napa kid, Burke thought he had a chance to see Texas. He picked up what pointers he could from Peter F. Lester, a fellow student and future professor of meteorology at San José State. Lester had seen the hammer thrown while he was in the military. When Burke could throw the hammer 160 feet, Coach Winter welcomed him to the traveling team. To young Burke's surprise, but not to his disappointment, the spring relays were at Mount San Antonio Junior College, which was in Walnut, Calif., and not in Texas. He went anyway. "It was terrific," Burke remembered in 1998. "I got to go on an airplane." Thus began a bountiful career that included three Olympic Games (1964, 1968, and 1984) and serving as American flag bearer for the opening and closing ceremonies at Los Angeles in 1984. Winter's runners, though, were the stars who broke the records, attracted the following, and inspired the sportswriters.

Winter's 1969 champions, heavy with Olympic gold and bronze, were highly politicized. *Track and Field News* in its pre-season pick projected San José State as the NCAA winner. But insiders wondered if the team could hold together until June. All of Winter's runners did not compete in every meet. At one meet, some declined to run out of sympathy for a strike by a Black Student Union. At the next it was a boycott in recognition of Philadelphia games honoring Martin Luther King, Jr. According to Evans, Winter dealt with the athletes in a spirit of respect and understanding. En route he let Evans deal with the political dimension, and together they created the formula for victory. The Winter-Evans team won the Pacific Coast Athletic Association meet without Carlos and won the NCAA title by three points over Kansas with Carlos. The Kansas triumph and the resulting NCAA championship became Speed City's greatest collegiate victory. In 1969, Evans and his fellow champions held 9 world records, 11 U.S. records, and 7 collegiate records.

Unfortunately for John Carlos and San José State, jurisdictional disputes took place frequently in the 1960s. Conflicts between the NCAA and the sponsors of some sporting events resulted in sanctions. What games an individual athlete could participate in were not altogether clear, even to those who simply wanted to follow the rules.

During 1969-1970, Athletic Director Robert T. Bronzan approved Carlos' participation in an invitational meet, which the NCAA subsequently maintained it had not sanctioned. Bronzan's action was, he maintained, based upon advance verbal approval from the NCAA. Bronzan's college superior, Academic Vice President Bert Burns, investigated, sustained Bronzan, and began preliminary efforts at legal action against the collegiate sports authority. The NCAA placed San José State on probation and, vindictively, in the opinion of Spartan insiders, prohibited San José State from defending its national title the following spring. The latter disciplinary action was specific to San José State. Other participants in the "non-sanctioned" meet and their colleges also were placed on probation, but only the national champion, San José State, was prohibited from defending the title. The athletic establishment had struck back against Carlos and against a college that, under Robert Clark's leadership, sustained Carlos and his accomplished colleagues when they stepped up into social protest.

Bud Winter suffered a fatal heart attack in 1985, one day before induction into the National Track and Field Hall of Fame. Speed City, likewise, with Winter's death, gradually faded. The actual track, once adequate to train the world's best, needed a quarter-million dollar overhaul, new stands, and facilities. The athletic booster organization contributed $56,050 toward the overall athletic budget, which marked another deficit, an additional $200,000 that year. Track gate receipts had shrunk to $1,200.

As funding from the state continued to fall short of campus needs, actual neglect of campus facilities became the strategic alternative to free-fall among the academic offerings. A backlog of deferred maintenance accrued for painting, plumbing, wiring, cement work, roofing, carpentry, and more. In response to this financial crisis, President Gail Fullerton abolished the track and field program, along with wrestling, men's gymnastics, and field hockey. Speed City had its own core supporters, and Fullerton ended up being sued.

Her files reveal that the heat was intense. Sports fans blistered her. Even usually uninterested professors asked if she had killed the wrong sports. Track and field enjoyed high visibility. Because of the Mexican Olympics and the NCAA championship and its traumatic aftermath, no other group of San José State athletes so captured broad public attention for themselves, for their cause, and for the college. Contentiousness, of course, shared that spotlight, but San José State runners were winners that no one could ignore. Further, the entire program enjoyed inexpensive and highly successful recruiting, all of which resulted in unparalleled name recognition. Americans who read about sports knew Speed City. And Speed City meant San José State and San José. Severely pressed financially, the president followed due process and exercised her rightful authority. The university prevailed over the suits, and Speed City became history.

Judo at San José State

The story of judo at San José State is a remarkable one, one which displays a niche within a vast and complicated system of values, conflicting trends, and even distinctly diverse cultures. A club sport, and therefore not an NCAA sport, San José State judo established the national standard and over the decades continued to perform at its own elevated level of accomplishment. Judo success at the national collegiate level became a standard of San José State's competitive best — 34 championship titles in 37 national competitions by 1998. This success rested upon the simplicity of its formula. The coaching was stable, prudent, capable, resourceful, and enlightened; the sport's values were in harmony with the academic goals of the university; best of all, coordination within the program was 100 percent effective. One man, Yoshihiro Uchida, was everything, even in semi-retirement. He was coach, mentor, role model, recruiter, donor, civic leader, an all-around likeable guy.

Yosh Uchida

Young Yosh Uchida came to San José State College as a student in 1940, one year before Bud Winter joined the physical education faculty. Uchida served in the U.S. Army from 1942 to 1945 and returned to graduate with a degree in biological sciences.

Judo was his major extracurricular activity. In 1957 Yoshihiro Uchida took and passed California's clinical laboratory bioanalyst's examination, which allowed him to establish a business of medical laboratory services without the supervision of a medical doctor. Thirty-two years later he sold the privately held company for $20 million.

Throughout the intervening years, Uchida coached, recruited, employed, and introduced generations of young men and women to competitive judo, personal goal setting and actualization of their own very best — in athletics and in their personal lives. He brought 34 National Collegiate Judo Association championships to San José State and coached the U.S. judo team for the 1964 Tokyo Olympics. His best San José State player later became a U.S. Senator, Ben Nighthorse Campbell. Other notable players include Mike Swain, gold medalist world champion in 1987 and bronze medal winner at the '88 Olympics, Olympic silver medalists Bobby Berland (1984) and Kevin Asano (1988). Individual and team success sprang from those values that all sports enthusiasts advocate and San José State judo illustrated.

On the personal word of those within the judo community, Uchida brought young and untested athletes to the university — some sight unseen. In doing so, he himself accepted an obligation to those on whose word the recruitment was consummated. If the recommendation proved to have been a mistake, Uchida had to, and did, create a competitor anyway. He could not expose the judgment or betray the trust of a friend or a respected colleague within the culture of the sport. Understating his sense of obligation, Uchida would not cut the player from the team. "My job at the university," he insisted, "is to improve the student." Participating in sport was wonderful, but preparation for the competitive world was far more important. Uchida did not run study halls or clock hours at library tables. He simply let his young men, and the women later, quietly know who was responsible for what. They observed his fulfillment of his responsibilities to them and to the program, and he gave them an insight into

San José State Judo Olympians

Kevin Asano, USA, 1988 Olympic silver medal

Sandra Bacher, USA, 1992, 1996 and 2000 Olympics

Bob Berland, USA, 1984 Olympic silver medal

Ben Nighthorse Campbell, USA, 1964 Olympics

Damon Keeve, USA, 1988 and 1992 Olympics

Paul Maruyama, USA, 1964 Olympics

Keith Nakasone, USA, 1980 Olympics

Gerardo Padilla, Mexico, 1976 and 1980 Olympics

Mike Swain, USA, 1987 world champion; 1988 Olympic bronze medal; 1980 and 1984 Olympics

Amy Tong, USA, 2000 Olympics

George Uchida, USA, 1972 Olympics coach

Yosh Uchida, USA, 1964 Olympics coach

Ben Nighthorse Campbell

BS, PHYSICAL EDUCATION, 1957

Ben Nighthorse Campbell
...elected to
U.S. Senate

BEN NIGHTHORSE CAMPBELL may have called Yoshihiro Uchida *sensei* while learning lessons of life and judo at San Jose State in the 1950s. But today Campbell is a venerated leader in his own right.

His first election to the U.S. Senate in 1992 was 10 years after he began his public career with election to the Colorado General Assembly. His progression from state legislature (1983-1986) to U.S. House of Representatives (1987-92) to U.S. Senate (1993-present) has been a steady climb. Now in his second Senate term, Campbell serves on key committees including Appropriations, Energy and Natural Resources, Veterans' Affairs, as well as Indian Affairs, which he chairs, and the Helsinki Commission. A Republican, he champions fiscal and budget constraint, conservation of public lands and natural resources, and zero tolerance for illegal drug use. In the 107th Congress, he sponsored and had signed into law more bills than any other U.S. senator.

But public service is just one facet of this Renaissance man. Campbell is a member of the Council of 44 Chiefs of the Northern Cheyenne Tribe, his father's heritage. He is a renowned jewelry designer, with more than 200 awards for his work. He enjoys motorcycling on his Harley as well, a hobby he shares with his wife, Linda, their grown children.

Campbell, who earned his BS in physical education in 1957, is also an accomplished athlete. At San Jose State, he was a three-time U.S. judo champion, earning All-American honors and a gold medal at the 1963 Pan-American Games. He captained the U.S. judo team in the 1964 Olympic Games.

Most recently, his judo training came in handy in Washington when he came to the aid of a U.S. Capitol Police officer who was struggling with a violent felon. This sort of valor follows suit for this recipient of the Korean Service Medal, the Air Force Air Medal and the Watchdogs of the Treasury "Golden Bulldog" award.

his larger university and community responsibilities as well. All his student-athletes understood that steady academic progress was their first responsibility; dedication to the team followed — and very closely.

The program thrived, and in appreciation, San José State dedicated Yoshihiro Uchida Hall to its loyal and generous son, the university's most enduring athletic success story.

In 1992 a grateful university recognized Uchida with its premier Tower Award. What was history making, though, was that its presentation constituted the largest banquet ever hosted in the 135-year history of the university. To enliven the festivities, Uchida had select casks of sake flown in from Japan and served them to the overflow of admirers. Former San José Mayor Tom McEnery captured the spirit of the occasion in his tribute to his own friend and supporter. He concluded with the obvious — every university deserved a moving spirit such as Yoshihiro Uchida.

Defining Athletics' Role on Campus

THE ROLE OF ATHLETICS within the metropolitan university remained to be redefined in 1999. How it was to emerge into the new century would be among the more interesting facets of university evolution. The belief endured that sports, particularly membership in the Division I-A football program, was a valuable public identifier of the university.

Even though fewer students, fewer faculty, and fewer administrators possessed sufficient leisure time for and personal interest in intercollegiate athletics, no one could terminate such well-established programs, particularly those with influential and articulate boosters. The combination of traditional forces was powerful and particularly hard to change within the shared-governance model that San José State had adopted for policy formulation.

As the student body changed, so, too, with time would the alumni change. Those whose student life at the metropolitan university did not allow leisure and did not include participation in sports, even as spectators, graduated with an entirely different perspective from that shared by older athletic boosters. At the turn of the century who could say what they would choose to support and what they would choose to endow?

CHAPTER FIVE

Beyond Academics
SERVING THE NEEDS OF A CHANGING STUDENT BODY

T HE GREATEST change at San José State in the late twentieth century was the demography of the student body. The students, for the most part, remained the children of the valley, but Santa Clara Valley had changed to Silicon Valley — from apricots and prunes to wafers and chips, from the children of European immigrants to children of the entire world. The mix of technical, economic, social, and cultural forces that constituted the vast transformation critically impacted the demography of San José State's service area and, therefore, the demography of the university. California's historic lure, plus the magnetic attractions of Silicon Valley opportunities, regenerated and redirected the flow of immigrants. In addition, numerous Vietnamese immigrants chose the region as their permanent new residence following the conclusion of the war in Southeast Asia. The generational effects of population mobility and growth impacted all regional institutions and their infrastructures. In addition, San José displaced San Francisco as the state's third largest city.

Student Body Demographics Evolve

Spartan Daily writers Jim Broady and Marsha Green first identified a new reality: "Increasing Minorities Changing [the] Face of SJS." During the spring of 1969, well in advance of California's and America's experiment with affirmative action, the *Daily* writers initiated a three-part series on ethnic and racial changes within the student body. They reported on a survey conducted by University Ombudsman Ralph Poblano, which collected ethnic self-identification data from 12,854 students, or 59 percent of those registering for spring classes. This survey data predated the university's government-mandated effort by a dozen years.

The largest "minority" group, according to Poblano's survey, consisted of foreign students who were not differentiated by race or ethnicity, followed by a short list of American minority students: "Orientals," "Mexican-Americans," "Blacks," and "American Indians." The categories and labels of later years had yet to evolve. The survey's conclusion estimated the college's minority component to be 20 percent of the student body. Efforts to validate the findings through records of the Foreign Students Office, the Educational Opportunity Program and ethnic activists of the day sustained the conclusion.

Student writers Broady and Green concluded, "With the sudden realization of racial identity ... on-campus activity and campus organizations have blossomed at SJS." Official and legally mandated enumeration of students' ethnic affiliations began in 1981.

From the first survey of 1969 to the enrollment statistics of fall 2000, San José State's student population grew from 21,997 to 26,698, a 21.3 percent increase. An all-time enrollment record, 30,338 students, was set in 1990, with the population falling during budget cuts in the mid '90s then beginning a swell toward new enrollment heights as the century turned. During those same years, 1969 to 2000, the white majority of about 80 percent became a white minority of about 28 percent. During the period of moderate overall growth, every minority category grew, except the small American Indian/Alaskan group. The white student population plummeted from a high of close to 18,000 students to about 7,500. Only somewhat less dramatic was the significant Asian increase. In fall 1999, Asians became the largest ethnic cohort of students, and by fall 2000, they numbered nearly 8,500.

Students' selections of academic majors affected the university's organization and structure. In the 1960s, white students registered in a broad array of courses. Foreign students, the largest of the "minority" groups, were directed by their sponsoring governments toward majors in engineering and science. New curricular patterns emerged at the end of the century, such that the once powerful College of Social Sciences and College of Humanities and the Arts adjusted to fewer majors, fewer students, fewer faculty and lower budgets. White students persisted as the predominant clientele of these colleges, though in diminished numbers. Enrollments in the College of Education, despite its outreach and public recognition of the need for minority teachers in large numbers, remained overwhelmingly white. These colleges held limited appeal to students of the new majority, except for political science majors, which attracted

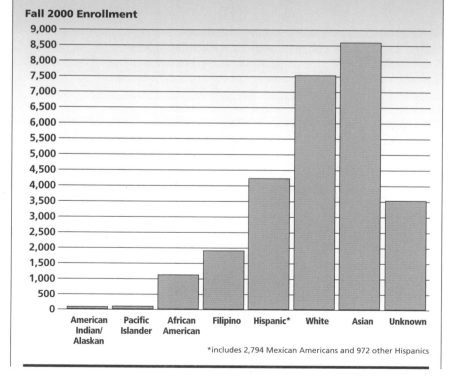

Door to higher education wide open for all

San José State achieved ethnic plurality — with no majority group — in 1991, reflecting the state's growing diversity, especially among its youth. Under the state's master plan for higher education developed in 1960, SJSU accepts high school seniors in the top third of their class. Many more students come to San José State as re-entry adults and community college transfers. Most of the university's growth has come in the Asian and Hispanic student populations. With a small percentage of African Americans in the university's service area, the number of African American students has remained relatively steady through the decades.

Fall 2000 Enrollment

*includes 2,794 Mexican Americans and 972 other Hispanics

Hispanic students, and psychology, which enjoyed a broad-based popularity. In humanities and the arts, the art and design major, heavily computerized by the 1990s, attracted minority students even out of proportion to their own large numbers. Asian and Hispanic students set the registration records, followed by significant numbers of Filipino students, then African American students. Courses in English literature and in the history of ancient civilizations contracted. Departments with growing enrollments could hire more faculty in specialized areas, but faculty within shrinking fields had to reduce or even relinquish teaching upper-division and graduate specialties as well as retool the required general education courses that served non-majors.

By the 1980s, the areas of overriding interest within the new student majority included business administration, engineering, and science — particularly mathematics and computer science. The College of Social Work began with a dedicated mission to the local Hispanic community, and Hispanic students continued to honor that mission through their selection of social work as a major. Within the College of Applied

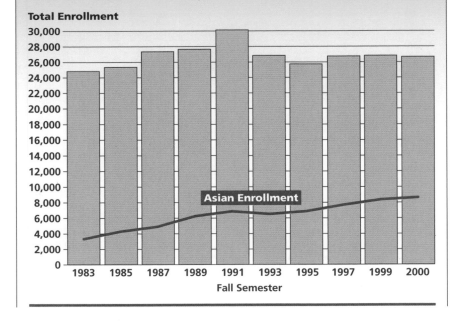

Asian students become largest ethnic group

ASIAN STUDENTS have been the campus's largest "minority" cohort since the university began keeping statistics in 1983. By 1999, Asian students made up the largest single ethnic group on campus, 31 percent of the student body. Adding the Filipino and Pacific Islander categories pushed the Pacific Rim impact to as much as 40 percent of the student body by 2000. In addition to the region's many residents of Chinese and Japanese ancestry, the Asian cohort was strongly influenced by the influx of refugees from Southeast Asia into San José in the 1980s following the Vietnam War.

Total Enrollment

Asian Enrollment

Fall Semester

Sciences and Arts, the School of Nursing enjoyed minority selection slightly above the minority portion of the university total — with strong enrollment among Asian, Filipino, Hispanic and African American students.

In 1997, the Mexican American and African American studies departments attracted only 10 and 13 majors each. Hispanic and African American students overwhelmingly opted for majors that prepared them for traditional careers in professional fields. Asian studies and women's studies, with considerably stronger enrollments, were organizationally assisted by being minor programs within the social science department and included a teacher-preparation track. Each ethnic studies program and women's studies also offered its courses to non-majors for their occasional elective selections.

The transformation of the San José State student body, and all of the institutional changes and individual adjustments that accompanied such a dramatic shift, took place within one generation, from the tenure of President Clark to President Caret. It was also a time of tight budgets and fluctuating student enrollments. Overall, San

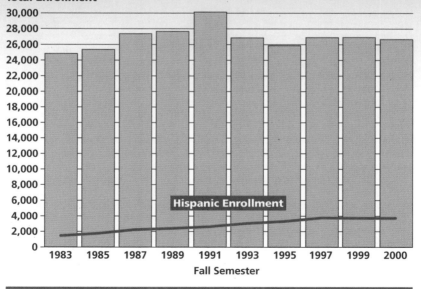

Number of Hispanic students on the rise

THE NUMBER OF HISPANIC students attending San José State has grown steadily since the university started keeping ethnic data in 1983. Measuring 14 percent of the student body in 2000, however, Hispanics may be the only ethnic group still considered "underrepresented." The 2000 census showed that Hispanics constituted 24 percent of the population in Santa Clara County. The recruitment and retention efforts begun in the 1960s under the Educational Opportunity Program retain a focus on the Latino population

Total Enrollment

Hispanic Enrollment

Fall Semester

José State did not meet all of the enrollment growth targets set with the Office of the Chancellor. Because budget support depended upon enrollment targets, low numbers affected every fiber of campus life.

Extended efforts to meet target enrollments meant that San José State had room for each person who was qualified. Under the state's master plan for higher education, state university campuses were required to admit the top third of graduating high school students. Recruitment among the valley's underserved population growth sectors helped to narrow the gap between actual and target enrollments. Special admissions increased more among non-athletes than among the recruits pursued by the coaches. Summer Bridge and the Educational Opportunity Program offered special help, academic and/or economic, for students who otherwise might not have been able to attend SJSU. The university's bottom line — the budget — demanded inclusion.

Another significant change in the student body demographics reveals a gradual

Black EOP 'hammered home' academic success

FROM DAY ONE, the focus of San José State's Black EOP program was graduation — not the Black Panther power politics that took hold at some other campuses. "Our EOP program was never captured by any group of individuals who were politically affiliated with any group that would have distracted us from our goal, which was to graduate," said Steven Millner, among the first 50 students in an experimental program in the spring of 1968. "We were inculcated with the idea that if we were not successful, the program would be jeopardized." Early leaders were committed "to helping the black students who came through to make the transition out of the ghetto and into the middle class.

"Right after Dr. King had been assassinated, America had begun to open doors, and some of those doors were here at San José State," Millner recalled. Bob Witte, psychology professor, was named interim director and started the Educational Opportunity Program, modeling it after UC Berkeley. Tim Knowles was hired as the first director in June 1968 and recruited 200 students for summer orientation and the official EOP kickoff in fall 1968. "We actually went out and drummed up business" from the Bay Area and Los Angeles, Knowles said. Some EOP students also served as staff through the work-study program.

"I went to the high schools and advised the seniors about enrolling in college," said Laverne (Washington) Richards, who earned her BA in political science in 1969 with an emphasis on international relations and eventually became a school principal in Houston. "I told them about the growing population of black students as well as the benefits of getting their education and the strong support that they would get" at San José State. That support included tutoring, financial aid, and special "block" classes in English, reading, and study skills.

"Our initial goal was to graduate 100 percent of the students," said Knowles, who earned his BA in secondary education and physical education with a minor in math in 1967, followed by his teaching credential in 1968. Knowles continued working in higher education, including recruiting for Central State University in Ohio. "We always wanted to show San José and the state of California that African American students could compete if they were selected properly, had a strong support system and were kept motivated. We hammered home academic success, retention and graduation."

increase in the ratio of female to male students. Throughout the early twentieth century, students had been mostly female and teaching-oriented. The GI Bill, which provided free college education to World War II veterans, changed this ratio, and with the emergence of the comprehensive university came a male majority. Female students constituted just 43 percent of the student body in 1972. However, the percentage of women students increased steadily through the decade and edged ahead to 50.1 percent in the spring of 1980. Women constituted 52 percent of the enrollment by 1990 and 54 percent by 2000. University records also show that women earned higher grades. The combined undergraduate grade point average for the fall of 1972 was a near high at 2.75. While that combined GPA fell to a near low of 2.69 in 1996, that GPA consisted of a men's average of 2.57 and a women's average of 2.81. Undergraduate men earned C+ grades; women earned B- grades.

Another change was the length of time to graduate. By the 1980s, receiving a degree

Chicano EOP program draws from local community

SAN JOSÉ STATE'S CHICANO EOP program traces its roots to a self-help approach called Project LEAP (Latino Education Advancement Program), developed by Arturo Cabrera in the mid-1960s. Cabrera, who taught in San José State's School of Education, wrote a grant to help bring a group of San José City College students, many of them military veterans, to San José State. The LEAP program included outreach and mentoring.

In 1969 the state legislature passed the State College Educational Opportunity Program, and San José State took advantage of the state funding and formed the Chicano EOP, with communications studies professor Elihu Carranza, an ex-Navy pilot, as its first director.

But state funding brought its own issues, including funding competition in 1970-71 between the university's Black EOP and Brown EOP, both of which were funded for 400 new students a year. While the university's black student activists had gained the ear of President Clark and taken advantage of a nationwide civil rights movement, Hispanic students were protesting farm workers' conditions but "had not risen to that (national) level of social consciousness," said Jose Carrasco, who graduated from San José State and began a teaching career at San José Unified School District.

One advantage the Chicano EOP had was widespread community support, organized as the Committee on Mexican American Affairs. The Chicano group's message was simple. "We said SJS has a service area that's not being served," said Carrasco, who by 1968 was back at San José State, teaching in the humanities department for three years before joining the Mexican American studies program, the nation's first such graduate program, begun in 1968 at San José State.

President Robert Clark sent the discussion of which group deserved how much funding to the Academic Senate, which recommended retaining the 50/50 split. The Chicano EOP filed a federal complaint with the Office of Civil Rights as the tug of war over funding, and serving more students, continued. The OCR's resolution of the problem ended the funding divisions by recommending that the two programs be merged into one in 1974. Gabe Reyes, director of the Chicano EOP since 1972, became the director of the combined program. St. Saffold, who had been directing the Black EOP, was named associate dean of students for special programs.

from any university following four years of attendance had become a thing of the past for most students in California. Alumni remained unaware of the new reality until their children registered for fifth and sixth years — usually in non-continuous semesters.

International students seek opportunities in America

SINCE BEING AUTHORIZED to accept international students in the 1950s, San José State served students from more than 100 countries. For the students, San José State was an opportunity for economic and social advancement. For San José State, the students were a cultural bridge to the wider world. In addition, international students paid the full costs of their education since they were not California residents; their non-resident tuition contributed to the university's bottom line. The International Program also included a Study Abroad program for U.S. students.

In the 1970s, the largest group of students on visas were from Iran. Then came a wave of students, especially graduate students, from Taiwan and other Asian nations, including Japan, India and Hong Kong. Sometimes the politics determined not just students' ability to get to the United States, but also their need to stay. "I counseled a lot of Chinese students who had suffered during the cultural revolution in the late 1970s," said Louie Barozzi (SJSU, BA Sociology, '59; MS Sociology, '64), who worked with international students for two decades before retiring in 1998. But as Chinese students poured into the United States in the 1980s, the Tiananmen Square massacre in 1989 created an immediate crisis. "Students in the U.S. were given permission to stay on afterwards, and it was easier for them to get green cards [to work]. They were very motivated to stay here," Barozzi said.

When the International Program began in the 1950s, with English professor Marion Richards as its adviser, the focus was on helping international students adapt to English instruction and American culture. The addition of the International House in 1978 created an opportunity for improved cultural exchange and integration. "The International House provided a place where students could live, but more importantly it provided a very rich living situation," said Barozzi. Designed to accommodate 76 students, a co-ed mix of international and American students, the house was named after alumna Phyllis Forward Simpkins, who donated funds to upgrade the house and hours of personal involvement in the program. In the 1990s, Simpkins and her husband donated the house to the university.

While the number of students from abroad on student visas averaged more than 1,000 a year, by the 1980s another phenomenon increased the number of foreign-born students at San José State to 20 percent of the student body. Immigrants, many of them refugees from Southeast Asia, flowed into northern California. San José State provided "a vehicle for them to integrate economically and socially into the society," Barozzi said. With its Pacific Rim location, San José State continued to attract many students of Asian ancestry, and by the turn of the century they constituted its largest ethnic cohort and some of its most successful alumni.

Reasons for not graduating "on time" multiplied: changing majors; stepping out for a semester or more, followed by the discovery of revised curricular requirements upon reentry; working fulltime; career relocation, and academic probation. Some majors extended the time to graduation simply because their department courses and general education requirements could not be squeezed into eight semesters. This became particularly true for mobile students of the 1990s, fewer and fewer of whom began and finished university degrees at the same institution.

Rising Costs of a University Education

FROM THE VANTAGE POINT of students and their parents, the cost of a San José State education and who paid for it changed dramatically from the 1960s to the end of the twentieth century. When President Clark left office in 1969, San José State's annual fees remained at about $200. Living in campus residence halls and taking meals at the Dining Commons came to an even $1,000 per year. Books and supplies added about $250 to this annual total. A student on a modest budget could manage a year at college for about $1,450. This was possible because actual costs of a public education were subsidized; in the place of tuition, the state of California, via the general fund, paid the actual costs of running the institution.

Because "tuition" had never been authorized, only the student "fees" increased. At the end of the century, the university's web site listed San José State fees at "just over $2,000 for the academic year." Books, supplies, and on-campus housing and meals were an additional $6,000. Theoretically, the same student on an equally modest budget could manage a year at the university for about $8,000.

Though fees had risen from $200 to $2,000 — 1,000 percent — the fee was still only $2,000 at the end of the century. Other expenses rose from $1,250 to $6,000 — 480 percent. Even considering adjustments for inflation, the increase was sizable. No longer did summer jobs and/or part-time work meet a full year's university expenses. Also, students tended to be older, more independent, and more fully responsible for their own support. For those students who otherwise could attend fulltime, more of them had to reduce the number of units taken and increase their hours of employment, which increased the number of semesters to graduation. The other option (sometimes both were pursued at the same time) was obtaining financial aid. Nearly 40 percent of the student body received some form of aid by century's end, with the result that degrees often meant debt obligations. Fifteen thousand dollars of debt was not extraordinary for bachelor's degree recipients, even when they spent their first years at community colleges.

The Emergence of Student Financial Aid

San José State's story of financial aid started in 1964 with a now-unknown amount of funding. Permanent record keeping commenced with annual reports to the federal government two years later. From then until 1998 the number of awards grew from slightly more than 3,500 to about 11,000. Funding grew from less than $5 million to well over $50 million per year. This funding became increasingly important as an education at California's state colleges and universities ceased being virtually free for residents of the state.

Financial aid was not part of public higher education until Congress, reacting to the Soviet's successful satellite launching in 1957, passed the National Defense Education Act of 1958 and the Student Loan Program. San José State immediately applied for funding. Vice President William J. Dusel took the initiative, and Dean of Students Stanley C. Benz and his assistant Robert Baron administered the embryonic program. Credit for the long-term success and thoroughly positive nature of the campus program goes to its first administrator, Donald R. Ryan.

Donald R. Ryan
...from student body president to 38-year career at SJSU

Ryan's time and position at San José State neatly paralleled the development of modern financial aid. He was student body president in 1957-58, taught in the public schools for a year, and began his 38-year professional career at State in 1959. First, he managed student loans and scholarships. Young Ryan grew with the program, founded the California professional organization of Financial Aid Administrators, and maintained close liaison with the national association in Washington, DC.

In 1964, Congress passed the Economic Opportunity Act as part of President Lyndon Johnson's War on Poverty. This included a work-study program whereby students could take jobs to help non-profit agencies. Funding was 75 percent from the federal government and 25 percent from the local nonprofit agencies being served. Community agencies had already responded favorably to Dusel's preliminary overtures, which put San José State one step ahead in the process when funding procedures were announced. That there were relatively few immediate applications nationally also contributed to San José State's initial full funding of $1 million. From the onset, under Ryan's attentive management, the college met the mandated requirement to demonstrate the administrative capability to manage such federally funded programs. In response to the maturing federal requirements, the CSU Chancellor's Office in 1965 established separate financial aid offices on each campus. Ryan became San José State's first director of financial aid.

Finding New Funding Sources

During the last quarter of the century, when a shift in public policy moved a significant portion of the costs of higher education from the general taxpayers to the recipients of the education, the university intervened and shared in the newly distributed burden. By 1998, the university had created and contributed an increase of 18 percent ($58 million) to its own annual budget. The major university-level offices involved included the University Foundation's Sponsored Programs, University Advancement, and Continuing Education. Income sources included governmental contracts, industry, foundations, educational clients, students, alumni, and parents. These funding sources improved the quality of the educational and campus experience in numerous ways, from scholarships and funding for faculty research to improved facilities and programs.

Entering the twenty-first century, San José State University was no longer fully state supported, but it was hardly self-supporting, either. State-assisted was, perhaps, close to the new reality. Student fees and university enterprise grew considerably following the "steady state" days of Governor Jerry Brown's administrations of the late 1970s and early 1980s. The enhanced state tax flow brought on by the California technology boom of the 1990s reduced the anxiety of university budget managers. The quality of California education became the number-one political issue in the 1998 election, resulting in voter approval of a $9 billion bond issue for schools and universities. In 1999, outgoing Governor Pete Wilson drafted a final budget with a five percent ($78 a year) reduction in 1999-00 student fees. At century's end, during the longest period of sustained prosperity in recent California history, the likelihood of a return to full state funding was remote.

Career Center

GROWTH AND EXPANSION OF SERVICES characterized the Career Center's placement function from the mid-1960s to the year 2000. That growth included new functions, services, and technologies as well as expanded numbers of students and employers served. Services expanded to include background preparation of students for job searches and for job interviews.

First, the Career Center refined its prep tasks for individual students through the use of videos, computers, and live exploration sessions with industry and business professionals. Second, the center expanded those successful techniques and applied them to the masses of career-minded students who flooded its offices and populated its hosted events. Third, an inevitable reversal of services took place; the huge growth in the numbers of local employers, most functioning in global markets, developed insatiable personnel needs. While serving the student jobseekers, the center reached out and served employers who regularly turned to San José State for volume and quality additions to their work forces. Over the decades, former San José State students recruited for Silicon Valley, national, and international companies. Returning to campus, these successful alumni displayed their fond affiliation by wearing Spartan blue lapel ribbons, often a welcome sight for first-time interviewees.

Much of the Career Center's record of growth and development rested upon the office's core staff. Key players provided stability, adaptability, and the astuteness to sustain innovation, all of which compelled the center's success through three decades. Preceded by Dr. Edward W. Clements and Jerry Brody, Cheryl Allmen-Vinnedge rose to the position of director from within the unit. Skilled at interacting with the deans who served on the center's board, she partnered with colleges and academic departments that wished to team with the center's ongoing success.

Assistant Director June Lim-Cullen, along with a team of counselors, had spent sixteen years advancing student and alumni careers by the end of the century, including preparation of students for successful interviews. Lim-Cullen changed the office from the basic coordination of qualified students and potential employers to a more comprehensive approach, seeing to it that San José State students promoted themselves well and actually received more job offers.

As the number of student applicants exploded and high tech employers helped standardize their side of the search process, Lim-Cullen linked the Career Center's placement challenges to the university's curricular reform. Courses that satisfied a new upper division writing requirement for all university majors allowed for an optional unit on resume writing. Professors of a more scholarly inclination who recognized practical reality found it easy to accept Lim-Cullen's quiet offer to conduct the sessions on resume creation. Lim-Cullen also introduced younger students to internships, volunteerism, summer jobs, and other building blocks for strong resumes and desirable career positions upon graduation. Lim-Cullen functioned with a team of center counselors who also educated the students on appropriate job search strategies along relevant career paths. All this was, of course, directly relevant to the economy of Silicon Valley and to the university's expanding metropolitan role.

Career Counselor Margaret Wilkes held the office record for length of service, service whose quality improved with the passing of the century and the expanding of services. Wilkes entered the Career Center in 1968, seeking advice about what to do

Business, engineering majors fuel Silicon Valley growth

IN THE 1980s and 1990s, students flooded the colleges of business and engineering, leaving disciplines in social sciences and applied sciences for careers in higher-paying fields. That career-building trend continued in the 1990s, with the colleges of engineering and science producing more and more graduates who fueled the Silicon Valley work force. The School of Library and Information Science, with its emphasis on technology, also grew in the 1990s. Many students continued to choose careers that support the region's infrastructure, services and education.

Majors by College	1977	1987	% change, 1977-1987	1997	% change 1977-1997
Applied Sciences & Arts	5,530	4,825	-13	4,078	-26
Business	4,650	6,004	29	4,722	2
Education	1,932	1,668	-14	2,422	25
Engineering	2,044	2,588	27	4,313	111
Humanities & the Arts	3,933	3,709	-6	3,481	-11
Library & Information Science	184	206	12	279	52
Science	2,428	2,604	7	2,882	19
Social Sciences	3,535	2,427	-31	2,815	-20
Social Work	474	342	-28	556	17
Other	3,599	3,176	-12	1,349	-63
Total	28,309	25,427		27,549	

with her degree in business administration, and she never left. As an energetic young employee, she worked on a new idea. The staff called it a "Job Fair," and she helped organize all 12 participating employers who shared the entire Student Union ballroom for the first event in 1971. By 1998 Wilkes, called the "Queen of the Job Fair" by her colleagues, had grown the event out of the ballroom and overtaxed the Event Center facilities, outdoor patios included. For her Career *Expo '98*, her 28th job fair, Wilkes gathered 180 employers to meet, talk, and recruit among 6,000 students who were approaching graduation and seeking professional positions. The real crisis for Wilkes and Allmen-Vinnedge was *Expo '99*. The Career Center's premier event had outgrown all campus facilities and, as the *Spartan Daily* observed, it continued to attract more students than rock concerts. Career Planning and Placement expanded

Graduates boost region's economy

S AN JOSÉ STATE awarded 5,492 degrees in 2000-01, making a huge impact on the region's educated work force. The large number of business and engineering degrees awarded continues to reinforce SJSU's image as the engine that drives Silicon Valley. The breadth of degrees offered also provides the region's professional infrastructure.

Top 20 degrees

Degree	Earned in 2000-01
Management Information Systems	369
Accounting & Finance	367
Mathematics & Computer Science	259
Education Administration & Leadership	258
Business graduate program	252
Organization & Management	249
Art & Design	226
Electrical Engineering	226
Library & Information Science	211
Child & Adolescent Development	172
Psychology	172
Marketing	168
Journalism & Mass Communications	157
Social Work	151
Humanities	146
Computer Engineering	144
Administration of Justice	141
Biological Sciences	111
Nursing	101
Mechanical Engineering	87

Earned in 2000-01

Expo '99 to two days, which allowed students to pursue internships, summer positions, and cooperative education opportunities.

Wilkes understood those repeat employers who made the job fairs so successful. They came from just about everywhere: Cisco Systems, Adobe Systems, IBM, Apple Computer, Amdahl, Hewlett-Packard, General Electric, Genentech, and Lockheed Martin as well as from the FBI, CIA, California Highway Patrol, KGO-TV, Kaiser Permanente, Coca-Cola, Disneyland, United Parcel Service, Visa International, and many more. Even San José State recruited at San José State. Wilkes' observed that, after 30 years of annual planning for the event, she had learned that corporate personnel officers liked to see a crowd, and the bigger it was, the better they liked it. For her part, Wilkes delivered the crowd — fresh, well-motivated, and well-qualified career aspirants, the very ones Lim-Cullen and the Career Center team had readied to work the room.

Disability Resource Center

PERSONALIZED AND EXPANDING service to students, staff, and faculty was the hallmark of the Disability Resource Center's 25th annual report in 1998. Over those two and a half decades, the DRC's client base grew from 64 students to more than 1,000. The campus program began as a pilot effort of California State University to address the needs of students with disabilities. It was an enlightened commencement, which preceded U.S. Congressional action and the nationwide public protests by the disabled to advance into law the long-pending and stalled national Rehabilitation Act of 1973. Mary Rogers, the first program "Enabler," worked with campus planners to remove the physical barriers that were impediments to those with mobility disabilities. As the years advanced, the portion of the university community with apparent mobility limitations remained substantial, while those with much less apparent learning disabilities greatly increased. By the fall of 1997, 56 percent of the Enabler program's students were in the learning disabled category. This constituted perceptual and/or cognitive problems that impacted learning. Those with mobility and visual impairments, and thus more immediately apparent within the daily life of the campus, were but 17 percent and 3 percent. The deaf and hard of hearing constituted 3 percent.

Martin B. Schulter became director in 1982 and immediately became a familiar sight traveling by his own wheelchair, usually at high speed, from meeting to meeting. Schulter extended services in coordination with the academic and business management areas of the university. All the while he was attentive to disabilities legislation, to CSU and campus policies, to the emerging professional understanding of disabilities, and to new strategies and technologies for addressing the problems.

The Disability Resource Center offered voice-activated computers, optical recognition scanners, a Braille printer, and access to the internet. The new technology built upon the previously acquired Kurzweil Reading Machine and earlier adaptive computers for the blind and physically impaired. Through these technologies, access to printed material and a sense of independence became possible for students for the first time. With more than 120 service providers each semester, the center significantly increased its paid note takers, readers, and service in the area of test facilitation.

Peter Ueberroth

BS, BUSINESS, 1959

A S A WORLD-RENOWNED ENTREPRENEUR who has led others to individual and group success, Peter Ueberroth remains a humanitarian who designs and implements change in the communities he serves. After making a try for the Olympics in 1956 in water polo, he graduated from San José State University in 1959. Ueberroth founded First Travel Corp., grew it into the second largest travel entity in North America, then sold it in 1980. Bursting back onto the Olympic scene in 1984, Ueberroth orchestrated one of the most successful volunteer efforts in history with the Los Angeles games. He launched a scholarship program for young athletes, the Olympic youth scholarship awards. He served as Major League Baseball's sixth commissioner, authored the best-selling *Made In America*, and received such accolades as *Time* magazine's 1984 Man of the Year and the International Olympic Committee's Olympic Order-Gold.

He has served on the boards of directors for Bank of America Corp., the Coca-Cola Co. and Hilton Hotels. As one of America's most enduring, trusted, and accessible business leaders, his basic message has always been clear — nothing can stop a committed group of people from making a difference. He truly believed there is no greater reward than doing well and doing good for others. Ueberroth pursued his individual path with determination and curiosity. Once describing himself as a contrarian, he offered this self-proclaimed definition: "One who is willing to consider alternatives to consensus belief."

On Campus: Lettered in water polo after attending SJSU on an athletic scholarship.

The guiding principle of the program was to provide accommodations to students who had documented their disabilities, without fundamentally altering the nature of their academic programs. Providing sign language interpreters and note takers to those who were deaf, extra test time and a facilitator for the dyslexic, and instruction and practice on customized computers for all disabled students far outstripped the need for elevators, ramps, and dry and safe entrance ways on stormy days. The growing program sophistication plus faculty education and cooperation made possible extensive services in the category of learning disabilities. The end result was that sensitive attention, even within what could be a large and impersonal metropolitan university, was given to the educational strivings of those with serious disabilities.

Continuing Education

S AN JOSÉ STATE'S 1857 beginning was due to a simple, practical need. San Francisco's post-Gold Rush populace was distinctly unhappy with the availability and the quality of its children's elementary schoolteachers. Prompted by the Board of

Education, George W. Minns implemented his teacher training night school, the first continuing education program.

Minns' school terms, three months each, consisted of modules within which he and his staff taught the teachers every Monday evening the specific subjects the teachers were already employed to be teaching during the day in the public schools. Unlike the motivation of late twentieth century teachers who voluntarily pursued continuing education for self-improvement and salary increments, Minns' teacher-students attended under penalty of being fired from their day jobs.

When Robert Clark assumed the presidency in 1964, two imperatives of the university's extension programs were to serve an adult public and to stay alive as a self-supporting enterprise. The office's strong line of modern administrators not only preserved and advanced the outreach function to adult learners, in time it created an income flow that attracted the attention of other divisions of the university, the Chancellor's Office, and the California State Department of Finance.

The highly regarded and personable Dean Joe H. West created and advanced the successful management of educational services and summer sessions. Thereafter, Dr. Leo P. Kibby, as dean of educational services, reorganized the operation and combined summer session and extension activities into a single administrative unit. Heavy commitment remained focused upon regional teachers and their continuing needs as the educators of the extraordinarily large and demanding generation of baby boomers.

When Dr. Ralph C. Bohn became dean in 1970, the office was named Continuing

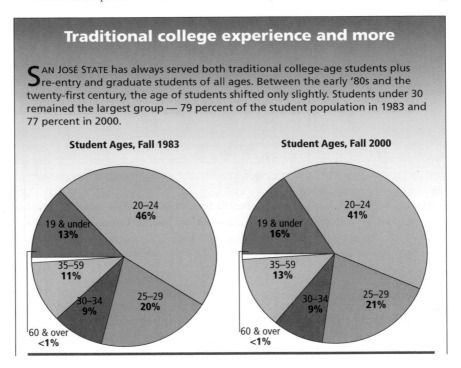

Traditional college experience and more

SAN JOSÉ STATE has always served both traditional college-age students plus re-entry and graduate students of all ages. Between the early '80s and the twenty-first century, the age of students shifted only slightly. Students under 30 remained the largest group — 79 percent of the student population in 1983 and 77 percent in 2000.

Student Ages, Fall 1983

20–24
46%

19 & under
13%

35–59
11%

30–34
9%

25–29
20%

60 & over
<1%

Student Ages, Fall 2000

20–24
41%

19 & under
16%

35–59
13%

30–34
9%

25–29
21%

60 & over
<1%

Education. Bohn hired the first fulltime marketing director for continuing education within the state system. The needs of teachers gradually slackened as local districts fulfilled their obligations to the baby-boom generation, closed schools, and ceased hiring significant numbers of new teachers. Shrinkage in the teacher market coincided with strong growth in other professional areas, which also required state licensing. In 1971, 43 state and professional licensing agencies required an estimated two million Californians to undergo extended education in order to maintain licenses. In time, the requirement extended from nurses and real estate agents to building contractors.

The emergence of Silicon Valley and its accompanying insatiable demand for education at all levels and in so many fields created a vast new market for adult education. Competing universities established programs or extended existing ones. Rivals even advertised in the *Spartan Daily* for student customers. Likewise, new education-for-profit enterprises arrived and claimed a share of the career-oriented adults who were struggling for promotions, for better jobs, and for changes of professional fields.

En route to successful participation amid such competition, San José State's Continuing Education Office became targeted as the goose with the golden eggs. In one swoop the State Department of Finance attempted to appropriate 50 percent of the revenue generated by one system-wide program, Open University, which allowed non-matriculated students to take university classes in which seats were available. During California's difficult budget years, the income from Open University had been going to the academic departments in which the courses were taken. The proposal of the Department of Finance was to siphon off half of the income. Continuing Education's statewide leadership won this battle, but still lost the war. Finance left the Open University funds in place, but the state adjusted the CSU budget downward, supposedly for a five-year period during which the reduction would shrink and then conclude, but by century's end the itemized reduction persisted.

During the interim leadership of Dean Paul Bradley (1992-96), a reformed revenue allocation system directed all surpluses from campus faculty-taught programs (summer, winter, Open University) to the academic departments, once all other charges had been paid. Payback charges continued to be levied by the state of California, the CSU Chancellor's Office, infrastructure elements of San José State itself, and the faculty and Continuing Education salaries. The operation went beyond being self-supporting. Continuing Education became a major contributor to the entrepreneurial sector of the university.

Continuing Education marketed its offerings to the point that they outgrew available space on campus, at community centers and local schools. The first off-campus Professional Development Center (3,000 square feet) opened in 1990 only to be superseded by 15,000 square feet four years later. This center was closed, and service continued at a Professional Development facility of 13,400 square feet, which opened in 1999.

Through summer, winter, and special sessions, career development stood out among the updated educational offerings for the adult community. Curriculum included both the pioneering and the long-popular programs that had established San José State as a leader in career development planning, including supervision and management, program and project management, construction specialties, purchasing

Carl Cookson

BS, BUSINESS ADMINISTRATION, 1957

CARL COOKSON began his distinguished career in the title business more than 40 years ago, after finishing a degree in business administration at San José State University. Cookson began his career at Valley Title Company, then moved on ten years later to start First American Guaranty Title. From there he purchased half of Santa Clara Title before it sold to the Alliance Title company. In short, he used his degree well and took decisive action, which led to his becoming a leader in the real estate business.

Today, Cookson's major activity is community service, and his interests are as wide and varied as his professional focus was targeted. Over many years, his numerous leadership duties have included service as president of the San José Symphony and Children's Discovery Museum and as chairman of the board for the San Jose Chamber of Commerce. In addition, he serves on the boards of organizations that represent his interests and the interests of California residents, including the San José State University Center for Beethoven Studies, the San Jose Chamber Political Action Committee, the National Conference of Christians and Jews, and Cupertino National Bank.

His many community awards include the prestigious Distinguished Alumnus Award from the College of Business, 1998. Cookson's professional life and community service reflect his passion for supporting the needs of a diverse community in all areas: the arts, healthcare, the welfare of children, aesthetic improvement, fund raising, and building partnerships among citizens.

On Campus: Added to his collection of frogs and clowns.

---

management, human resources, technical writing and communication, marketing communications, meeting planning, nonprofit management, and telecommunications/ network technologies. The 1999 academic year saw the start of more technology programs, including the first e-commerce management certificate program in the world. Other technology programs included client/server technology, internet, systems engineering, web developement, Linux, NetObject Fusion, ColdFusion, Perl, UNIX system administration and other computer programming and database programs.

University Foundation

SAN JOSÉ STATE TEACHERS COLLEGE initiated a non-profit entity, the San José State College Corporation, in 1932. The purpose was to be able to transact business that supported the larger educational mission of the college, but which state bureaucratic rules or organization simply did not facilitate or allow in the college's capacity as an agent of the state. The San José State College Corporation's first major project was the construction of the original football stadium.

The corporation's second large enterprise of the Depression was its reacquisition of the corner property at Fourth and San Fernando streets from the city of San José, which had constructed its Carnegie Library there in 1902.

In 1961 a revived corporation was renamed the San José State College Foundation, its purpose being to advance the interests of the college in an agreed-upon manner and in a way beyond its limitations as an agency of the state. In 1975, in keeping with the institutional name change, it became the San José State University Foundation. Scholarly, scientific, technological, and applied research conducted by a faculty built upon President John T. Wahlquist's upgraded standards could hardly function without the modern foundation. The enabling legislation, policy considerations, and regulations were far less restrictive for the foundation than those governing the university. The foundation enjoyed greater fiscal flexibility and ease in contracting. In the areas of sponsored research, property and equipment acquisition, project personnel, and sub-contracting, the administrative burdens confronting university managers were negotiated more easily via the separate incorporation of the foundation. Consistent with the role of other major American university foundations, the San José State foundation remained an efficient instrument with which to advance the university's educational mission and its general wellbeing.

Of the four basic sources of funding for San José State University in 1998, the foundation's sponsored programs ranked second by contributing 10 percent ($32.2 million in cash) to the total. The first was the state of California general fund, 82 percent ($260.6 million). The third, following the foundation and also growing, were private contributions at 4 percent ($13.7 million). University Continuing Education was fourth at 3 percent ($10.6 million). Both the foundation and Continuing Education met their own overhead costs.

Remarkably, the foundation facilitated academic research in the face of the California Master Plan for Higher Education, which officially assigned the research function to the University of California. Clearly, the faculty who engaged in research and who involved their students in that same research followed the promptings of scholarship and the intellectual life. Additionally, the resulting, indirect revenues became important resources in the ongoing quest for enhanced external funding.

University Advancement

IN ITS MOST LIMITED AND DIRECT FORM, University Advancement means fundraising. Robert L. Caret recognized the need for an expanded, more effective fundraising office as early as the interviewing stage before his appointment as the twenty-third president of San José State University. In due time, during his second academic year in 1995-96, Caret elevated the advancement function to vice-presidential level and committed his administration to the expansion and the professionalization of that division. The predominant reason for this quiet decisiveness was the obvious widening of the disparity between the modern educational needs of the university and the level of California state funding. San José State, like her sister campuses in the CSU system, was no longer fully funded by the state General Fund. Professional self-help

Leigh Weimers

BA, JOURNALISM, 1958

L EIGH WEIMERS is a popular, widely read columnist for the *San Jose Mercury News* who began his journalism career by writing for the local weekly paper, the *Napa Journal*, for a mere 10 cents an inch. When he was only 18 years old, he joined the *Napa Register* as the youngest sports editor of a daily newspaper in California. Graduating from SJSU in 1958, he signed on with the *San Jose Mercury News*. Nine months later, he was drafted into the U.S. Army. When he returned, he continued a professional journalism career that would span more than 40 years, writing columns for the *Mercury* for 37 of those years. In 1993 he published *Leigh Weimers' Guide Book to Silicon Valley*, a companion for any traveler who wants to understand the history, sites, and companies of the region. Involved in the local community, Weimers served on the boards of directors of the SJSU Alumni Association, the Centre for Living with Dying, and the Redwood Mutual Water Co. He is also a member of the Rotary Club of San Jose and Sigma Chi Fraternity. Weimers believes he has the best job at the newspaper. He delights in the creativity, the daily changes in the way business is conducted, and the exciting and talented people who make it work. Speaking about Silicon Valley, he said, "It's been as earth-shaking as the developments in the Renaissance. So being here and writing a small portion of the history, day by day, has been the reward for me."

On Campus: Joined the staff of the *Spartan Daily,* serving as editor. Graduated, then several years later returned to campus to attend Homecoming and met his future wife, student Geri Stone (BS, marketing, '62).

became the most attractive alternative to long-term erosion of the physical and academic structure of the university.

The university's first development officer, Robert Ringe, began a fundraising effort in 1985. Complicating and limiting his efforts were the relationship of the Alumni Association to his own office and the size of his own staff. At that time, each dean was to develop and manage a decentralized Alumni Association. Each dean held a non-profit organization and was required by the Internal Revenue Service to report annually. The flaw in the system was that many deans did not consider alumni affairs to be their job. They were academic administrators, not alumni administrators.

In the early 1980s Alumni Association President Gary Olympia, a local attorney, devised a decentralized scheme to provide graduates easier identification with their schools and majors. In this plan, which enhanced the total membership and support to the university, alumni joined a university-wide Alumni Association. They also became members of college-specific alumni chapters, designed to provide more interaction with faculty and discipline-related events.

Daniel Buerger, an English professor who was to become the administrative assistant to successive presidents, restructured the advancement office on a university relations model: public affairs, alumni, and development. Into this fragile organization President Gail Fullerton appointed a director of university relations to lead the office. When President Caret arrived, bringing a deeper appreciation of the need for advancement at a higher level, the stage was set for office and function growth with accompanying professional staff.

The public affairs division became proactive in its media relations rather than reliant upon the "no comment" approach to university problems. The deans were cut loose of their former alumni/fundraising nexus and invited and encouraged to participate in fundraising via the advancement office, now headed by a vice president appointed by President Caret. Among the results were coordinated efforts, supported by software and databases, managed by university professionals who identified potential donors capable of advancing the university mission at specific levels of giving. By the century's end, not only did the president, his vice president for advancement, and deans start asking donors for large contributions, they actually achieved results. Perhaps equally welcome with the reorganization was the cooperation within the university. Dean Marshall J. Burak initiated the College of Business plan to renovate its instructional building. Cooperatively, the dean, the president, and the vice president for advancement prepared the groundwork and solicited the donors with satisfying results. Likewise, the Annual Fund, alumni memberships, and special capital projects became accepted as regular features of university operations.

By the turn of the century, soliciting a million dollars or more from wealthy alumni was uncommon, but hardly bizarre. In fact, after the first few university supporters said "yes," President Caret welcomed each opportunity. The high-profile gifts added excitement and brought valuable public attention to the fundraising enterprise. Public recognition of such generosities helped to identify San José State and to include the university within the broadening vision of emerging Silicon Valley philanthropists. This welcome change in thinking among individuals with discretionary wealth, in turn, facilitated the planned giving dimension of University Advancement. By 1999 the changed university courted the embrace of a changed community. Enhanced wealth and emerging philanthropy promised the support San José State required to advance beyond the limits of state funding and state formulas.

STATE NORMAL SCHOOL, SAN JOSE, CAL. Birdseye view of new State Normal School, San Jose, Cal., the finest Normal School in this country, which cost the State of California $325,000. It numbers over 700 students and has a faculty of thirty-four. President, Morris Elmer Dailey.

CHAPTER SIX

Beyond Washington Square
GROWING THE PHYSICAL CAMPUS

EMERITUS FACULTY long remembered President Wahlquist (1952-1964) and his annual addresses to the university community. They were loaded with building statistics, cubic yards of concrete poured, and number of feet of new plumbing and electrical wiring. Development was high among Wahlquist's priorities, and thus emerged the antiseptic new state buildings within the once park-like, hacienda environment. Growth in student population was immense, and those students had to be educated in safe buildings with enough classrooms and sufficient educational equipment and furnishings.

According to the campus oral tradition, Wahlquist was able to build so much because it was easier then, particularly when he was content to abide by the standard architectural guidelines of the state. But these oral traditions miss the truth when they characterize Wahlquist with such freedom of action. As early as 1961, bureaucracy and administrative process slowed any individual action John Wahlquist could take. The new California State College Board of Trustees defined campus planning and authorized each campus president to appoint committee members "...to give him assistance and advice in developing a master plan and building program for his college." Accompanying this standardization came a new set of players beyond the campus president and the legislative funding sources. This mandate included the campus committee members themselves, consulting architects for master plans and landscaping, individual project architects, administrators and staff of the expanding Chancellor's Office, and the trustees via their own committee system. Navigation through these entities had to precede any specific approach to the state legislature; no longer would the president approach the legislature for enhanced funding, uninvited by the Chancellor's Office. Simultaneously, the state legislature, with its expanding committees and staffs, had become more professionalized and bureaucratized as well. The overall intent was to switch from dealing with so many individual presidents to dealing with a system of higher education.

San José State's campus master planning became, by CSU mandate, a permanent process that required an official update every five years. University planner Alan Freeman, during a 1998 interview, defined the master plan as "a process, a dynamic model used to meet the physical needs of the university in support of the academic mission." The standard driving force was the enrollment goals set by the Chancellor's Office. Higher enrollments required greater physical capacity, and the master plan included models intended to accommodate those system goals. Long-time planner and Acting President J. Handel Evans characterized the master plan as a set of guidelines offering a "speculative venture into the future...."

Under Wahlquist, the modern campus jumped east of South Seventh Street with the construction of the engineering and music buildings. When Robert Clark assumed the presidency in 1964, the old and romantic inner quad had been demolished, leaving little but the saved Tower Hall. From Clark to the presidency of Robert L. Caret, the eastern and southern sectors of the main campus were consolidated under major construction projects and attractive street closings. The added facilities represented balanced growth by supporting three functions.

- Instruction (MacQuarrie and Duncan Halls, Business Complex, New Engineering, and Clark Library)
- Recreation and student life (residence and dining halls, Student Union, Event Center and Aquatics Center, and Simpkins Stadium Center)
- Infrastructure (Parking Garages, Power Plant and Corporation Yard)

Meanwhile, the state college system continued to add new campuses, some of which in Southern California enrolled more students than San José. Since growing institutions had a higher funding priority, San José was increasingly disadvantaged. The mandated master plans continued to be updated, but implementing them without meeting commensurate enrollment growth became more difficult.

Aging facilities challenged campus professionals charged with daily operations and continued development of the campus's physical facilities. They liked old buildings as much as the alumni did; they especially liked those with architectural merit, functioning systems, and support budgets to keep them at a comfortable standard of safety and cleanliness. During the 1970s and 1980s, however, the capital improvements budgets buckled and threatened to collapse. As a result, with concurrent reductions for ordinary maintenance and repairs, a chronic campus problem received a new name — Deferred Maintenance. In 1985, the immense and ever-growing backlog of repairs achieved a new budget line. But isolating the problem did not solve it, and neither did subsequent funding efforts.

By the end of the twentieth century, San José State's main campus consisted of more than 50 major buildings occupying 92 acres (19 square blocks) of downtown San José. The additional 62 acres of the South Campus included Spartan Stadium and its surrounding cluster of athletic facilities, student housing, Simpkins Stadium Center, and the Simpkins Athletic Building. The problem area was the main campus, where modern restoration work addressed only the most attractive among the oldest buildings constructed between 1910 (Tower Hall) and 1933 (Old Science, later Washington Square Hall). By the last quarter of the twentieth century, the major classroom buildings and residence halls, and even the first high-rise garage on Seventh Street were in jeopardy. The legacy of the Wahlquist era of growth, 33 major buildings, erected on modest construction budgets during 1950s and 1960s, required extensive maintenance and renovations by the 1970s and 1980s.

San José State was disadvantaged for two reasons. First, an old campus meant heavier maintenance. Second, no new replacement buildings were forthcoming from state funding because the university was not meeting its assigned enrollment growth targets. The growth campuses were receiving much of what little new construction funding became available.

Buildings with Spanish tile roofs and chronic leaks, for instance, were extremely costly to restore. The 1932 Men's Gym at Fourth and San Carlos had to be re-roofed twice because the leaks persisted. Between the efforts of the hard-pressed contractor, the campus staff displayed the ingenuity characteristic of campus responses to the serious problem confronting all state agencies. Workers, to preserve the gymnasium floors, suspended a huge sheet of lightweight plastic from the dripping ceiling above the basketball courts. They tapered the plastic down the west wall and into rain barrels, which the custodians emptied. Other common deferrals included painting, electrical, carpentry, cement and tile, plumbing, heating, ventilating, and air conditioning systems. On top of all of these unmet needs emerged the new requirements of computer connectivity.

Instead of offering real money for the real problem, in 1987 the California State Department of Finance injected more bureaucratic activity by requiring a report from the CSU describing the deferred maintenance problem. Not only did the CSU define

Campus development by president

Washington Square

1910 Tower Hall
1911 Dwight Bentel Hall
1920 Morris Dailey Auditorium
1924 Central Classroom Building
1932 Spartan Complex West
1933 Washington Square Hall
1941 Wahlquist Library South
1948 Spartan Stadium
1949 Building FF (Alumni Building)
1950 Spartan Complex East

Wahlquist

President John Wahlquist presided over the largest construction in San José State's history, adding buildings and faculty to keep up with student growth. The student residence halls constructed during his tenure would serve more than 40 years until being scheduled for replacement by high-rise facilities in the 21st century.

1952 Spartan Memorial
1953 Music Building
1954 Hugh Gillis Hall
1955 Computer Center
1957 Administration Building
1957 Dudley Moorhead Hall
1957 Science
1957 Wahlquist Library Central
1958 Cafeteria
1959 Art Building
1959 Art Foundry
1959 Building BB (Athletics)
1959 Faculty Office Building
1959 Building G (UPD)
1959 Health Building
1959 Building Q
1959 Building X
1960 Allen Hall
1960 Hoover Hall
1960 Industrial Studies
1960 Markham Hall
1960 Moulder Hall
1960 Royce Hall
1960 Washburn Hall
1961 Wahlquist Library North
1962 Aviation Building
1962 Engineering Building
1962 Field House (East)
1962 Instructional Resources Center
1962 Seventh Street Parking Garage
1963 Spartan Complex Central
1963 Sweeney Hall

Clark

1965 MacQuarrie Hall
1967 Dining Commons
1967 Duncan Hall
1967 Joe West Hall
1969 Student Union

Bunzel

1970 10th Street Parking Garage
1971 Business Complex
1972 Central Plant

Fullerton

President Gail Fullerton turned to non-state funding for key building projects: the Engineering Complex, funded in part by corporate donations; the Event Center, using student fees; and Spartan Stadium expansion and renovation, with alumni and community support. She also laid the groundwork with the San José City Council for closing San Carlos Street through campus.

1980 Corporation Yard
1982 Clark Library
1985 Fourth Street Parking Garage
1989 Engineering Complex
1989 Aquatics Center
1989 Event Center
1989 Modular Buildings
1990 Block House

Evans

1994 Simpkins Stadium Center

Caret

The turn of the century under President Robert Caret was marked by city-university cooperation, from the final closure of San Carlos Street to the beginning of the university/city joint library project.

1996 Paseo de San Carlos
1997 Alan B. Simpkins Intercollegiate Athletics Administration Building
1998 Modulars A-G (located in old parking lot near ATM, corp yard)
1999 Heritage Gateways
2000 Student Services Center (first floor of 10th street parking garage)

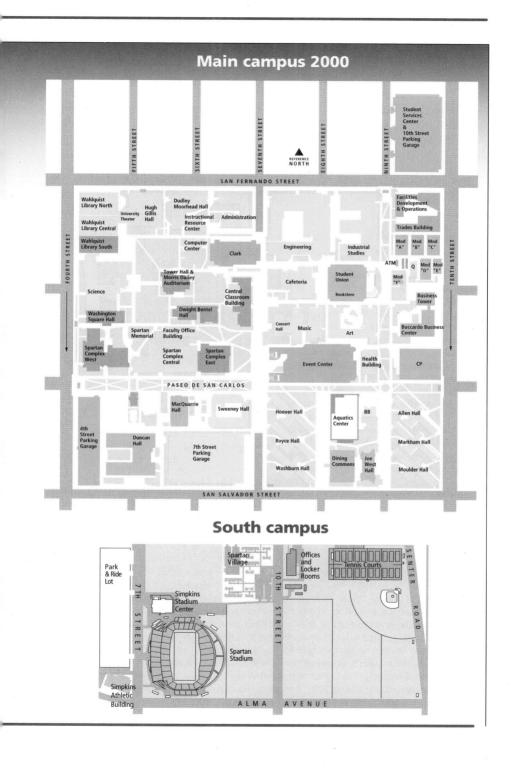

Main campus 2000

FIFTH STREET · SIXTH STREET · SEVENTH STREET · EIGHTH STREET · NINTH STREET

REFERENCE
NORTH

Student Services Center & 10th Street Parking Garage

SAN FERNANDO STREET

FOURTH STREET

Wahlquist Library North
University Theater
Hugh Gillis Hall
Dudley Moorhead Hall
Instructional Resource Center
Administration
Facilities Development & Operations

Wahlquist Library Central
Trades Building

Wahlquist Library South
Computer Center
Engineering
Industrial Studies
Mod "A" Mod "B" Mod "C"

Clark
ATM Q Mod "D" Mod "E"

Tower Hall & Morris Dailey Auditorium
Cafeteria
Student Union
Mod "F"

Science
Central Classroom Building
Bookstore
Business Tower

Washington Square Hall
Dwight Bentel Hall
Concert Hall Music
Art
Boccardo Business Center

Spartan Memorial
Faculty Office Building

Spartan Complex West
Spartan Complex Central
Spartan Complex East
Event Center
Health Building
CP

TENTH STREET

PASEO DE SAN CARLOS

MacQuarrie Hall
Sweeney Hall
Hoover Hall
Aquatics Center
BB
Allen Hall

4th Street Parking Garage
Duncan Hall
7th Street Parking Garage
Royce Hall
Markham Hall

Washburn Hall
Dining Commons
Joe West Hall
Moulder Hall

SAN SALVADOR STREET

South campus

Park & Ride Lot

7TH STREET

Simpkins Stadium Center

Spartan Village
10TH STREET
Offices and Locker Rooms
Tennis Courts
SENTER ROAD

Spartan Stadium

Simpkins Athletic Building

ALMA AVENUE

the disastrous backlog, the drafters subdivided deferred maintenance into three stages of priority. First were non-funded repairs that blocked instruction and direct support operations. Documented health and safety code violations were on file, and liability problems awaited potential suits. Second were potentially critical campus physical problems. This priority level included systems functioning at the time of the report, but which had been dysfunctional previously. The report stated that the "liability factors include[d] an anticipated citation upon the next official inspection, and an Environment Health & Safety report is expected to be placed on record." Priority three included elements in need of replacement or repairs, as the option to advancement to

Red-tile renovations keep campus look intact

WHILE PRESIDENT JOHN WAHLQUIST raced forward with new construction, President Gail Fullerton had the opportunity to look back at the institution's history and make sure it didn't get erased. Three beautiful, old buildings were renovated under her watch, ensuring that the flavor of the early campus would remain a key ingredient in future planning.

Fullerton successfully engaged the university master planning and state financing systems for the preservation of three vintage and architecturally respected buildings: Central Classroom Building, Dwight Bentel Hall, and Washington Square Hall. The result was a restoration to an even higher quality than the original while preserving and enhancing the artistic merits of each.

Central Classroom Building
...built in 1924 and housed the home economics program

The Central Classroom Building was built in 1924, its exterior of pale stucco walls and red tile roof matching the Spanish-style architecture of the Tower Hall quad. Originally home to the home economics program, it was remodeled at a cost of $1.4 million in 1976, while Fullerton was executive vice president, to house the nutrition and food science program.

Dwight Bentel Hall was built in 1911, with an addition that doubled its size in 1929. Home to the journalism and mass communications department, it was named in honor of Dwight Bentel, who retired as chair of the journalism department in 1967 and taught until 1974. It was remodeled in 1961 and then again in 1991 at a cost of $4 million.

Washington Square Hall, built in 1933, bore the name of Old Science Building until its remodel in 1991. The $7 million renovation restored the gleam of the last old jewel on the Tower Hall quad, maintaining the historical integrity of the building's exterior as well as its amphitheater-style lecture hall. Classrooms and offices were renovated for the colleges of Humanities and Arts, Social Sciences and Social Work. Structural and health and safety measures were corrected.

One more landmark campus building — Tower Hall — and its adjoining Morris Dailey Auditorium were renovated before the turn of the century. The $1.4 million project added steel columns and shear walls and strengthened the roof as part of a seismic upgrade in 1997, ensuring the continuation of the red-tile roofs and Spanish arches that defined the early campus.

a higher priority. To spend more time and money estimating the costs of repairs that were not to be funded had become an expense no facilities manager would authorize, and neither would campus presidents. As deferred maintenance skyrocketed, the gap between the problem and its documentation widened as well.

By 1995, San Francisco State, though a newer campus, received a state grant under which Rich Stevens Consulting calculated its deferred maintenance at $66 million. In 1999 Daniel R. Johnson, San José State's associate vice president in charge of Facilities Development and Operations (without benefit of grants or consultants) estimated the San José State problem at $125 million. In the larger perspective, California budgeted an immense amount of funding for higher education, yet the system these budgets supported never reached the standard of health and safety legislated by the state itself.

Unable to solve the problem to which it had conferred definition, the Chancellor's Office reversed its earlier action and simply enveloped the deferred maintenance category within the annual base budget. By the year 2000, deferred maintenance compounded to and remained at an estimated $115 million, but during this same period university managers received only $10.3 million to placate the problem.

Student Union

PUBLIC DISCUSSION of the need for a Student Union building dated at least back to 1927, but talk never became reality, even as the number of students rose to 20,000 in 1963. Instead, students continued to meet over coffee and plan their events in cramped and transient facilities awaiting demolition. San Diego State and Fresno State, however, were planning their student unions by the early 1960s. Nearer to home, Berkeley, San José City College and Santa Clara had built their own handsome models.

The Associated Students retained an attorney in 1963, drafted a ballot measure, and boldly asked one question: Shall the student body finance, for a total of $5,500,000, a new student center and pay for it from reserves and through bonded indebtedness not to exceed $20 per student annually?

The student Democratic Club and the Young Republicans both opposed the measure. They feared that the facility would not be run by students for students, but would become just another building controlled by the administration and used as the administration saw fit. Additionally, the student political clubs did not like the uses proposed for the facility. They thought that the balance of recreation to culture was backward — too much recreation and not enough culture. The cost factor was peripheral. The 9,134 valid ballots set a record for the number of votes cast in any campus election, with a voter turnout of 47 percent. By the required two-thirds majority of votes cast, in November 1963, the college students voted to tax themselves and their successors for 40 years to pay off the principal and the three percent interest federal loan of $3.24 million. Spartan Shops received the two-story southeast corner for Spartan Book Store in exchange for $1.1 million to bridge the gap between the federal loan and the cost of construction and furnishing.

Basic campus harmony characterized the planning and the decision-making processes for the Student Union. The architect was E.J. Kump Associates, who had designed the very well regarded Foothill Community College in Los Altos, and high quality architectural drawings appeared with favorable articles in the *Spartan Daily*. The *Spartan Daily* described the attractive building: "three distinct levels...of 135,000 square feet. Light sandblasted concrete, red brick and selected dark wood trim will characterize the building's exterior." The interior seemed even more promising with "an open central core with a sunken lounge on each level as well as oak paneling, textured concrete and carpeting. A minimal amount of paint...."

Naming the public rooms of the Student Union building may not have been the students' method of enhancing culture over recreation, but that was the result. Respect for the Native American and Hispanic heritage of the community won out. Those who have ever attended a function in the *Umunhum Room* (pronounced oomoonoom) had to have wondered what the word meant — historians report that it is a Costanoan Indian word meaning resting place of the hummingbird. *Guadalupe*, from the Virgin of Guadalupe, was a popular place name in the Santa Clara Valley in the 1700s. The Guadalupe River is an important geographic feature that runs near campus. All the original room names — *Pacheco, Loma Prieta, Costanoan, Diablo, Almaden, Laguna Seca, Pacifica, Madrone, Manzanita* and *Verde* — reflected the area's valued cultural life with words borrowed from California's indigenous and Mexican past. The exception is the ballroom, named after the long-time director of the Union, Ron Barrett. He made the building work by sound professional competence and a friendly, easy, but very wise manner in dealing with his annually rotating student bosses. Barrett was the sort of professional who did well on a college campus. He understood the youth culture and quietly enjoyed being at its edge.

The Event Center and Aquatics Center

IF THE FUNDING, planning, construction and management of the Student Union was the model, replicating it in the Event Center became far more than just a challenge. A center that offered recreation, entertainment, and competitive athletics all under the same roof was in vogue at other campuses. Physical Education Professor Daniel W. Unruh recognized the need for modern facilities and had suggested the idea for San José State back in 1972. He resurrected it again in 1976 with support within student government.

The men's and women's swimming pools were archaic, intercollegiate basketball had to be played off campus at the San José Civic Auditorium, and intramurals suffered from a lack of facilities. Taking a PE class seemed to be the only easy way to schedule ordinary exercise on campus. Unruh also recognized that student lives were changing, that more students spent less time on campus because of busy schedules. To Unruh this represented an unattractive change in college life, and he thought that having their own recreation center would encourage students to hang around longer in the afternoons.

President Gail Fullerton favored construction of a recreation and sports facility and approved its inclusion in the university master plan of 1983. Academic Vice President Hobert W. Burns announced that the state would not be funding this building. Therefore, financing would be by student fees, just like the Student Union. The initial cost estimate was $8 million for a structure that would cost students an additional two to fifteen dollars on top of their $10 special fees per semester.

Event Center (top) and Aquatics Center
...voted on three times

The first questions to come up became enduring ones, those of control and of cost. President Fullerton's decision to advance the construction plan, supported by Academic Senate action, marked an advocacy that was new to campus development. As it turned out, three elections would be necessary, and each election was highly contested. The process became highly politicized. Larry Dougherty, associate student body vice president, organized the "Stop the wRECk" Committee, and the committee's coverage in the *Spartan Daily* exceeded that of pro-center advocates. The university administration and athletic personnel who most desired the facility were not capable of financing it, and prominent alumni were not asked. Dougherty's reaction to the first election, a 59 percent victory for the proponents of the center, was to launch an initiative drive for a second vote. With heavy campaigning, Dougherty and the anti-REC committee turned the voters around with a 55 percent defeat of the proposed center.

Reaction to Dougherty's referendum, which popularly rejected the center, was simple denial. Directors of the Student Union, who arbitrarily displaced student government officials as the decision makers, moved ahead. En route they authorized four architectural drawings of the planned, but contentious, facility. They then circulated the conceptualizations for students to select their favorite one among the four.

President Fullerton wanted the new building, as did every campus professional who dealt with facilities. So, too, did the coaches and those associated with student services. Basketball Coach Bill Berry felt that the new facility would help him recruit better players who would elevate the quality of play and attract more fans. President

Fullerton said that a third election was appropriate to conclude the matter of building an Event Center and Aquatics Center.

At this point the directors of the Student Union appeared to act as advocates for a pro-center vote. Their expenditure for the third election far outpaced Dougherty's no-wRECk resources. The architectural drawings were interesting and engaging, and advocates took the drawings into classrooms for students to see and register an opinion. This unprecedented intrusion into instructional time required faculty cooperation or acquiescence, at least. Additionally, prominent alumni such as Peter Ueberroth, the director of the 1984 Los Angeles Olympics, endorsed the project.

With the narrowest of election margins, 51 percent favored the construction of the center. By the fall of 1985, the cost had risen to $21 million and the student fee to $81 per semester. Included among the positive side effects were an expansion of women's athletics and movement of aquatic sports to modern outdoor facilities, with summer swimming available to neighborhood families. Even the academic side of the university grew to appreciate the facility. Spartan Stadium's 30,000 seating capacity remained necessary for annual commencements, but the Event Center allowed the Honors Convocation to recognize president's and dean's scholars in comfort and style.

The Clark Library

BY THE CONCLUDING YEARS of the 1960s, a new library was needed by anyone's standard. San José State had continued to grow by all contemporary measurements, including library budgets that substantially added to the collections of books and journals utilized by both faculty and students. At the core the need was  space — for growing numbers of students as well as the growing collections. The drawings projected an 18-story campus library, the theme structure within a new master plan. In the spring of 1969, the projected cost to the state for this building was $11.4 million. It was the central new building for the planned campus of closed streets, landscaped walks, fountains, and open space.

Executive Dean C. Grant Burton, a holdover from the Wahlquist administration, announced in the *Spartan Daily* that he expected state funding for the Clark Library, "...due largely to the building's high priority in the statewide State College budget." That confidence was misplaced. Not only was funding not forthcoming, but four years later, in 1973, building costs had escalated from $11 million to $15 million. From this point on, the financial difficulties became much worse.

The longer funding remained unavailable, the worse the prospects became. Stagflation became a national phenomenon. Virtually no major construction was taking place in Santa Clara Valley, and construction costs continued to escalate rapidly with general inflation. By 1978, for an additional half-million beyond the original price tag, all that could be constructed was five of the original 18 stories.

Ten years following the original drawings of the library, California state bond money became available for construction, and the legislature authorized the expenditure of $12 million. While the original high rise would have cost $11.4 million had it been built in 1969, construction bids for a five-story library came in at $15 million. By then, J. Handel Evans presided over campus planning. The options, as he saw them, were to bring the project in at or very close to the approved amount or forget altogether any library construction.

During the era of Governor Jerry Brown, the heating and cooling systems of the concrete and steel buildings were required to be of natural energy, ecology-friendly and experimental in design. Solar panels, a water tower, fans, and circulation systems were to heat and to cool the building. Even the energy radiating from the internal lighting and the body temperature of the patrons found its way into the equation. To bring the project in at the prescribed cost limits, Evans had to forego the backup, standard heating and air conditioning hook up.

But the natural system simply did not work in the Clark Library, and no back-up system existed. As a result, patronage lagged and librarians suffered through the changing seasons. In the end, the Chancellor's Office had to assist the campus in connecting the library to the overall campus energy system, all of which was subsequently overhauled. Worst of all, Clark Library did not replace Wahlquist Library as originally intended. It only shared the housing and management functions of what had to become a two-building operation with split collections. Subject matter collections of books came to be divided between buildings mostly by date of publication. Plans to reintegrate the collection accompanied the designs for a new library, a turn-of-the-century joint project between the university and the city of San José.

Clark Library construction took place between the two modern student-financed facilities (the Student Union and the Event Center and Aquatics Center). As a result, informed observers did not have to wonder which process resulted in better buildings. The university obtained first-class facilities when the planners could spend non-state funds.

Library Stability and Innovation: A Difficult Relationship

Transitions are seldom easy. Miss Joyce Backus, with a recent degree from Simmons College, had accepted her appointment as college librarian in 1923. She resigned in anger 42 years later, in 1965. During the intervening years Backus served dutifully, but the university changed while she did not. She retained a fixed understanding of a teacher's college even after the professionalization of the faculty under President Wahlquist. She had persisted in spending library funds on textbooks since the Great Depression.

When Backus regularly proclaimed, "This is not a research institution," she was officially correct. Unofficially, she resisted the expansion of knowledge development as an innovative force in knowledge acquisition. Also, she resisted students who wanted the library opened longer, and the faculty who

Miss Joyce Backus
...college librarian
42 years

wanted monographs and journals in science and the arts.

Post-Backus library leadership became the reverse, progressive but temporary. Through the remainder of the twentieth century, the average tenure of directors was three years. James Schmidt, who planned the blending of city and university libraries into a joint library, held the record, seven years in office. The professional staff was largely responsible for the major advances from textbooks to information age technologies, all the while extending student and faculty services. The magnitude and the uniqueness of the joint library plan looked to both innovation and stability for the new century ahead.

Spartan Stadium

A MONG THE PRESIDENTS and acting presidents from Wahlquist through Caret, Gail Fullerton bore the heaviest and most demanding burden in the area of campus physical development. Only the Engineering School's successful Project '88 began and ended within her administration and benefited from her full commitment and support. Each of the other major construction projects originated before her appointment to the presidency, and she saw them to conclusion. The longest and most difficult project was the Spartan Stadium expansion. Preliminary planning began in 1963, the last year of the Wahlquist presidency, and it continued in various stages of hope and desperation until Fullerton saw construction concluded in 1985.

The university's long tradition of intercollegiate sports has in the modern era benefited from organized sports boosters who constituted a core advocacy for athletics, mainly football. For them and for others at San José State, Division I-A status, the top of the NCAA scheme, was critical. The occasional spectacular successes on the gridiron sustained this core even as attendance figures shrank, and the student body shifted from Greek and on-campus living to part-time enrollments and commuting. Stadium expansion, like construction of the Student Union and the Event Center and Aquatics Center, was approved by the system trustees, but without funding.

John Bunzel's administration (1970-1978) obtained the trustee approval and then worked on interesting the San José City Council in a stadium partnership. This was a decade before Tom McEnery arrived in the mayor's office, a decade before Mayor McEnery and San José Redevelopment Agency Executive Director Frank Taylor would embark on downtown San José's ambitious redevelopment program. The San José Arena and the Sharks NHL ice hockey team were not yet even a dream. Though Bunzel's personal relations with the city fathers and mothers had not been the best, the city's first response was favorable. Time, inflation, and lack of progress resulted in setbacks followed by periodic resuscitations. But a decade later, the San José City Council withdrew any offer of support as new leadership under McEnery began developing its definition of urban renewal.

On its own, the university persisted with fundraisers and proclamations of success followed by extending campaign deadlines. When campaigns fell distinctly short of the goals, the university made do once again and decided to expand the stadium in three stages as money could be extracted from non-state sources. The plan focused upon expanding Spartan Stadium from a seating capacity of 18,000 to 30,000. Annual commencements were the events that assured capacity crowds; games did not. Nevertheless, improved football facilities became the argument for enhanced player recruitment, winning teams, and larger attendance.

Additionally, the threat that the National Collegiate Athletic Association would terminate San José State's Division I-A status worked its way into the public discourse by expansion advocates. Simply put, San José State needed a bigger stadium because the NCAA required it. Once having the larger stadium, more and better athletes could be recruited to win more games and create a greater spectator demand. The advocates' plan to fund stadium expansion included fund drives, alumni and other individual donors, the boosters, the sale of luxury boxes, and multiple low-interest loans to be redeemed through higher gate receipts. Supporters of San José State athletics worked hard and contributed a great deal, but the equation was loaded against their easy success. Dean Pinson raised a third of Project '88 from industrialists and chief executive officers who presided over discretionary budgets and who already understood the product their contributions were to improve. President Fullerton and the boosters needed to gather the total costs for the stadium expansion from among sports supporters who could not

Campus childcare center grows into new building

THE IDEA OF BUILDING a childcare center for San José State parents did not mature quickly. In 1972, education professor Frances Gulland helped a group of students establish the first campus childcare center in rented space at a church across from campus. By the 1990s, there was strong demand for a new, purpose-built center.

A proposal to fund a new center through a student fee first appeared on the ballot in 1993. "I remember children campaigning on campus, passing out fliers. They came into the Board of Directors of Associated Students, and they brought cookies," said Alfonso De Alba, then AS director of business affairs. But it took several attempts before Associated Students President Blair Whitney finally accomplished one of his main goals, overwhelming passage of the student fee — $5 for construction and $3 for operation — in 1994. Collecting the fee each semester proved to be just a baby step.

"It took several more years to convince the university to find us a space, arrange financing, and get the university's OK to operate a center," said De Alba, now executive director of AS. "For the land, we have to thank the University Foundation, who sold us the site. For the financing, we have to thank Spartan Shops and the Foundation, who floated the bonds and put in financing." More help came from the David and Lucile Packard Foundation, which awarded a $100,000 grant for the center in 1998.

The new $2.3 million AS Child Development Center, built at 460 S. Eighth St., opened in September 2000. The new building allowed the center to double its capacity (to 100 children) and add infant-toddler rooms. The center was licensed by the California Department of Social Services and accredited by the National Academy of Early Childhood Programs.

disperse discretionary awards from corporate budgets and who would not accrue any financial return.

En route to the expansion project's conclusion, the president had to call in virtually every chip the university had among the boosters, less-focused alumni, foundations, and the local financial community. Fundraising proceeded resolutely, and loans from understanding friends and alumni in the local financial industry patched the project together, concluding in the fall of 1985 with a new seating capacity of 30,844 seats.

School of Engineering: Project '88

JAY PINSON ARRIVED at San José State in 1979 when vast, accelerated growth and change occurred in Silicon Valley business and technologies. In fact, his years as dean of the School of Engineering coincided with the conversion of Santa Clara Valley into Silicon Valley. The School of Engineering was in a state of crisis due to anti-

The engine that drives Silicon Valley

ENGINEERING DEAN JAY PINSON showed industry leaders the best-kept local secret: San José State was the "leading university in the U.S. in providing engineers to Silicon Valley." He also showed the chief executives that their out-of-state recruiting funds could be more effectively spent on upgrading the local program.

Pinson's pitch, done as a slide show, located San José State at the center of the worldwide electronics industry where over 1,500 electronics firms resided within the university's assigned service area. In sheer numbers, San José State provided two times more of the valley's engineers than any other university. He listed 1,427 SJSU graduates at Lockheed, 1,008 at IBM, 788 at Hewlett-Packard, and another 635 at General Electric. At Lockheed Missiles and Space Co., which hired 217 engineers in 1985, half of the hires were from San José State.

Jay Pinson
...secured Silicon Valley help for Project '88

Pinson used his basic set of 14 slides in early presentations before CSU Chancellor W. Ann Reynolds and her staff, before the state legislature, and before the potential industrial donors whose support he was intent on capturing. His opening slides identified his Resource Development Committee, chaired by Dan Tellep (president of Lockheed Missiles and Space Co.), with David Packard (Hewlett-Packard), Robert Noyce (Intel), Jerry Sanders (Advanced Micro Devices), Charles Sporck (National Semiconductor), Don Beall (Rockwell International), and Ray AbuZayyad (IBM). This committee also included political and media mainstays San José Mayor Tom McEnery, U.S. Congressman Norman Y. Mineta, and *San Jose Mercury News* Publisher Tony Ridder.

Pinson's recommended minimum level of giving was $250,000, with higher amounts provided by members of his leadership committee. Since the new laboratories had to be outfitted with cutting-edge electronics, Dean Pinson also accepted donations of equipment. Not only was Project '88 successful, it overshot the objective. The $13 million goal was committed by the time construction began in the spring of 1987. By August 1988, when faculty moved in, donations of money and laboratory equipment totaled $17 million and state funding $30 million.

quated school facilities, a curriculum that was behind the local innovative curve, and a faculty heavy in part-time instructors. In addition, Pinson found the apparent invisibility of the engineering school somewhat of a mystery. It was true that San José State provided engineers to valley companies, but no one seemed to know or care.

Project '88, conceived in a meeting of the school's Industry Advisory Council, became the largest capital undertaking in San José State's and California State University's experience at that time. Original brainstorming and a bit of data gathering suggested that the combination of mostly new construction and dedicated laboratories, along with some limited renovations, would realistically cost about $40 million. Because the state could not fund such a large, costly project, advisory council members and Pinson gingerly adjusted the figure to $39 million so that it would be divisible by three. The plan was for the state to put up two thirds and for private industry to put up the other third, about $13 million. In the end, Dean Jay D. Pinson worked his magic on industrial donors, alumni, and friends of engineering. The result was a modern, new facility that was a unique university-industry joint venture, the first public-private capital project in the CSU.

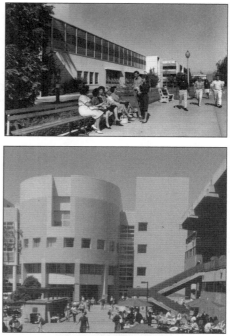

Engineering Building
...before and after Project '88

Street Closures

THROUGHOUT THE LAST HALF of the century, campus master planners persisted in one clear, overall goal — closing city streets that still carried auto traffic through the expanded campus. After the campus construction during the Wahlquist administration vaulted Seventh Street — Music (1953), Cafeteria (1958), and Engineering (1962) — internal pressure for a unified campus naturally followed. Large numbers of students, staff, and faculty crossing and re-crossing through the moving traffic endangered themselves and annoyed auto and truck drivers of San José. The college planners thought beyond basic safety, however. They also looked to utility and beauty, noting that closing streets to vehicular traffic added to the university's real estate, i.e., the actual streets and sidewalks, which the planners believed could be used to create landscaped pedestrian malls.

The city of San José agreed to close South Seventh Street in 1963, one year before

Clark arrived. By the time South Ninth Street closed in 1974, an entire new eastern echelon of buildings had vaulted that thoroughfare. But the university's promise to landscape the area remained long delayed due to the failure of another state bond election. That reversal's most debilitating result from the university's point of view was reduced trust among city planners, those who had the major say-so on the university's next plan — closure of San Carlos Street.

Success of San José State's master planning objective — a contained campus — took a full generation, from 1962 to the end of the century. Fullerton's strategy was meticulous and unrelenting. San José Councilman David Pandori saw the problem from the university's perspective and appreciated what community open space within a contained campus would mean for the neighborhood and for the advancement of the downtown renaissance. Equally important was the upturn in the California economy and the popular recognition that education needed better funding. A large statewide bond issue provided funding from which San José State was able to meet its accumulated landscaping obligations. Along with the San Carlos mall, the other former streets received well-appointed landscaping, fountains, and paths. When Councilman Pandori spoke at the warm summer ceremony at which he tied a bright red ribbon across San Carlos at Seventh Street, a member of the small crowd asked him how he overcame all the opponents of closure. With a knowing smile Pandori replied, "We bored them all to death!"

Pedestrians finally get campus right of way

PRESIDENT WAHLQUIST oversaw campus growth beyond the original Washington Square onto the south side of Seventh Street, which resulted in conflict between pedestrians and cars. The university narrowly won city approval to close Seventh Street in 1963 and Ninth Street in 1974. But promises of grass, trees, walkways and outdoor seating — required by city officials who thought the closed sections of asphalt an eyesore — were delayed by

President Caret officially closed San Carlos Street with Mayor Susan Hammer and Councilman David Pandori.

budget problems for two decades. While these numbered streets running north-south had been absorbed in campus construction, San Carlos Street continued to bisect the university. It would take President Gail Fullerton and her executive vice president J. Handel Evans a decade to win city approval for the closure of San Carlos in 1994, accomplishing a campus master plan detail on the books since 1962. Councilman David Pandori, a graduate of San José State (BA 1980, environmental studies), was instrumental in working with neighborhood groups on traffic mitigation and parking concerns. Also important was funding — finally — for the landscaping that would transform Seventh, Ninth and San Carlos streets into tree-lined pedestrian malls. The Paseo de San Carlos was dedicated in 1996.

By the time of President Robert Caret's inauguration in 1995, the physical integrity of the campus had been assured and the long-delayed, comprehensive landscaping was well underway. The campus looked good and would get even better.

Parking Garages

RISING ENROLLMENTS at San José State seriously impacted neighborhood parking, university garages, surface lots, and community relations. While these enrollments oscillated between 20,000 and 30,000 students, one factor remained steady, the institution's conversion into a commuter university. The first high-rise parking garage opened on Seventh Street in the fall of 1962 and inaugurated what was to become a familiar process, far more cars than slots at peak class hours.

Through the 1980s, continued campus building and the downtown renaissance eliminated the safety valve of vacant lots. In 1981, for example, the city reclaimed 800 parking spaces. Additionally, the Naglee Park residents (faculty included) objected to their neighborhood being appropriated as street parking for students and implemented permit parking available to residents only.

Bonds paid for the construction of new parking garages, and parking revenues paid for the bonds. The openings of the Tenth Street Garage in 1970 and the Fourth Street Garage in 1985 coincided with the start of decade-long enrollment increases. From the professional planner's point of view, this was brilliant. But from the frustrated driver's point of view, nothing was happening.

Frustration peaked during the 1998-99 academic year. Good things for the long-term were bad for the short-term. The closure of San Carlos Street, the renovation of Business Classrooms, the landscaping of Seventh Street, the relocation of administrative offices to the first floor of the Tenth Street Parking Garage pending the demolition of Wahlquist Library, and the construction of a child care center by the Associated Students were desirable improvements, but each shrank parking further. The university's problem, of course, continued to spill over into the neighborhoods and to aggravate local traffic.

Although the vast majority of commuting students and faculty did find campus

Formula for parking was simple addition

RISING ENROLLMENT and lack of affordable off-campus housing led to more and more commuter students. The first high-rise parking garage opened on Seventh Street in 1962, but cars still outnumbered parking spaces. The Tenth Street Garage opened in 1970, and the Fourth Street Garage in 1985. In the 1990s, the university opened new parking lots at South Campus and initiated shuttle service to the main campus. The plan took hold, however, when the university made parking at South Campus free in an introductory offer in 1999.

New buildings, new band uniforms on their list

As Kappa Kappa Gamma president in 1964, Phyllis Forward Simpkins helped architects design the sorority's new house at 360 S. 11th Street. Little more than a decade later, the building was just one of a line of half-way houses along the campus's east side, until Simpkins and her husband, Alan, came to the rescue.

"The halfway house went bankrupt, and we saw an opportunity to obtain this fine building for use for the university," she said. "While watching the half-time show of a football game, we saw a picture of a house in Alabama that

Alan and Phyllis Simpkins
...gave with pride and joy

resembled the San José house, and it housed international students." They bought the property, painted the rooms, bought new beds and bedding, and opened the International House to 40 students in September of 1978. Phyllis personally made sure that the new residents found the house to be the comfortable home she had envisioned years before. Nearly 80 students, most of them on student visas from around the world, fill the house each semester. In January 1997, the Simpkins donated the Phyllis Forward Simpkins International House, valued at $1.7 million, to the university. It was not the only time the Simpkins added to the university's physical infrastructure.

In 1994, smiling proudly, the Simpkins helped dedicate the Simpkins Stadium Center, a brand new building they funded at the South Campus. The center, which also had general use meeting rooms, was the beginning of a revitalization of athletics facilities. In May 1997, they found another property on the market adjacent to campus. The 1.7-acre property and 22,700-square foot building at Seventh and Alma streets, valued at $3 million, became the Alan B. Simpkins Intercollegiate Athletics Administration Building.

When Alan passed away later that same year, band director Scott Pierson (SJSU, music) reminded band alumni of Simpkins' generous spirit: "As most of you probably know by now, Alan Simpkins passed away on September 10. Each of you has enjoyed your time as a member of the Spartan marching band, for without pressuring SJSU in 1978, there would be no band. Without their constant generosity, most of the trips you took would never have happened, you wouldn't have gotten new uniforms, new drums, nor would a lot of other good things have happened to the band. It is important to understand that all of the good things Alan did for the band came unsolicited. I never asked them for assistance of any kind; Alan would call up every August and ask how things were going. The budgets, of course, were always terrible, and he'd laugh and say, 'They just don't get it over there, do they? Well, Phyllis and I are going to send a little something over to help out with the season. We'll see you at the first game.' That was it, and you know the rest."

Phyllis earned an AB in home economics and marketing in 1946. Alan received his BS in physics in 1948. They were Tower Award recipients and were awarded honorary doctorates from San José State.

parking and did settle into their routines, those who could not constituted the problem — for themselves, for campus managers, and certainly for the neighbors. New university leadership and a revived cooperative spirit drew the campus and neighborhoods together in 1997-98. Meetings were attended by as many as 400 participants, and they resulted in the University Neighborhoods Revitalization Plan. The most promising community recommendation, intended to reduce student demand for on-street parking, was actually a refinement upon what the university had tried with only limited success — parking near Spartan Stadium to the south. The Revitalization

Business education gets high-speed transformation

IT TOOK A LOT OF ALUMNI to transform San José State's Business Classroom building into a high-tech teaching facility for the twenty-first century. The renovations, in fact, were unveiled at the dawn of the new century in January 2000.

More than $6 million was raised from private sources for the Business Classrooms Renovation project, a total redo turning the traditional building (circa 1971) into a state-of-the-art facility with theatre-style classrooms, a robust computer network, open-access computer labs, and a student advisement and tutorial center. An additional $10 million came from the state and the College of Business to complete the project. "Not only did we renovate the campus's largest classroom facility," said Business Dean David Conrath, "we also turned it into a centerpiece model of technology-assisted instruction on the backbone of its computer network."

Marshall Burak
...initiated
Business
Classrooms
Renovation
project

Leading the alumni charge was Richard Previte, then-president of Silicon Valley's Advanced Micro Devices and chair of the campaign. Previte earned his BS in business administration in 1956 and his MS in 1957. Setting the funding benchmark were James F. and Lorraine Boccardo, who chose the college's 1997 alumni association awards banquet as the perfect setting to announce their pledge of $2 million to the project. The Boccardos received the university's highest honor, the Tower Award, in 1998, and the renovated building now bears his name, "The James F. Boccardo Business Education Center." James Boccardo earned his BS in chemistry in 1931 at San José State, then headed for law school and a high-profile career, founding the Boccardo Law Firm in San Jose.

The Business Classroom Renovation was one of two major fundraising campaigns at the end of the century. Cooperation between then-Business Dean Marshall Burak, who initiated the project, President Robert Caret and the university's advancement staff led to dual gifts from the Boccardos. They also made a $250,000 leadership gift to the Heritage Gateway Campaign, funding a gateway at South Fourth Street and Paseo de San Carlos. Many other San José State alumni followed the lead of the Boccardos on these two campaigns, leaving a lasting legacy on the campus.

"San José State has always been my primary love," James Boccardo said of receiving the Tower Award. "My feeling is that I owed the university something in appreciation for what it did for me."

Plan encouraged "SJSU to expand this program by reducing parking rates for those students using the shuttle service and by increasing the number of shuttles used."

For the fall of 1999, when campus construction projects minimized parking and enrollments increased, the university parking managers went a step further and refined the Revitalization Plan's refinement. Those who used south campus parking received the introductory offer of free parking and free shuttle service. That innovation, plus enhanced garage access and attentive enforcement of parking regulations, improved conditions to a level at least equal to earlier years when fewer students hunted slightly more parking spaces. The university's cooperation with the community, in this case, generated the most promising immediate and long-range solution to one of San José

Brandenburg partnership started at State

LEE BRANDENBURG had $35 in his pocket when he and another San José State student, Diane, headed for Reno more than 50 years ago to elope. He was a Sigma Nu senior, she "a lowly freshman." They finished school living in an apartment on Seventh Street that they rented for $37 a month, including utilities.

Always one who believed in leverage, Brandenburg grew his $35 into a very successful property development company, Brandenburg, Staedler & Moore. The Bran-

Lee and Diane Brandenburg
...made leadership gift to library

denburgs are widely respected patrons and supporters of numerous community arts, sports and children's programs. Their development projects, from golf courses to housing sites, have helped shape the growth of Silicon Valley.

Five decades passed before Lee and Diane returned to the site of that Seventh Street apartment. Their inspiration was the transformation of San José State into an outward-looking metropolitan university and their decision to be a part of that movement. "We were really talking about how much (SJSU President) Bob Caret was doing to bring the university and the community back together," Diane said. The Brandenburgs are a key part of that city-university reunion. Their leadership gift to the joint library will fund the browsing library near the first-floor entrance. The library, a joint project between the city of San José and San José State University, will be the first such collaboration between a major city and university in the nation as well as a high-tech model supported by Silicon Valley's innovators and leaders.

"When Diane and I attended San José State in the last century, the library was a remnant of the college's early days as a teacher's college," Lee said. "No more! We are well on our way to something grand and exciting. This is not going to be just another library. This is going to be a first-of-its-kind in the U.S." Not only will it feature the latest technology appropriate to Silicon Valley, "it's going to be a fun place to go" for schoolchildren and college students alike.

The Brandenburgs received the university's 1988 Tower Award and are long-time supporters of Spartan athletics, especially the golf team and the Walk for Women of Sparta.

State's most aggravating and persisting modern problems. South campus parking was not close or convenient, but it was fully available for the significant numbers of students and faculty who still enjoyed the luxury of some flexible time.

The Joint Library:
City of San José and San José State University

FROM THE MOMENT of its unveiling, the Joint Library Project assumed gigantic proportions: physically, financially, and symbolically. The plan was to replace the city's Dr. Martin Luther King, Jr. Main Library downtown and both the Clark and Wahlquist libraries on campus. In addition, the outcome was to be a public statement validating the reconciliation of campus and community. The project called for a unique state-of-the-art library befitting the nation's world-renowned Silicon Valley. The joint library would confirm the "metropolitan university" concept, serve as San José State's bridge to the revitalized city and Silicon Valley, and symbolize the vibrant advance of San José into the twenty-first century. The library would provide more on-campus book space (475,000 square feet) and

Architectural rendering of joint library

cutting-edge information technology than could ever become available under state or city funding alone. The model from which all of this would arise existed nowhere else. But if the project fulfilled the expectations of its advocates, then this plan could be offered to California and the world as the model for the new millennium.

Campus critics depreciated the joint library project as an unplanned brainchild of President Caret and Mayor Susan Hammer. The traditionalists depicted the big idea as springing spontaneously from a random conversation between the two. In actuality, interest in joint projects had been around for some time. President Fullerton had attempted to draw the city into the redevelopment of Spartan Stadium, and before Caret's arrival on campus in 1995, several deans had become acquainted with Frank Taylor, the city's redevelopment chief. Acting President J. Handel Evans and Frank Taylor, both trained architects, were comfortable in discussing the possibility and wisdom of joint projects. For his part, Caret wanted to implement the metropolitan university concept, and he discussed with the city the possibility of joint facilities: an art gallery, performing arts center, tennis courts, and softball diamonds. As he made himself acquainted with city officials, these subjects continued to surface. A joint library was within the mix.

Caret joined and became active in the San José Chamber of Commerce, Joint Venture Silicon Valley, and the Silicon Valley Manufacturing Group. He functioned easily and naturally within the revitalized role of external advocate president, seeming to enjoy each opportunity to advance San José State into the larger affairs of the community.

At receptions and meetings alike, Caret summarized for city representatives the list of possible collaborations they had discussed. He would typically add, "If any of these come up on your radar screen, give me a call and we can talk about them."

Hammer shared Caret's interest in a joint library, and she included the subject in her next major address. Both leaders launched the idea in February 1997 and formed committees to research location, funding and operational issues. Hammer dealt with the members of the City Council, who also served as the governing board of the Redevelopment Agency, which would be contributing financially. Caret had to sell a very new idea within the university community.

With the reliable assistance of supportive vice presidents, Caret had to convince the Council of Deans, the professional librarians, and the broader campus community, including students, staff, faculty, alumni supporters, donors, local and state holders of key political offices, and the CSU chancellor. Specifically, and most important of all, Caret had to convince San José State's Academic Senate, which was officially responsible with him for the formulation of university policy.

'More pleasure...than anything I have ever done'

LOCATION. LOCATION. LOCATION. Phil and Susan Boyce paid $125,000 for a gateway at Ninth Street. Billye Ericksen invested $100,000 in a fountain across from the Business Tower. James Boccardo put $250,000 on the gateway at San Carlos and Fourth streets. These high-profile business leaders all expected an excellent return on their investment in San José State. Joining in their optimism: San Jose National Bank, Comerica Bank, Bay Networks, and many others.

Seven entrance gateways, three fountains and 43 park benches are not only lasting legacies for alumni and corporate neighbors. They are also visual landmarks of a university proud of its heritage but ready for an active role in the twenty-first century. Opening the campus up to the community, the gateways reversed the walled-in feel created in the 1970s, replacing it with welcoming entrances for coming and going between a redeveloped downtown and a revitalized university.

The $1.5 million Heritage Gateway project, dedicated in 1999, marked the first university-wide capital campaign. It drew support from 1,000 alumni, students, faculty, staff, corporations and community members. Phil Boyce, who earned his business degree in 1966, and Susan (Eastburn) Boyce, with a 1965 sociology degree, chose a central location for their gift. Phil, who chaired the campaign, said the volunteer support he saw arise for the project is the difference between a good university and "a really wonderful university."

"My fountain sits in the shadow of the Business Tower," said Ericksen, who earned her accounting degree in 1982. "This school has been a fountain of information and resources for me. Business students of the future will pass by that fountain."

James Boccardo, who graduated from San José State in 1931 and made his name nationally as a tough litigator and diligent businessman, said, "I have derived more pleasure out of these gifts (for the gateway and the business classroom project) than anything I have ever done."

What he presented, in coordination with Mayor Hammer, was a revolutionary new proposal budgeted at $171 million. It would be the largest single construction undertaking within the California State University system and would have no conceptual parallel anywhere in America. Caret's selling job turned out to be far more difficult and prolonged than Hammer's. As president of San José State and with the cooperation of the Chancellor's Office and partial funding from the state, Caret could enter into the joint agreement. His presidential authority allowed him to do so over campus opposition. But he understood that university presidents do not enjoy happy administrative after-lives once they reject the considered advice of their university communities, especially when expressed by an Academic Senate.

Opposition to the Joint Library Project within the university community was substantial and vocal. The traditionalist view saw the purpose and function of a university and a city library to be simply different. The Clark and Wahlquist libraries served a student and faculty community engaged in professional and learned pursuits at the university level. The city's library served children, the general public and, to some degree, the business and commercial interests of San José.

From a distance, negative campus opinion appeared overwhelming. It was broadly based, but its leadership and strength came from the departments of history and English. E. Bruce Reynolds, chair of the history department and a well-published Asian scholar, was the strongest and most visible of the anti-joint venture forces. He was ably assisted by Scott B. Rice, a professor of English with decades of experience in campus union and activist causes. The entire concept of a shared library seemed so abhorrent to the intellectual traditionalists that determining which parts of the metropolitan concept they disliked most was difficult. Both professors were philosophically opposed to the joint library.

With a nucleus of support from departments that relied heavily upon library services in the delivery of their curriculum and for graduate level and faculty research, Reynolds organized SOUL, the Save Our University Library movement. The major dissatisfaction focused upon faculty fear that there would be an insufficiency of academic books to satisfy both the assignment needs of the university students and the supposed-massive reading interests of the local public.

The Academic Senate was the campus body that would deliver the heaviest input. Since the senate was not under Caret's direction, SOUL organized a highly successful petition campaign requesting the senators (some of whom were SOUL members) to recommend against the president's proposed new library. The SOUL petition opposing the project carried more than 3,550 campus signatures, which Reynolds delivered in person to the Academic Senate on the day of its critical vote. SOUL also organized its own rallies and demonstrations. Articulate faculty delivered critical presentations at public hearings scheduled by the administration in order to air the proposal. The university had its own web server and home page that explained and advanced the joint library idea. SOUL responded with its own page, which included documentation and volumes of criticism. SOUL generated flyers, posters, and letters to editors of the *Spartan Daily* and to the *San Jose Mercury News*.

After the full campus debate, the Academic Senate, in a voice vote and in a clearly strong majority, approved the Joint Library Project and with it validated Caret's metropolitan university concept. Later, Caret admitted that he would not have gone against the Academic Senate's vote — if that vote had been substantially opposed to the joint library. If the senate had been split or had the opposition margin been very thin, then he would have advanced the proposal. He felt that the joint library was best for the university and for the community.

A December 9, 1998, editorial in the *San Jose Mercury News* concluded that, "There is no place like a university campus to stir up controversy. So the idea got the full university debate complete with public demonstrations worthy of the 1960s." Though of little solace to SOUL believers, their powerful and insightful criticism forced the plan to address every imaginable weakness and unexplored issue from every perceivable perspective. The dialogue that preceded the highly contested approval created a blueprint for potential success at what the metropolitan university and the Silicon Valley dared to offer as a world model.

Next in the cavalcade of progressive actions, California voters approved a mammoth $9.7 billion bond issue for education that contained the state's share of the library costs. On top of that, the San José Redevelopment Agency unveiled its massive new plans for extending the already successful downtown renaissance into the North Campus neighborhood, within four blocks adjacent to the campus. The projection included the relocation of the San José City Hall, a symphony hall, new elementary school, three to four new parking garages, and several new office buildings. The Redevelopment Agency also provided for major residential and retail improvements within the North Campus area. At 2000, San José State welcomed a new departure.

CHAPTER SEVEN

❖

The Campus and its Community

FROM COMPREHENSIVE TO METROPOLITAN UNIVERSITY

CHANGE HAS BEEN nowhere more evident than in the relationship of the university to its community. Mid-century, President John T. Wahlquist inaugurated his administration with civic pageantry, a full academic procession from the campus quad through downtown to the Civic Auditorium, where he delivered his inaugural address. Influential members of the Rotary Club had all but determined his appointment, and the new president shared this bond with the city of San José.

From the 1960s forward, however, the town changed, the college changed, and the defining components within each changed. Community leaders ceased to determine college presidents. Their small-town clubs and local interests became less influential entities amid the growing interests and influences of the defense, space, electronics and information industries. The college became a university, and its focus as trainer of teachers blurred. The campus suffered from its location on the eastern edge of the downtown San José business district, formerly the valley's center of commerce. By the mid-1960s, however, downtown was the picture of urban blight, having succumbed to post-WWII suburban housing sprawl and the development of suburban shopping centers.

Amidst the changing relationship in the 1960s, the San José Police Department, over the firm opposition of the college administration, sent its tactical squad to physically subdue students for what Vice President Hobert Burns termed minor student infractions. Certainly, the flow of academic-robed faculty who followed Wahlquist through downtown San José and the counter-flow of combat-equipped police across San Fernando at Seventh Street constitute symbolism that requires little analysis. The relationship of the town and the college had gone from good to bad, from the tranquil and sedate 1950s to the uproarious '60s and '70s. The respective cultures and interests of the town and the campus diverged, and the participants gradually drifted apart.

Even architecture played a role. The row of concrete buildings lining Fourth Street to the south of San Fernando came to be popularly called San José State's "great wall." Critics saw it as the manifestation of the university's siege mentality, which not only physically separated the campus from downtown San José, but also symbolized social division, psychological defensiveness, and cultural separatism. It reflected a two-way divide, also, to the extent that the neighbors feared or disdained what they perceived as ill-behaved, ungrateful students, and sometimes faculty, as well, who dressed poorly and failed to present themselves as role models. For its part, the campus population had its own list of dislikes: the physically decaying downtown and the depreciating neighborhoods, the ever-present and growing number of street people and halfway house residents, many of whom were disruptive and occasionally even dangerous when not medicated, and the physical violence inflicted by criminal predators who seemed to surround the urban campus, some of whom even ventured behind the wall and into the sanctuary. With the advent of the commuter campus, the grounds became deserted and foreboding as night fell.

When Professor Terry L. Christensen arrived in San José as a newly recruited political scientist in 1970, he drove around trying to figure out how to enter the campus. San José State had plenty of buildings, but no welcoming entrance, certainly no endowed gate or portico to focus the attention of a new arrival. When Frank Taylor left Cincinnati for his new position as director of downtown redevelopment for San José in 1979, he had not heard of San José State until he arrived. Reflecting back on it all in 1999, Taylor thought that the university had closed in on itself and that a "we and they" mentality persisted. Tom McEnery, San José mayor and political godfather of Taylor's downtown renaissance, was a local boy who had always been aware of San José State's presence. When Santa Clara College stopped playing big time football, his father took him to the San José State games. With a Bellarmine preparatory education and Santa Clara undergraduate and graduate degrees, he was far more attentive to the state university than might otherwise have been expected. He learned about the problem areas in which city and campus met and those over which they contended. Where Christensen and Taylor initially saw a still-photo shot capturing the college and the city at the moment of their arrival, McEnery saw San José State and downtown San José as a motion picture. His major criticism was that it was all playing in slow motion and without color.

Progress began slowly, but like most everything else in the region, it gathered momentum until it became a challenge to direct rather than to propel. The ongoing story of town and gown relationships evolved within a complex mix of city and campus leaderships, the agenda priorities of each, and the larger economic and cultural changes, which revolutionized local life, creating Silicon Valley and its metropolitan university.

Campus Neighborhoods

THE GREATEST CHANGE to campus residential neighborhoods at the end of the twentieth century was the rebirth of cooperation and outreach between the university and the community. When the *University Neighborhoods Revitalization Plan* appeared in 1998, its existence was as noteworthy as its contents were insightful. San José city staff, campus neighbors, and university representatives actually gathered together on the campus in productive meetings where they reviewed their shared problems and envisioned a future of cooperative improvements. The diverse players developed a plan of action and obtained start-up funding from the city, initiative and expertise from the university, and cooperative participation from the neighbors.

The neighborhoods for which San José State was the predominant institution and focal point were easy to characterize. They appeared as if a shadow of Tower Hall were casting itself mostly to the southeast. Immediately south as far as Interstate 280 and east through Naglee Park to Coyote Creek, these largely residential neighborhoods constituted the bulk of the adjacent population and land. South Fourth Street to South First Street to the west, along with the area between San Fernando and Santa Clara to the north rounded out the western and northern quadrants. But most of San José State's neighbors lived to the south and east, where most of the land and homes were.

Through the 1950s and 1960s, as the campus grew to the east and to the south, neighborhood speculators at the edges of the college boundaries bought property in order to sell to the state during the successive expansions. While they waited, they rented to students and to the occasional new faculty and staff members who opted for the convenience of strolling to campus. Maintenance and appearance were not high priorities for these owners, particularly after the recession-induced halt to campus expansion caught some speculators overextended. Naglee Park held up better, and presidents Wahlquist and Clark chose to reside in the southern end of this once-grand, turn-of-the-century neighborhood. Faculty sprinkled the neighborhood, but far more often, younger faculty and staff chose to pay somewhat more for newer homes in appreciating sections of San José, Cupertino, Los Gatos, and Saratoga.

In 1968, a standard two-bedroom home on South 14th Street, 60 years old, with attractive woodwork and appointments, and an antique furnace dug into the dirt basement, sold at $17,000. New, two-story Almaden homes sold for $32,000, while highly appreciable houses in Los Gatos were still offered at below $30,000. San José State salaries at that time qualified potential buyers for all areas throughout the valley. The housing costs were still manageable on a university salary.

Naglee Park
...homes increased in value

Over the years after WWII and into the early 1980s, the direction of neighborhood change was downhill. Some homeowners fought the trend by establishing the Campus Community Association, a membership organization of neighborhood residents — owners and tenants — in the early '70s. In addition, many homes fell to heirs who became absentee landlords. Larger, older, formerly elegant single-family homes became apartments and cheap rooming houses renting by the week to alcoholics, parolees, and other poor people living one step away from homelessness. Many large homes became halfway houses, and the campus neighborhoods housed the largest concentration of such facilities in Santa Clara County.

In the mid-1960s, sororities and fraternities, with their spacious, well-maintained buildings, crested in popularity and financial soundness. Other large, privately owned housing units were officially sanctioned by the college as student residences. Though the influence exercised by the office of the dean of students over the owners and resident managers of these properties was informal, an official relationship did exist, and managers (sometimes "house mothers") resided on the premises. The spirit of the times prompted tidiness, lawfulness, and respectability as defined by middle-class assumptions. The student revolution of the late '60s contributed to the seriously diminished status of Greek life. It marked the termination of the college's registration and approval of private housing providers. Also, the student revolution and the new realities of student emancipation brought about the reversal of the established college policy of *in loco parentis*. In time, new state laws addressed discrimination in housing, but the quality of that housing remained largely unaddressed.

The quality of student accommodations in the East Campus neighborhood along 10th and 11th streets deteriorated along with the rest of Naglee Park. The official findings of the *University Neighborhoods Revitalization Plan* charted an increase in crime, trash, traffic hazards, and the use of what had been landscaped front yards to park the overwhelming number of automobiles. Absentee landlords generally failed to reinvest profits in the maintenance and appearance of the campus neighborhoods. Noting the impact, the *University Neighborhoods Revitalization Plan* addressed the problem with a grants scheme intended to reverse or at least mitigate this problem. With university and city help and their own organized self-help, neighborhoods to the south and east made progress.

Over the long run, even as the quality of housing declined, the dollar value of the properties increased. By the 1990s, all San José real-estate values had greatly appreciated, and the homes in Naglee Park were hardly an exception. Some 1,500-square-foot

Craftsman homes, in fact, sold for more than $500,000 before being renovated by new owners. In 1999, Naglee Park resident Professor Christensen concluded that faculty and staff previously not wanting to purchase near the campus no longer enjoyed the option to do so; they had been priced out. Most students commuted and placed greater demands upon the freeway system, parking facilities, as well as themselves. Those who did live within the neighborhoods crowded more densely into aging accommodations and paid the vastly higher rents with augmented student loans. Those loans, plus credit card obligations, became their post-graduate debts.

The success of Frank Taylor's urban renewal of downtown San José, accompanied

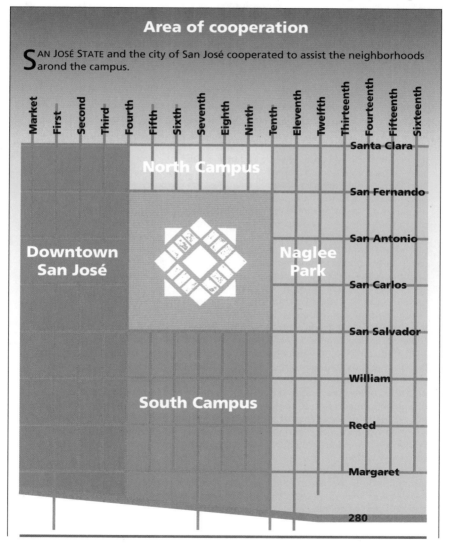

Area of cooperation

SAN JOSÉ STATE and the city of San José cooperated to assist the neighborhoods arond the campus.

University police look after the neighborhood

SAN JOSÉ STATE POLICE committed themselves to the concept of community service years before the term "community policing" was coined. The evolution of campus police grew from campus security officers in the 1950s, to certified officers in the 1970s, to a professional force focusing on community service in the late 1980s. By the turn of the century, their community leadership would reshape not just the campus, but the surrounding communities.

Ric Abeyta
...implemented community policing

When Ric Abeyta donned the police chief's hat in 1988, he began a program to transform the force into a more responsive unit, starting with training not only on police tactics, but also on cultural sensitivity and community needs. "I wanted professional high-profile police officers out there in the community being seen and solving problems," Abeyta said. He also wanted visible results.

One of the department's first community efforts was a holiday food drive where UPD collected donations and delivered food and toys to needy families in the campus neighborhoods. "When you go up carrying a sack of toys into an apartment complex that's fairly spartan, and Santa Claus knocks on the door...kids with eyes wide open ...it touches the heart," Abeyta said. The program grew to serve 60 families each year and included participation from across campus, including football players and fraternities and sororities.

In 1996, President Robert Caret and San José Mayor Susan Hammer authorized Abeyta to delve further into problem-solving in the neighborhoods surrounding campus. Abeyta chaired the South of Campus University/City Task Force to reduce crime, gang activity and visual blight adjacent to campus. The first order of business was neighborhood cleanup. Police cadets did a "blight survey" that helped identify city code violations. A massive cleanup day was scheduled, and 350 campus and community members pruned, painted and filled 42 large trash bins. In cooperation with city police, UPD took a more active role in law enforcement in the area, from undercover drug arrests to street crime bike patrols and graffiti abatement. UPD officers received joint jurisdiction with city police in a one-mile radius around campus.

When additional resources were needed in 1997, the task force lobbied for the city's Project Crackdown to designate the neighborhood as a target area. A plan of action emerged — the University Neighborhoods Revitalization Plan — in 1998, and the university obtained a U.S. Department of Housing and Urban Development matching grant of $400,000 ($460,000 in university funds) to create permanent community cooperation. Abeyta also applied for and won four federal COPS (Community Oriented Policing) grants to add four sworn officers and two dispatchers. In addition to the university's leadership, community groups were encouraged to take charge of their neighborhoods, and eventually the University Neighborhood Coalition and the South University Neighborhood groups were working hand-in-hand to improve livability in the downtown area. The results were very visible.

Throughout, Abeyta focused his staff on continuous improvement, with core values that include professionalism, responsiveness and respect. The campus, he said, has become "very safe.... We have a lot of people watching out for the students." The UPD staff of 60 includes 34 sworn officers. Dozens of students also serve as cadets and assistants.

by the transformation of the regional economy into the world's information technology engine, fueled the transformation of much of Naglee Park. Likewise, west-side change had been long in coming and, because so much time lagged between demolition and the renaissance that blossomed into the Paseo Condominiums on South Fourth Street, the university was able to use the wasteland for parking. In time, the Colonnade apartments, street-level shops, and the Paseo Condominiums assumed full occupancy of the land along Fourth Street from San Carlos to San Fernando. The new, high-end real estate promoted gentrification of the university's buffer with downtown which, itself, had become definitely upscale with the Fairmont Hotel, Children's Discovery Museum, Tech Museum of Innovation, light rail transportation, San José McEnery Convention Center, San José Repertory Theatre and a good number of trendy and successful restaurants. The Paseo Condominiums had its own homeowners association, and Naglee Park and South Campus homeowners and tenants also were represented by neighborhood associations.

For its part, San José State organized its own positive response to the revitalization challenge. President Gail Fullerton had ensured the restoration of Washington Square Hall to its better-than-original 1930s elegance. She retained its openness to downtown through tiled entranceways on Fourth Street. In the 1990s, the Heritage Gateways Campaign, initiated by the university's Advancement Office, raised the funds to construct university gates to welcome campus pedestrians. The closing and landscaping of San Carlos, from Fourth Street to Tenth Street, and the city-university joint library venture went much further. Both cooperative ventures marked immensely improved relations between the campus and the city.

By 1999, three of the four neighborhoods (east, south, and west) surrounding the campus had some form of grassroots organization to advance their interests. From the university perspective, the disaster zone was the north campus neighborhood, seven lateral square blocks south of Santa Clara Street that bordered the campus at San Fernando Street. The Lucky supermarket parking lot was the focal point, complete with drug dealing, panhandling, and vagrancy. The neighborhood's remainder was an unorganized mix of small businesses and mostly inferior housing.

Among the few bright spots was the John XXIII center for the elderly on San Fernando and South Fifth streets, with its adjacent high-rise, subsidized, affordable apartments. Much of the rest of the neighborhood suffered from parking congestion, panhandling, and street drug deals. East Santa Clara Street had one of the highest crime rates in the city, a fact that received much publicity when a police officer was fatally shot at a donut shop.

The worse the neighborhood sank, the more likely became its ultimate transformation. Depressed property values, dysfunctional and transient residents, and proximity to an incredibly wealthy and expanding downtown were the features that prompted the city to designate the north campus area for the most ambitious urban renewal project within the San José renaissance. According to the plan put in place before the retirement of Frank Taylor and before the end of Mayor Susan Hammer's second term as mayor, north campus would house the city's new and relocated city hall in an expansive civic center.

At the threshold of the twenty-first century, this depressed neighborhood promised to become the most exciting enhancement to the physical life of the university. The new San José mayor, Ron Gonzales, elected in 1998, adopted a slow-but-sure approach to this major advance, which included his own progressive initiatives. Gonzales persisted in his attempt to have Bay Area Rapid Transit (BART) extended from Fremont, past the San José State campus, and into the transportation hub of downtown.

By the turn of the century, substantial progress had been made in addressing neighborhood problems, which had been largely neglected since the days when the college became a fortress. The plans and visions for the twenty-first century seemed bright, not just because of strong and continuing economic growth for the Silicon Valley, but also because San José State had accepted its own leadership role. It did so in a more organized and focused manner; its commitment was substantial and promised to be enduring.

Robert Caret becomes the "External Advocate" President

PRESIDENT ROBERT L. CARET arrived at San José State at a time when transition in community relations was becoming possible. His predecessor Gail Fullerton believed that the university had been stereotyped for too long as an isolated institution, one not interested in community interaction or outreach. Fullerton knew that the characterization was simply unfounded and initiated an institution-wide investigation. Exactly what did San José State do in cooperation with the community? The resulting publication *San José State University: Community Involvement* began life as a database to which Caret contributed a "Partnership for the Future" introduction and noted that the 71-page listing was incomplete. The involvements extended from memberships on community boards of directors to consultancies, internships and volunteerism, through health, environmental, and cultural affairs affiliations. Sample organizations crossed the spectrum: Opera San Jose, Salvation Army, Joint Venture

Cadets serve as national model for campus safety

WHEN SAN JOSÉ STATE needed some highly visible efforts in the 1970s to battle crime and downtown blight, two key programs emerged — the blue light phone system and one of the nation's first police cadet programs on a college campus. President Gail Fullerton had 178 phones with blue lights above them installed across campus — inside buildings and along walkways — to provide immediate access to the University Police Department. New blue light phones were planned at the turn of the century.

The cadet system was designed to help serve as UPD's eyes and ears and became a model that other universities would follow. The well-trained cadets also became UPD's feet, walking and biking the campus and providing services such as evening escorts for students. Many cadets graduated into law enforcement careers, including local agencies and the FBI. One cadet, Chris Riffel, even found his way to the Royal Canadian Mounted Police.

James Boccardo

AB, Chemical Engineering, 1931

A S A PRACTICING LAWYER, James Boccardo declared: "I love law. I love what I'm doing."

Born in San Francisco and raised in San José, Boccardo started his San José-based Boccardo Law Firm in 1934. Building a successful practice specializing in personal injury cases, his reputation grew as one who worked on behalf of, and sought justice for, "the common man." But what he found in the courts appalled him. Juries were all white, selected from a group of names offered by the county board of supervisors. Boccardo pushed back, going to the state judicial council and protesting. The county was forced to change its jury selection process to one in which names were pulled from the registry of voters, assuring a truer cross section of the community in the jurors box.

He went on to become co-founder and president of the Inner Circle of Trial Advocates, a member of the International Academy of Trial Lawyers, and charter president of the Santa Clara Trial Lawyers Association. In 1996, the Consumer Attorneys of Santa Clara County named him lawyer of the year. In 1998, Boccardo received the prestigious Tower Award from SJSU. With a generous leadership gift in the university's Heritage Gateway Campaign from James and his wife, Lorraine, and an additional $2 million for the Business Classrooms Renovation Project, two structures on campus bear his name: the campus gateway at Fourth and San Carlos Streets, and the James F. Boccardo Business Education Center.

On Campus: Majored in chemical engineering. Hoped to find a cure for cancer.

Silicon Valley, Software Business Cluster, South Bay Water Recycling, Women's Housing Connection, Teens for Success Tutoring, Sacred Heart Community Services, San José Beautiful, and Community Concepts/Community Service. With a student body, staff, and faculty in excess of 30,000, the university naturally contributed to the networks that held the region together. For the most part, what was so unsurprising also remained largely unknown.

Worse, publishing the results of the inventory seemed to make little public relations impact. Fixed and stubborn popular opinion overshadowed reality. Outdated factors such as the Fourth Street "wall," proximity to crime, and inner-directed leadership constituted the public's lingering perception of the university. Even the construction of the community-subsidized Engineering Building and the publicity associated with San José State's contributions to the new economy failed to change the broadly held public opinion. That the region's leading engineer-producing university and the engineer-consuming Silicon Valley cooperated at such a level remained little noticed beyond the engineering community itself and seemed an exception to San José State's alleged isolationism.

During his three years, Acting President J. Handel Evans tried to change the outdated stereotype, but few beyond local officialdom noticed. He stepped out into the community, and he enjoyed doing so. As a caretaker president, though, he did not redefine the nature or the scope of the community relations he was attempting to advance. Evans authorized an image survey, which confirmed the unscientific views of insiders. The university lacked high visibility in the community and appeared as an undifferentiated, mass educational institution. Self-evaluations, consultants, and high-level brainstorming reached the same conclusion. The university lacked definition, and no one knew what San José State's niche within the community should be. But some positive actions were taking place.

During Evans's interim presidency, Dean Marshall J. Burak initiated the College of Business's outreach to the community, the Business Classrooms Renovation Project. His objective was to acquire financial support to underwrite a major renovation of the Business Classroom building. The off-campus MBA program already had established positive links. Beginning in 1995 the Office of University Advancement initiated the Heritage Gateway Campaign. The design and erection of six campus gateways would identify major access routes into the university, symbolize openness to the community, and invite public access. These two funding drives, business and advancement, carried over into the Caret administration. Though university-serving, they reflected administrative desires for continued improvements in community relations.

The concept of the metropolitan university, which Caret brought to San José State, offered a new definition of self. The metropolitan university concept implied a mission, a role, and a guidance system. The old category, comprehensive university, implied that the university did everything. As a result, prioritization and planning lacked cohesiveness and continuity. The comprehensive university model accepted all good ideas, even when they pulled in different directions. The concept of the metropolitan university provided a more refined guidance system.

Obtaining acceptance of that concept and its consequences became Caret's basic challenge. Since Robert Clark's time, San José presidents shared policy formulation with the faculty's Academic Senate. Caret was free to direct his administrative activities in line with the metropolitan concept. What he could not do without Academic Senate approval, however, was convert his own understanding of the university and the larger Silicon Valley into university policy. Also, he could not wisely initiate a major project that followed from the metropolitan concept when the rest of the university community still thought in terms of the comprehensive university. By winning Academic Senate validation for the metropolitan university concept, Caret could broaden the scope of university-community relations and still sharpen San José State's definition and focus.

Metropolitan University

FACULTY AND ADMINISTRATORS who were not well attuned to the major developments in higher education at the national level assumed that their new president either invented the term *metropolitan university* or merely appropriated it from his previous employer, Towson State University in Baltimore.

Actually, Caret had been a junior founder of what was to become an organization of 55 institutions of higher education that proclaimed the concept of the metropolitan university. The father of the idea was Page Mulholland, president of Wright State University in Dayton, Ohio. President Mulholland's problem was his discomfort with the generic category, comprehensive university. The category simply did not sufficiently identify Wright State or differentiate it from the likes of the Ohio University and Ohio State University. As long as his university remained within the broader category dominated by major, high-profile institutions, it would remain less focused on its own mission and less able to satisfy its own specific educational obligations. So Mulholland called a meeting of 20 kindred university presidents who gathered at Towson State. He brought his own provost, Charles E. Hathaway (subsequently president of the University of Arkansas, Little Rock), and there they met Towson's provost and vice president for academic affairs, Robert Caret.

At the Towson State meeting, the participants founded the organization of metropolitan universities. Their journal, *Metropolitan Universities: An International Forum,* followed. From the mid-1980s, the organization made clear its intent: not to challenge established national leadership groups within higher education, but to be a subset of the comprehensive universities group. They shared a special and defining interest and organized themselves as the Coalition of Urban and Metropolitan Universities.

The applicability of the metropolitan university concept and philosophy to San José State became immediately apparent to Caret when he read about the city and the university at the time of his presidential recruitment. He had been seeking a metropolitan presidency, and he felt comfortable in the fit that San José State allowed.

The metropolitan concept committed its universities to addressing community needs and to using university resources and leadership in combating urban problems through teaching, research, and service. Appropriately, the metropolitan university was to seek opportunities to link its own investigations with practical applications for addressing complex urban problems. Accordingly, the metropolitan university was to develop creative partnerships with public and private enterprises that engaged its intellectual resources in ways that benefited the university and the community.

Caret introduced the words *metropolitan university* to the San José campus and community at his inauguration as San José State University's twenty-third president. He intended the term not solely as a tool to change the university, but as the idea to define what it had already become. The advantages, he thought, were numerous. First, it gave definition to a large and often unwieldy institution. In dealing with the general public, the two words offered a streamlined way to talk about a very complex organization. Second, the two words encapsulated the mission and the vision of San José State. Beyond the education of the people in general, San José State, as a public institution, should serve society. In a broader sense, it should be reaching out so that the community and the university could grow and improve together.

Caret's immediate mission was not to persuade the university community to formally adopt the metropolitan university philosophy. It was to explain what it meant and to demonstrate how San José State already fit that category. In part, he did that through innovations that reflected the official declarations of the Coalition of Urban and Metropolitan Universities.

Phillip Boyce

BS, Business Administration, 1966

Phillip Boyce never thought his first job at a bank would launch his career. In 1966, Jack Holland, a professor at SJSU, spoke to him right before graduation and told him that the local banks offered a training program. He signed up and learned fast. By the time Boyce was 30, he began a founders group and started the Pacific Western Bank. There he managed the bank through a merger with Comerica Bank-California and took pride in the fact that he could direct and maintain control of an actual "community" bank.

Retirement in 1994 left Boyce with time on his hands and many interests to accommodate. Always active in the nonprofit sector, he threw himself into philanthropy. He chaired the Valley Foundation, which provided more than $3 million a year to worthy non-profit organizations in Santa Clara County. He served on and chaired the SJSU President's Advisory Board, and served on the boards of the Community Foundation of Silicon Valley, Villa Montalvo, American Leadership Forum, and the San Jose Chamber of Commerce. "I've been involved in fund-raising in the hundreds of millions of dollars," Boyce said. "I've been doing it for 25 years." In addition, his personal generosity set an example for others to follow. Boyce received the highest honor bestowed by SJSU, the Tower Award, in 1997, reflecting the university's gratitude for his unfailing support and volunteer efforts on behalf of future students.

On Campus: Member of the Theta Zi fraternity. Hung out at Lenny's on Santa Clara Street. Went to every football game.

His first actions included organizational adjustments in consultation with the Academic Senate. He converted the former office of academic vice president into that of provost and vice president for academic affairs. Dr. Linda L. Bain accepted that new appointment and became Caret's second in command at the university. Where President Fullerton had looked to J. Handel Evans, the administrative vice president, Caret conferred primacy upon the academic function of the university. Caret reserved for himself the role as ambassador to the community (neighborhood, city, region, and nation) and looked to Bain to serve as his primary campus representative.

Next, Caret upgraded the entire alumni, community relations, and fundraising arm of the university by creating the office of vice president for university advancement. Thereafter, and with special CSU system funding, Caret initiated the campus infrastructure project, which "wired" acres of university buildings for the information and communication requirements of the twenty-first century. Opportunely, as the deep crevasses widened and cut their ways across campus, the facilities planners used the openings to replace century-old plumbing lines and overhaul heating and update air-conditioning.

Far more visible than the greatly improved infrastructure was the growing list of community partnerships that coalesced under Caret's new metropolitan university umbrella. The Community Outreach Partnership Center began facilitating neighborhood improvements within the 360 blocks surrounding the campus. With funding from the U.S. Office of Housing and Urban Development, matched by the university and private sources, the faculty, staff and students joined the efforts. At the same time the University Foundation supported three San José business incubators that drew the colleges and schools of the university into cooperative undertakings in software development, environment preservation, and international business. The metropolitan university concept provided for the advancement of the interests of the university and the local business community, in several cases, through technology transfer. Before the end of the century, San José State's neighbors included software giant Adobe Systems, which had located its corporate headquarters downtown along the Guadalupe River. Symbolic of university outreach, the colleges of business and engineering offered the world colossus in internet technology, Cisco Systems, customized programs, which included the MBA and master's degree in electrical engineering. Engineering built upon the already well-established College of Business model.

Given San José State's historic role in training teachers for the public schools, outreach initiatives of the College of Education and the local schools also fit comfortably within the metropolitan university concept. The Metropolitan San José Collaborative for Academic Excellence drew together district educators and the dean and faculty of the college. Clear recognition of the great challenges confronting public education in California and America prompted numerous sponsored projects, most of which attracted the participation of campus educators. Additionally, in his welcome to the faculty in the fall of 1999, President Caret noted the university's broad and growing educational participation with the National Hispanic University in San José.

Campus-community cooperation in the immediate neighborhood was most apparent within the police-related initiatives such as Project Crackdown and Clean-Up Days. The South Campus Task Force and the Neighborhood Revitalization Plan were broadly based and cooperatively advanced. Less visible, but at least equally valuable to the participants, was the work of practitioners from the nursing faculty who managed community health clinics. Across San Fernando Street from Hugh Gillis Hall, nursing faculty member Gail Marculescu managed the John XXIII Neighborhood Clinic and Nursing Center. The health facility, combined with subsidized housing for the elderly at Jeanne D'Arc Manor on South Fifth Street, advanced under the watchful administrative eye of Alvin C.K. Lau, who had earned his master of social work at San José State. Owned by the Catholic Church, the center functioned under policies determined by a board that included two Catholic priests and Professor Manuel Fimbres, stalwart of the College of Social Work.

These numerous advances into the community did not emerge from the metropolitan university concept. They preceded President Caret's arrival and constituted the cooperation he observed and identified as not only appropriate to that concept, but also one of the most enticing reasons for him to accept the position of SJSU president.

CHAPTER EIGHT

❖

The Reason for Being
ACADEMIC LIFE OF THE UNIVERSITY

L YN NOFZIGER had good reason to value San José State's hands-on approach to career preparation. Under the GI Bill he earned his journalism degree in 1950. He advanced from crime reporter on the *Glendale News Press* to stalwart within Ronald Reagan's two administrations, first as California governor, next as president of the United States. San José State's practical approach propelled Nofziger to the upper limits of an idealized career, and Dwight Bentel, his professor and founder of the journalism department, undoubtedly appreciated his famous student's words of tribute: "You never taught me anything I couldn't use."

A Practical Curriculum

THIS SHARED UNDERSTANDING between Nofziger and Bentel symbolized a specific type of education that San José State had always provided its students. The San José State education was practical and intended to qualify generations of students for entry-level professional positions within the expanding industries and institutions of the region and the nation. In exceptional cases, remarkable talent, timing, and good fortune could take the graduate over the top.

Leon C. Dorosz, professor of biology and university administrator, drew two interesting observations regarding the totality of courses San José State faculty offered to its students. First, the undergraduate curriculum package was practical; it equipped each year's graduates to step directly into relevant employment at the entry level of their professions, and employers recognized and appreciated their immediate readiness. Second, the curriculum, by stressing the applicable and the utilitarian, slighted the theoretical and the abstract.

There were positive reasons why the San José State education became more practical than theoretical. The bulk of American students go to colleges so that they may experience upward economic mobility. Parents hope their children may achieve better jobs and a more abundant life. In that sense, San José State blended with the American pattern. But for the most part, the generations of students who came to San José State lacked a family history of higher education. Dwight Bentel knew his students, and his students knew him. Because Bentel initiated his career at San José State as a student himself, and because he matured within its intellectual environment, he affirmed the college's practicality. He knew why Nofziger enrolled at San José State under the GI Bill. The future presidential adviser wanted to become a journalist, to qualify for an entry-level appointment. Nofziger wanted to do things, and Bentel equipped him to do them.

University Curriculum

BY THE TIME of President Robert D. Clark's arrival in 1964, the department system of academic organization had already matured. Specialized faculty, through the committee system, determined which courses their departments offered. They created the sequences of courses that became a student's major or minor. The drive to professionalism led committees to assume that the more courses students had in their field, the better they would be as beginning practitioners. The minority point of view was that education had to go beyond job training.

Faculty who arrived in San José with the expectation that they would teach as they had learned, at an elevated theoretical level, frequently experienced shock and dismay. Some became depressed, some left, some adjusted to their new mission — preparing entry-level professionals. Long-term Academic Vice President Hobert W. Burns understood this quite well, and he had made his own adjustments early. Burns noted in

Michael Deaver

BA, Public Administration, 1960

Michael Deaver led a life under both the glare of political limelight and the illumination of self-awareness. In his first life, with a degree from San José State, he began working for then-Governor Ronald Reagan, launching a professional relationship that would last for 18 years. Serving as deputy chief of staff under President Reagan, Deaver was responsible for setting Reagan's daily schedule and deciding the themes and events the president should emphasize. He was a confidant to Reagan and a close friend to Nancy Reagan. As one of the Reagans' inner circle of friends, he was in the line of fire during the 1986 assassination attempt against Reagan, but Deaver crouched low and missed being shot.

After leaving the Reagan administration, Deaver launched a successful consulting business as a beltway lobbyist and was featured on the cover of *Time* magazine. By 1987, however, his world came crumbling down around him—alcohol was to blame. Confronting his own alcoholism launched his second life. A life he now controls, relishes, and enjoys. He talks to teenagers and college students about his rise to power—and his fall. His message is clear and succinct and touches on the cornerstone of alcoholism: that it is a disease, one that needs to be treated, monitored and recognized. "I used to be somebody that was on television and in the magazines. Today, I'm also Mike Deaver, recovering alcoholic."

Deaver served as a Republican strategist and was back in front of the camera as a guest analyst on the *Today Show*, *NBC Nightly News*, *CBS Evening News*, and the *Mac-Neil-Lehrer News Hour*.

his oral history that the best students at San José State compared favorably with those he had encountered at top-ranked universities. Many others, however, required basic help. As the first to occupy the new position of academic vice president, Burns accepted his challenge and set out to reorganize the curriculum, particularly the general education program.

While the purpose of general education was to provide students with the knowledge and skills needed to understand and to contribute to society, when Burns surveyed graduation requirements in 1966, he discovered significant inadequacies. From hundreds of courses, students chose as they pleased and satisfied general education requirements by taking 32 units of course work in just about anything. In Burns's opinion, "students could take all 32 units of general education and not have a general education!" He shared his views with the Academic Senate, where professors David H. Elliott and David K. Newman arranged for Burns to chair a committee charged with reviewing general education. There Burns drafted the general education redesign that, with modifications, became San José State's modern plan. The Burns model increased general education from 32 units to a 52-unit maximum and also junked the smorgasbord approach.

Burns' basic assumption was that it was "insane to ask students to major in something until they were sound in the fundamentals." The Burns plan put heavy emphasis on writing skills, breadth of reading, and critical thinking. He insisted that

Tom and Dick Smothers — The Smothers Brothers

ADVERTISING MAJOR, 1957-59; EDUCATION MAJOR, 1959, RESPECTIVELY
EACH RECEIVED AN HONORARY DOCTORATE OF FINE ARTS, 2000.

TOM AND DICK SMOTHERS entertained, educated and inspired an
entire generation and remained icons
of comedy and political commentary
for more than 40 years. *The Smothers Brothers Comedy Hour* debuted
in 1967 on CBS-TV and immediately
became the focus for the duo's satirical
and thought-provoking humor. Bringing national attention to counter-cul-
tural perspectives on issues of the day
— war, drugs, sexuality, religion, politics, race relations and civil rights — the show
was under constant pressure of censorship and was canceled after a three-year run.
Their successful lawsuit, considered a struggle for the First Amendment right of free
speech, not only paved the way for future political satire on television but became a
point in civil liberty history studied in classrooms across the country. Still performing
with their unique style of comedy, a blend of satirical folk singing, sibling rivalry, and
yo-yoing, the brothers also operate a successful vineyard near Sonoma. The Museum of
Broadcasting in New York produced a retrospective and seminar series of their work.
Tom said in 1969, "Seventy-five percent of the 26 shows we've done this season were
censored." As CBS tried to dictate the content of their show, the Smothers continued to
push the boundaries of free speech.

On Campus: First performed as duo in 1959. Polished up their live act and took it
off campus to the Purple Onion in San Francisco.

the laundry list of GE satisfiers be replaced with subject matter conceptually different
from what departments offered to their own majors as introductory courses.

Simultaneously, California State College Chancellor Glenn S. Dumke recognized
that the entire system needed a general education overhaul, and he appointed Burns
to the statewide committee which, in turn, accepted Burns' San José State model as
its working document. The final draft came close to the Burns original and was implemented throughout the multi-campus system.

Academic Vice President Burns created a rational model that significantly advanced
general education throughout California. Starting with the conviction that "there is
a natural relationship between all subject matters," the vice president concluded that
general education should be a series of interdisciplinary or multidisciplinary courses.
For example, the intellectual relationships of nineteenth century literature, nineteenth
century history, and the advancement of science and technology should be taught in
harmony. Naming the concept *cognate structure,* Burns years later could not recall if
he had coined the term or had encountered it previously in his own studies.

Even among those who understood the concept, some opposed it. This resistance, however, may actually have facilitated statewide implementation of his more basic general education reform. *Cognate structure* assumed a large and sophisticated curriculum, like San José State's. Few other campuses within the decentralized California State system enjoyed that curricular richness. Additionally, the other colleges within the system presumably shared San José State's practical-careerist approach to education. Burns himself was gratified by the broad impact of his reform, though he remained displeased with the awkward and abstract name he had given to his most advanced curricular innovation.

As Silicon Valley's demand for young professionals grew to insatiable levels, business leaders wanted more from their new hires than what their majors had taught them. They sought women and men who could not only work in teams, but could share ideas, understand colleagues from diverse cultures, and communicate well in person at meetings and electronically. In time, even the accrediting agencies for the professional colleges joined the cavalcade for greater improvements in general education. The result, only slightly less a mouthful than *cognate structure,* became "outcomes assessment." What had to be assured was student outcome, not faculty input.

The new academic problem, therefore, was not what to offer as general education. New thinking and new organization simply required that what the general education program taught was actually learned. Meeting such a challenge had become more difficult by century's end when the student body included an increased number of students with a limited grasp of English, but with professional goals as strong and focused as the university's traditional students. And as the student body and the high tech work force it provided became all the more diverse, graduates too often seemed to lack multi-cultural perspective and understanding.

Academic Vice President Arlene N. Okerlund, whose own field was English literature, accepted this redefined challenge in the late 1980s and sensitized the faculty to the new thinking surrounding "outcomes assessment." As she diversified the faculty through new appointments, Okerlund worked to persuade senior faculty to embrace outcomes assessment. What she needed, but did not have at that time, was the backing of accrediting bodies in support of her innovations. That came by the mid-1990s and took hold when President Robert Caret converted and upgraded the position of academic vice president to that of provost and vice president for academic affairs. His appointee, Dr. Linda L. Bain, turned to the university stalwart in curriculum matters, Professor Leon C. Dorosz, for implementation of outcomes-assessment reform. She appointed him as her interim associate vice president for curriculum and assessment.

On his home page on the web, Dorosz provided step-by-step models for how faculty could design new courses and redesign old ones with outcomes assessment built into the structure. "Younger faculty," he said in a 1999 interview, "accept as self-evident that what students learn is the vital ingredient." Senior faculty, most often in the professional departments that once had been most resistant to general education, were coming around, too. They had gotten the word from their own outside professional evaluators during accreditation reviews. High tech professionals, too, needed to be liberally educated, sensitive, and articulate.

The 8,200 class sections offered each year, which satisfied the requirements of 30,000 students, were for the most part non-controversial and constantly evolving. These courses fueled the university's degree programs, which at their apex totaled 280 and constituted an over-extended financial burden. President Robert Caret and Provost Linda Bain cooperated in reducing the number of programs to 190 by 1999. Characteristically, though, the curricular heart of San José State's academic life remained big, strong, and productive.

Impact of Technology

Technological revolution entered San José State's curriculum from the bottom up. The initial costs of hardware and software acquisition were such that members of the campus community who could equip themselves were the ones who first advanced into the field. Organizationally, department chairs could do little to help or hinder, because their budgets simply had not been constructed to anticipate the heavy costs associated with the new technology.

The schools of engineering, business, and science took the lead, and engineering dean Jay D. Pinson established the standard. He included dedicated computer laboratories within his major overhaul of facilities in 1988. Dean Marshall J. Burak initiated much the same for business students and faculty through his networking with valley businesses and with income from off-campus programs. Science deans Lester H. Lange and Alan C. Ling advanced the technological component for the department of mathematics and computer science through a combination of grant funding and state budgeting.

Since these early advances took place during the years of lean state college budgets, deans with access to non-state funding did what the state should have done. Without adequate centralized funding, the deans became entrepreneurs with limited goals. The early result was an uneven distribution of new technology across the university and an uneven impact upon the university curriculum.

By the 1980s, virtually all of the business and library services of the university were computerized. Appropriate sectors of the curriculum, likewise, were catching up. Technology was revolutionizing the student and faculty approach to learning. Information literacy, the new buzzword, embraced a new reality, actual or virtual. By 1999, technologies were prominent in the delivery of instruction, as the subject matter of instruction, and in a limited manner they were the object of research and development.

Within the concluding years of the century, enrollments doubled (2,300 to 4,600) in the programs of computer science, computer engineering and management information systems. The art curriculum experienced a similar explosion as it adopted a computer-based curriculum in graphic design, industrial design, and interior design. Engineering had long since converted from constructing prototypes based upon mathematical formulations to computer modeling.

Leon Dorosz, the university's best articulator of this innovation and the challenges technology brought to the academic life of San José State, put San José State's 1999 status this way:

The use of electronic information systems is transforming many curricula. Material that used to require a great deal of classroom time is now relegated to computer interaction. In Molecular Biology and Biochemistry and Virology, for instance, the three-dimensional interactions of molecules that once had to be described verbally by instructors, at great length, can now be seen and manipulated by students in three-dimensional visualizations, directly from web pages.

This change is more profound than we might think. The use of words to outline the cycle of a heartbeat, for instance, is no longer required, as students see and manipulate the intricate cycle of valve opening and closing in active 3-D visualization. Students (and instructors) are increasingly less likely to place into the verbal realm material that is now so easily visualized.

The ability of more senior traditionally verbal instructors to communicate with visually-oriented students has diminished markedly, while the younger generation of students is very comfortable sharing information with peers graphically and visually. Newer faculty have some degree of difficulty in communicating with senior faculty about the use of information tools; the idea that there are faculty who don't routinely use e-mail is simply impossible for younger faculty to grasp — and this interferes with their ability to use the same language in talking about curriculum development. *Words aren't going away, but their role in the curriculum is changing*, both within the curriculum itself, and in the nature of the communication among professionals....

To the anguish of those who prized verbal (written and oral) skill, the advent of the technology age appeared as a mixed blessing. Would the ability to understand and to manipulate images simply bypass and ignore the need to understand and to articulate ideas? San José State educators, including those committed to career preparation, worried about how best to prepare professionals for the next century.

Academic Life: Artistic and Intellectual Outreach

THE EDUCATION OFFERED at San José State was for careers in the professions, and most faculty and administrators realized this and functioned accordingly. Some, aided by community supporters, extended their reach without obstructing or frustrating entry-level careerism as the mission of the university. Talented faculty, alert administrators, and generous patrons reached beyond curriculum to engage more deeply the university's intellectual and artistic potential. Many community components of artistic and intellectual outreach existed before the arrival of President Robert L. Caret, and these extensions of university academic life into the community facilitated his application of the metropolitan university concept to San José State and Silicon Valley.

Opera San Jose

IRENE DALIS had wanted to be a music teacher ever since her older sister gave her piano lessons. When the young and accomplished Dalis graduated from San José

State in 1946 in music, she enjoyed family support that allowed her to venture to New York, where she completed a master's degree at Columbia University Teacher's College. Thereafter, a Fulbright scholarship to the Giuseppe Verdi Conservatory in Milan, Italy, and recognizable talent launched her career in opera.

Through the 1950s and 1960s and into the 1970s, Dalis commanded center stage with the New York Metropolitan Opera as *mezzo-soprano* and principal artist. In 1976, one year prior to her retirement from grand opera, the vivacious and celebrated performer accepted an appointment in San José State's music department. With the university's invitation, began the story of Opera San Jose, the cultural start-up that Dalis launched from her San José State professorship. Over the subsequent decades of her academic career, Dalis developed the university's Opera Workshop, sustained its transformational season in 1981 as the San Jose Community Opera Theater, and presided over its rebirth as Opera San Jose in 1984.

Opera San Jose became firmly established and, based on nearly $70 million in funding from the San José Redevelopment Agency and the Packard Humanities Institute, Dalis planned the company's second transition, a move from the Montgomery Theater to a restored Fox Theater.

Interviewed for a *San Jose Mercury News* entertainment article in 1999, "Women in the Arts," Dalis clearly projected the same vision of the university's prevailing concept of its academic life. "It was always a dream of mine," she said, "to help entry-level professionals develop their craft and performance…. Opera San Jose is that company. You can build a singer in a studio, but the only way you can develop a performer is to offer them the stage." The dramatic *mezzo-soprano* remained true to her first calling, teaching. "I never changed," she maintained. "I believe in bringing this art form to young people and to all people. There's something in opera for everybody."

Opera San Jose's new home — a classic

DESTINED TO REGAIN ITS STATUS as a crown jewel of downtown San José, the Fox California Theatre was undergoing renovation in the last years of the '90s to become the new home of Opera San Jose and other performing arts. The $70 million renovation project was funded two-thirds by the San José Redevelopment Agency and one-third by the Packard Humanities Institute.  Renovations underway at the end of the century restored the classic look and feel of the theater, built in 1927, when vaudeville shows and films were the major forms of entertainment. The Packard Humanities Institute provided a restored Wurlitzer organ for the theater. The project design included a three-story building for performer support facilities, a courtyard, and a two-story building with public spaces including a café. In addition to Opera San Jose, San José State choirs, theater groups and musical productions planned to use the new theater, further integrating university productions and the city arts scene.

Irene Dalis

BA, Music, 1946;
HONORARY DOCTORATE, 1999

INTERNATIONAL OPERA STAR, professor, director, and mentor, Irene Dalis honed her talents at San José State University as a music major. She then went on to have a distinguished career and bears the distinction of having sung every major role for dramatic mezzo-soprano composed by Verdi, Wagner, and Richard Strauss.

In 1977, after 20 years with the Metropolitan Opera in New York, she retired from the stage and returned to SJSU, where she launched a second career. Accepting a professorship, she began to consider how to showcase the talent she coached, which resulted in the founding of Opera San Jose, an innovative company that supports and promotes new talent. Serving as executive and artistic director, she has brought professional artists and students together, creating a nationally known, regional opera company that has become a prominent fixture in the Bay Area arts arena.

As part of her teaching mission, Dalis also created an extraordinary set of educational outreach programs, including the "Let's Make an Opera!" project in which local children write and star in their own productions. Dalis has always believed her mission is to teach, to nurture and to provide the environment where her pupils can achieve their potential. "When talent is discovered, it must be developed. There is always room at the top. Where it gets crowded is at the level of mediocrity."

On Campus: Did not think becoming a professional singer was possible.

The Martha Heasley Cox Center for Steinbeck Studies

EDUCATED IN ARKANSAS, English Professor Martha Heasley Cox arrived in San José in 1955. She implemented her vision for the creation of a research center at San José State, which a grateful university in 1997 renamed the Martha Heasley Cox Center for Steinbeck Studies.

When interviewed by San José State alumnus and *San Jose Mercury News* columnist Leigh Weimers in 1999, Cox maintained that John Steinbeck was America's greatest writer "when it comes to portraying America. He pictures the country so well and so beautifully."

Cox also had an additional and practical reason for developing her Steinbeck interest — the proximity of his subject matter to her and to San José State. Promptly, she advanced her own academic expertise in the field of Steinbeck studies and moved the subject beyond the specialty courses that she regularly offered in the English department. She became an established figure among Steinbeck scholars, spoke and wrote about the Nobel Prize-winning author, and popularized San José as the gateway to Steinbeck Country.

Her enhanced position within the field allowed her in 1971 to organize and host at San José State a three-day celebration of the life and works of John Steinbeck. Cox offered the event to international scholars, to devotees of Steinbeck's works, and to casual readers. Her conference included the traditional scholarly papers presented for the experts, a film festival of the major movies made from Steinbeck's books, and a field trip to Monterey, Cannery Row, and Salinas.

That 1971 conference was, for Cox, merely a first step. She had already positioned San José State to assume an advanced role in Steinbeck studies. Next, she created a research center for the study of Steinbeck's life and his works.

San José State's initial acquisitions of Steinbeck materials, 180 items, included all principal published works and several rare, limited editions. By 1999 this collection had grown through purchase and gifts to over 15,000 items: photographs, letters to and from the author, reviews, films, editions of books autographed by the author, some of his unpublished writings, as well as portraits and other materials relating to his life and work. By century's end the center had become one of the most important Steinbeck archives in the world.

In 1995-96 the colleges of humanities and the arts and social sciences sponsored the "Year of Steinbeck" in which issues of labor, gender, ethnicity and race served as an organizing and energizing theme. The films *Of Mice and Men, The Grapes of Wrath,* and *Viva Zapata* served as departure points for assessing the continued relevance of Steinbeck's work.

The single Steinbeck Center event that drew extraordinary popular attention was the benefit performance of "The Boss," popular singer Bruce Springsteen. Not a habitué of rock concerts, Martha Heasley Cox nonetheless proclaimed her delight while accepting Springsteen's generous donation of the campus concert proceeds. At the reception, the retired Professor Cox, then in her late 70s, beamed graciously while being photographed at the arm of "The Boss."

Springsteen's overflow concert at the Event Center coincided with his acceptance of the first annual Steinbeck Award, "In the Souls of the People." The high-energy performer received the recognition for two reasons. First, the overriding working-class themes in his music matched those themes that characterized Steinbeck's writings and for which the writer had received the Nobel Prize in 1962. The second reason was due to the name of Springsteen's hit album, *The Ghost of Tom Joad,* which had appropriated the name of Steinbeck's fictional character in *Grapes of Wrath*. Springsteen's

Martha Heasley Cox gives Bruce Springsteen the first "In the Souls of the People" award.

performance energized San José rock devotees, and his generosity of spirit infused the center's budget. Additionally, the center inaugurated its annual Steinbeck Award by associating it with its high-profile recipient. Best of all, the message of the music was the message of Steinbeck.

Choraliers take world by song...San José State's Choraliers won their seventh international competition resoundingly in July 2000. The 1999-2000 Choraliers were awarded the Grand Prix in Miedzyzdroje, Poland, with 22 points out of 25, the next closest choir with just 14 points. The chamber choir performed American spirituals and gave renditions of Latin motets by Polish composers, earning the special Musica Sacra award from the Catholic Church, which had never before been presented at the Polish competition. The Choraliers' European performances included 13th century churches and cathedrals. "The 34 singers loved performing for the audiences in Poland and Berlin as well as in Liepzig, in the Nicolai and St. Thomas churches where Bach worked, and in Wittenberg, where Martin Luther tacked his 95 theses to the door," according to Choraliers director Charlene Archibeque.

The Center for Literary Arts

MARTHA HEASLEY COX's young and energetic dean, Arlene Okerlund, lamented to Cox that big-name authors often spoke at Stanford, but not at San José State. Okerlund was conscious of the working-class perspective at San José State, and she appreciated the way Cox celebrated the labor theme of Steinbeck's works. Okerlund was convinced that classroom instruction at San José State was as good as any of the top-ranked universities, and had the advantage of being more personalized — no immense lecture halls with squads of teaching assistants to shield the single professor from hundreds of students. Her lament was for the wherewithal to bring major authors to San José State as inspiration for students. San José State students needed to have their vision broadened; they needed to see and experience the extent of the possible. Her comments to Cox hit the mark.

That semester Cox was teaching the American novel, and the idea of hosting major authors greatly appealed to her. Martha Heasley Cox had earned royalties, which she invested wisely, from a successful textbook, *A Reading Approach to College Writing*. It underwent seven revisions, numerous printings, and enjoyed multiple publishers from its first appearance in 1959 through the 1970s. Her initial endowment and her continuing support resulted in what became San José State's Center for Literary Arts, with the Martha H. Cox lectures at its nucleus.

Authors who have appeared at The Center for Literary Arts

Edward Albee (Pulitzer Prize [four times] and Tony Award)
Sherman Alexie
Isabel Allende
Margaret Atwood
Russell Banks
John Barth (National Book Award)
Ann Beattie
Robert Bly
Eavan Boland
T. Coraghessan Boyle
Ernesto Cardenal
Lorna Dee Cervantes
Lucille Clifton
Andrei Codrescu
Billy Collins (U.S. Poet Laureate)
Pat Conroy
Robert Creeley
Diane di Prima
Mark Doty
Stephen Dunn
Lawrence Ferlinghetti
Carolyn Forche
Barry Gifford
Molly Giles
Allen Ginsberg
Mary Gordon
Jessica Hagedorn
Barry Hannah
Robert Haas (U.S. Poet Laureate)
Seamus Heaney (Nobel Prize for Literature)
Garrett Hongo
David Henry Hwang (Tony Award)
Gish Jen
June Jordan
Garrison Keillor
William Kennedy (Pulitzer Prize for Fiction)
Ken Kesey
Maxine Hong Kingston (National Book Award)
Galway Kinnell (Pulitzer Prize for Poetry)
Carolyn Kizer (Pulitzer Prize for Poetry)
Maxine Kumin (Pulitzer Prize for Poetry)
Tony Kushner (Pulitzer Prize and Tony Award)
Anne Lamott
Ursula K. LeGuin
Elmore Leonard
Denise Levertov
Peter Matthiessen (National Book Award)

Jay McInerny
Terry McMillan
William Meredith (Pulitzer Prize)
Diane Middlebrook
Arthur Miller (Pulitzer Prize and Tony Award)
Jane Miller
Czeslaw Milosz (Nobel Prize for Literature)
Toni Morrison (Nobel Prize for Literature)
Walter Mosley
Bharati Mukherjee
David Mura
Joyce Carol Oates (National Book Award)
Edna O'Brien (National Book Award)
Sharon Olds
Mary Oliver (Pulitzer Prize)
Tillie Olsen
Michael Ondaatje
Grace Paley
Cecile Pineda
George Pimpton
James Ragan
Adrienne Rich (National Book Award)
Richard Russo
David Sedaris
Carol Shields (Pulitzer Prize)
Jane Smiley
Gary Snyder
Gary Soto
Shelby Steele
Wallace Stegner
Gerald Stern
Oliver Stone
William Styron (Pulitzer Prize)
Amy Tan
Paul Theroux
Luis Valdez
Victor Villasenor
Sarah Vowell
Derek Walcott (Nobel Prize for Literature)
Wendy Wasserstein (Pulitzer Prize and Tony Award)
Bruce Weigl
John Edgar Wideman
C.K. Williams
Tobias Wolff
Lois-Ann Yamanaka
Yevgeny Yevtushenko
Al Young

She endowed the author series in 1986 in order to bring to the campus Wallace Stegner, one of the most distinguished American writers of the time and author of *Angle of Repose*, which won the Pulitzer Prize. By 1998 the thirteenth Cox lecturer was Norman Mailer, followed at century's end by playwright Arthur Miller. In between appeared such distinguished literary figures as Toni Morrison, William Styron, and Paul Theroux.

Following Okerland, Dean John K. Crane enveloped Cox's lecture series within the larger organization of his creation in 1989 — the Center for Literary Arts. Crane assumed broader fundraising responsibilities that supported a perpetual calendar of major authors. Over the years the Center for Literary Arts hosted four Nobel Laureates in literature and more than a dozen recipients of Pulitzer Prizes and other national book awards. Dean Crane fondly recollected the evening during which Irish poet Seamus Heaney shared his poetry with an enraptured, overflow audience. Heaney's devotees jammed the aisles and the exits and engulfed their idol on stage, literally at the feet of the future Noble Laureate. To that appreciative audience the Irishman whispered his words of enchantment. At the conclusion of his program the audience refused to allow the night to end. The poet read on.

The Ira F. Brilliant Center for Beethoven Studies

U NLIKE OPERA SAN JOSE, literary arts, and Steinbeck initiatives, the Beethoven center originated from an outside stimulus. Ira F. Brilliant was a Phoenix real estate developer and a Beethoven collector who wanted to place 75 first editions of Beethoven's music with a university that would participate in co-developing an academic center for research, performances, educational programs, and additional collections. He approached San José State through a friend, David Shapiro, who taught in the economics department. Dean Arlene N. Okerlund immediately warmed to the opportunity and discussed it with President Gail Fullerton.

Ira Brilliant
...devoted to Beethoven scholarship

The Ira F. Brilliant Center for Beethoven Studies opened in 1985 and secured its presence through sound personnel actions. Senior professor of American history and life-long Beethoven devotee Dr. Thomas Wendel accepted what became his second San José career, impresario of all things symphonic and Beethovenian. Selected for permanent director of the center (and professor of music) was a new PhD recipient, William R. Meredith. Meredith and Wendel projected the image of the center through their lectures, publications, and public relations initiatives. Meredith, with the board of directors over which Wendel came to preside, set goals, acquired funding grants, identified projects, and organized events, all of which advanced under the watchful eyes of Ira Brilliant.

By the end of the century, the center's scholarly collections were online via its Beethoven Bibliography Database project and available through the university library and the internet. Original manuscripts became regular display items at the center. The

Outstanding Professor Award Recipients

Year	Recipient
1965-1966	Brant Clark, Professor of Psychology
1966-1967	Charles Burdick. Professor of History
1967-1968	Dwight Bentel, Professor of Journalism
	W. Gibson Walters, Professor of Music
1968-1969	Francis Huang, Professor of Mechancial Engineering
	Jack Holland, Professor of Business
1969-1970	Peter Koestenbaum, Professor of Philosophy
1970-1971	Epaminondas "Nondas" Panagopoulas, Professor of History
1971-1972	Harry Gailey, Professor of History
1972-1973	Hans Guth, Professor of History
1973-1974	Edgar Anderson, Professor History
1974-1975	Richard Ellefsen, Professor of Geography
1975-1976	B.J. Scott Norwood, Professor of Marketing and Quantitative Studies
1976-1977	H. Thomas Harvey, Professor of Biological Sciences
1977-1978	Albert Castro, Professor of Chemistry
1978-1979	Charles Burdick, Professor of History
1979-1980	Fay Bower, Professor of Nursing
1980-1981	Ted Hinkley, Professor of History
1981-1982	Alan Ling, Professor of Chemistry
1982-1983	Ruth Yaffe, Professor of Chemistry
1983-1984	James Smart, Professor of Mathematics & Computer Science
1984-1985	Charlene Archibeque, Professor of Music
1985-1986	James Freeman, Professor of Anthropology
1986-1987	Artice Davis, Professor of Electrical Engineering
1987-1988	Robert Bornstein, Professor of Meteorology
1988-1989	John Baird, Professor of Marketing & Quantative Studies
1989-1990	Irene Miura, Program Director of Child Development
1990-1991	Herbert Silber, Professor of Chemistry
1991-1992	Kuei-Wu Tsai, Professor of Civil Engineering
1992-1993	James Asher, Professor of Psychology
1993-1994	James Stull, Professor of Marketing & Quantitative Studies
1994-1995	Kathleen Cohen, Professor of Art History
1995-1996	Kevin Jordan, Professor of Psychology
1996-1997	Alice Carter, Professor of Art and Design
1997-1998	Terry Christensen, Professor of Political Science
1998-1999	Chris Brenigar, Professor of Biological Sciences
1999-2000	Shawn Spano, Professor of Communication Studies

collection of Beethoven materials contained about 300 first editions of the composer's music, more than 1,500 editions published during his lifetime and shortly thereafter, as well as 2,700 relevant volumes published since 1800. The center collections included recordings and even a more popular item, a fortepiano replica modeled after a c.1795 instrument by Munich craftsman Jean-Louis Dulcken. The instrument contained 66 keys (rather than the modern piano's 88) and, therefore, accommodated Beethoven's early works and some later sonatas.

The Beethoven center's public events, usually staged on campus, included performances by the Julliard String Quartet, pianist Richard Goode, and some more light-hearted renderings. Within the national membership of the American Beethoven Society was the long-time media personality, conservative journalist and popular author, William F. Buckley, Jr., who with Wendel shared undergraduate enthusiasms for Beethoven at Yale in the 1940s. Buckley's celebrity status enhanced a fundraising event where they performed on harpsichords with Barbara Day Turner, the conductor of the Chamber Orchestra of San Jose, and Craig Bohmler, composer and pianist.

More serious performances included the Young Pianists' Beethoven Competition, which celebrated its thirteenth anniversary in 1999. The center also hosted weeks of Beethoven, which included concerts, parties, and accommodations, from which developed a large portion of the membership in the American Beethoven Society. The Beethoven Center published the semi-annual, award-winning *Beethoven Journal* for the American Beethoven Society.

A small consortium led by Arizona physician Dr. Alfredo Guevara and including Brilliant and the American Beethoven Society, purchased at auction at Sotheby's, London, what became known as the "Guevara Lock" of Beethoven's hair. The publicity value exceeded the cost ($7,300) for what turned out to be 582 individual strands of hair trimmed from the composer at his death in 1827. The lock's provenance and test results thereafter appeared on the Beethoven web pages.

When interviewed in the summer of 1998 at his center, Ira F. Brilliant remained deeply engaged in collection development. He was highly pleased with the support of San José State and supremely confident in the twenty-first century success of Beethoven studies. His enthusiasm fixed upon the cultural and artistic dimensions of the enterprise.

Mineta Transportation Institute

THE NORMAN Y. MINETA International Institute for Surface Transportation Policy Studies, founded in 1991, emerged from a confluence of interests in local, state, and national transportation problems shared by two prominent experts who were well placed in politics and who were long associated with San José State.

Norman Y. Mineta served two terms as San José's mayor and 20 years representing San José in the U.S. Congress before retiring in 1995. After a brief period as a vice president at Lockheed Martin Corp., he was named U.S. secretary of commerce by President Bill Clinton. Throughout his political career, Mineta was attentive to the needs and aspirations of the university. He participated regularly in campus events, and his staff expedited challenging interactions of the university and federal bureaucracies.

Rod Diridon had been equally attentive and even closer at hand. He earned his bachelor's and master's degrees from San José State, and members of his family held four additional degrees from the university. Diridon pursued a successful career in local politics, serving 20 years, 1975–1995, on the Santa Clara County Board of Supervisors and the County Transit Authority Board. Throughout, he remained active with the university on local issues and even drew faculty and students into various research projects that benefited Santa Clara County.

Norman Y. Mineta
...named U.S. Secretary of Commerce

Both Mineta and Diridon developed expertise in the field of transportation during their public service. In addition to serving six times as chair of the Santa Clara County Transit Board, Diridon chaired the San Francisco Bay Area Metropolitan Transportation Commission and the California High-Speed Rail Authority. He was knowledgeable about planning and policy formulation relating to freeways, light rail, railroads, and rapid transit. Mineta had chaired the Surface Transportation Subcommittee in the U.S. House of Representatives and developed the enabling legislation, the Intermodal Surface Transportation Efficiency Act (ISTEA), from which 18 transportation institutes developed across America. The institute at San José State became the only one on the West Coast. With the passage of years and his retirement from active politics, Diridon became executive director of the institute. Mineta, as honorary chair, continued to participate on a voluntary basis in the organization's policy formulation.

With renewable federal and state funding of $1.5 million per year, the Mineta Transportation Institute addressed three distinct duties in the field of surface transportation: policy research, management education, and technology transfer. Basic to each area was the early realization that quality-of-life issues were critical, and that international economic advantage in the new century would be enhanced by America's ability to move its citizens and their products efficiently. By the end of 1999 the Mineta Transportation Institute had engaged 52 post-doctoral-level researchers, completed 11 projects and had 22 in progress.

The educational function of the institute, to prepare surface transportation leaders of the twenty-first century, took the form of a graduate degree program offered by San José State, the master of science in transportation management. The incoming students were the mid-echelon transportation professionals from whom would emerge the next leaders in the mass transit field. Dealing with policy issues, it was the only such program in the United States. The master's students focused on the business and management aspects of transportation systems, not technology and engineering. Students resided throughout California and participated in interactive conferencing at the 12 statewide facilities of Caltrans and at San José State, the originating instructional site.

Moss Landing Marine Laboratories

SINCE ITS HUMBLE BEGINNINGS in an old cannery on Monterey Bay in 1965, Moss Landing Marine Laboratories (MLML) put more than a few marine science

Rod Diridon

BS, Accounting, 1961; MBA, 1963

AFFECTIONATELY CALLED MR. TRANSPORTATION and the Father of Light Rail in Silicon Valley, Rod Diridon actually resented the train system in his early life. From his point of view, trains were what kept his father, a railroad brakeman, away from home. But later in life, transportation issues would become central to his career in public service. After serving as the youngest member ever elected to the Saratoga City Council and the youngest member elected to the Santa Clara County Board of Supervisors, he went on to spearhead a 20-year plan to build light rail in the South Bay.

He has received many awards throughout his distinguished career, including the American Public Transit Award in 1995. As executive director of the Mineta Transportation Institute at San José State University, he works to focus graduate student research into numerous areas of transportation, including planning and designing mass transit; assessing the needs of the elderly; seeking quick response to terrorism attacks and natural disasters.

Driven, passionate, and forthright, he is proud of his many contributions and unwaveringly supports the projects he believes in, saying, "I'm not here to curry favor with the rich and famous who want to protect the status quo, who are in the way of those who want to lead. I am here to work."

On Campus: Worked his way through SJSU as a brakeman for the Southern Pacific Railroad.

---

discoveries on the map; its international reputation expands along with its important scientific findings.

Operated by San José State, the facility now overlooks Monterey Bay from new $21 million research facilities just south of Moss Landing. The facility was reconstructed after the 1989 Loma Prieta earthquake, thanks to local leadership and grants that made the new construction possible. Total funding of $23.6 million came from the David and Lucile Packard Foundation, MLML, and federal agencies (FEMA and OES). MLML students and faculty moved into the new facility in January 2000.

San José State leads a consortium of seven California State University campuses — including San Francisco, Fresno, Hayward, Monterey Bay, Sacramento, and Stanislaus — that send more than 120 students a year to study marine sciences in the oceanside setting. Faculty led nine MLML research groups in benthic (deep sea) ecology; biological, chemical, geological and physical oceanography; ichthyology; invertebrate zoology; ornithology and mammalogy, and phycology (study of seaweed).

With research grants totaling $8.8 million in 1999-2000, much of the MLML research takes place at sea. Students and faculty head to sea from Moss Landing on the 135-foot research vessel *Point Sur*. MLML students pursue their master's degrees in the waters of Monterey Bay, as well as all the world's oceans, from the Antarctic to the Arctic. MLML graduates, nearly 30 percent of whom earn PhDs, play prominent roles in marine science research, teaching and environmental management throughout California and beyond. MLML also houses the University National Oceanographic Laboratories System's nationwide coordination of research vessels.

In the mid-1980s, at a lecture at the Woods Hole Oceanographic Institution, Moss Landing Marine Laboratories former Director John H. Martin quipped in his best Dr. Strangelove accent, "Give me half a tanker of iron, and I will give you an ice age." But he was deadly serious in his quest to find a solution to the greenhouse effect and global warming — via the world's oceans. He offered his "iron hypothesis."

Shortly after Martin's death in 1993, Moss Landing colleagues Ken Johnson and Kenneth Coale sailed to the Galapagos Islands from Miami with a cargo of pharmaceutical grade iron sulfate to fertilize a 64-square-kilometer patch of ocean

President's Scholar Award Recipients

Year	Name	Department	College
1973-1974	Arthur Fallico	Philosophy	Humanities & the Arts
1974-1975	Charles Burdick	History	Social Sciences
1975-1976	Albert Castro	Chemistry	Science
1976-1977	Aiko Onishi	Music	Humanities & the Arts
1977-1978	Peter Koestenbaum	Philosophy	Humanities & the Arts
1978-1979	Harry Gailey	History	Social Sciences
1979-1980	Fletcher Benton	Art	Humanities & the Arts
1980-1981	Edgar Anderson	History	Social Sciences
1981-1982	Juana Acrivos	Chemistry	Science
1982-1983	Robert Hicks	Psychology	Social Sciences
1983-1984	James Freeman	Anthropology	Social Sciences
1984-1985	Howard Shellhammer	Biological Sciences	Science
1985-1986	Gabriele Rico	English	Humanities & the Arts
1986-1987	Ellen Weaver	Biological Sciences	Science
1987-1988	Brent Heisinger	Music	Humanities & the Arts
1988-1989	Allen Strange	Music	Humanities & the Arts
1989-1990	Douglas Greer	Economics	Social Sciences
1990-1991	Shelby Steele	English	Humanities & the Arts
1991-1992	Rupert Garcia	Art and Design	Humanities & the Arts
1992-1993	Charlene Archibeque	Music	Humanities & the Arts
1993-1994	Joseph Pesek	Chemistry	Science
1994-1995	John Gruber	Physics	Science
1995-1996	Stanley Baran	Theatre Arts	Humanities & the Arts
1996-1997	Patrick Hamill	Physics	Science
1997-1998	Randall Stross	Org. & Mgmnt.	Business
1998-1999	William Shaw	Philosophy	Humanities & the Arts
1999-2000	Tommy Lott	Philosophy	Humanities & the Arts

considered high in nutrients but low in chlorophyll. They wanted to prove in nature what Martin had earlier proved in controlled lab tests — that algae needed trace amounts of iron in order to grow. As Martin had predicted, algae bloomed off the Galapagos Islands, feasting on the nutrients and sucking carbon dioxide out of the atmosphere. The introduction of iron to these waters doubled phytoplankton populations.

John H. Martin, former director, MLML
...*"I will give you an ice age."*

Coale refined the experiment in 1995, this time increasing phytoplankton production 30 times above normal. The algae, with a biomass equal to 100 redwood trees, used more than 2,500 tons of carbon in photosynthesis. Martin's earlier work had shown that algae, when they died, took the carbon to the ocean floor with them, thus depleting the atmosphere of one of its troublesome greenhouse gases. Martin's idea of using the ocean to recycle carbon remains pertinent as the world addresses global warming. The National Research Council ranked the iron hypothesis and the experiments that tested it among the top three scientific discoveries in ocean science during the last 50 years.

Martin was director of Moss Landing Marine Laboratories for 18 years. His body of work ranged from the early quantifying of trace metals in the Earth's oceans to his experiments on the amounts of atmospheric carbon recycled into the ocean by algae and is chronicled from the cover of *Nature* and *Newsweek* to the archives of NASA. Other MLML researchers added to the scientific base of knowledge — and Moss Landing's prestige — including Dr. Valerie Loeb's discovery of significant changes in the krill and salp populations in Antarctica, featured in *Nature* and *Newsweek*. And Dr. James Nybakken, the lab's first fulltime professor, who put into the scientific lexicon the *mosslandica* name of a mollusk species discovered in the shallows of Monterey Bay.

Moss Landing Marine Laboratories have quietly advanced scientific knowledge along with the careers of new scientists.

Celebrating Academic Life

SAN JOSÉ STATE enjoyed the presence of a distinct group of faculty, an elite of talent and productivity. Secure in their world of accomplishment and reinforced by a work-a-day system that admired and envied excellence, they constituted the celebrated ingredient of the academic life.

President Robert D. Clark was the first to take official note of the best among the faculty. In 1965 he initiated the Outstanding Professor Award, a tradition that has continued. In 1973 President John H. Bunzel initiated the President's Scholar Award to honor published scholarship or artistic or scientific accomplishment. By the end of the century, both awards had been conferred upon 55 individuals. Of this elite, identified by faculty committees and chosen by successive presidents, six were doubly recognized with both awards, Outstanding Professor and President's Scholar.

Albert J. Castro

Professor of Chemistry, 1949 to 1986
President's Scholar, 1975-76
Outstanding Professor, 1977-78

PROFESSOR ALBERT J. CASTRO received both honors, President's Scholar and Outstanding Professor, because of his original contributions to the field of organic chemistry. He was a senior, esteemed scientist whose work peaked during San José State's transition from teaching college to comprehensive university. Born locally in the city of Santa Clara, Castro earned degrees in chemistry from San José State College (BA) and Stanford University (MA and PhD). His initiative and his commitment to science prompted his quiet eclipse of the non-research tradition that permeated the college through the presidency of Thomas W. MacQuarrie.

Professor Castro's selection as President's Scholar rested upon a large and significant body of scientific research, published from 1942 into the 1970s, with his greatest productivity in the later years. Almost always the primary research scientist and the lead writer, Castro published his findings in the best relevant journals: *Journal of the American Chemical Society, Journal of Organic Chemistry, Journal of Chemical Education,* and *Journal of Medical Chemistry.* Mingled within his research articles were the occasional patent and his co-authored textbook, *Essentials of Modern Organic Chemistry,* which Reinhold published in 1965. The Spanish language edition, published by the Alhambra Press, Madrid, enjoyed three more editions.

Castro's crossover distinction in teaching was, in significant part, derived from his scholarship. He conceived and advanced the use of modern physical methods in qualitative organic analysis. His breakthrough methodology resulted in the publication of *Spectrometric Identification of Organic Compounds* by Stanford scientists R.M. Silverstein and G.C. Bassler, who credited Castro in their preface. The course embodying this subject became a staple offered to professional chemists throughout the country by the American Chemical Society.

Professor Castro's standard university teaching load, four courses of 12 semester units, included the department's introduction to chemistry, general chemistry, and all courses in organic chemistry. He took his turn at chairing the graduate committee and developed the graduate curriculum in chemistry. A 1954 article in *Journal of Organic Chemistry* appeared to be the first publication that was based upon chemical laboratory research carried out in any substantial degree within a state college laboratory. By 1969 Castro was the repeat recipient of unsolicited and unrestricted funding for his research and scientific activities, with support from Merck, Sharp and Dohme research laboratories. Doctoral and post-doctoral students came to study with him from The Johns Hopkins University (Baltimore), the University of Saskatchewan (Canada), the University of Bari (Italy), and the University of Basel (Switzerland).

By awarding both top faculty awards to Professor Albert J. Castro, San José State demonstrated its own change from a basic conveyor of knowledge to an institution participating in the creation of knowledge.

Charlene P. Archibeque

Director of Choral Activities, 1970 to 1999
President's Scholar, 1992-93
Outstanding Professor, 1984-85

CHARLENE P. ARCHIBEQUE was well prepared to assume her responsibilities at San José State upon her arrival in 1970. She had attended the Oberlin Conservatory and earned a bachelor's, a master's, and the doctorate in musical arts at Michigan, San Diego State and the University of Colorado, respectively. Her expertise consisted of the preparation and application of choral music for performance, including the organization, instruction, and direction of choral groups. Archibeque's talent and energy, plus her organizational and inspirational skills, constituted the soul of the university's choral excellence, which she first put on international display in Greece, Italy, and Germany during her 1971 European Tour. In 1999 she conducted her students in

The valley is alive, with the sounds of SJSU

IT'S HARD TO IMAGINE the Silicon Valley without all the SJSU music grads," said Charlene Archibeque, director of the world-renowned Choraliers. "We have trained hundreds of musicians who are teaching music in our public and private schools, performing and conducting in orchestras, serving on arts boards, working in churches, singing in choirs, running music stores, and attending cultural events." San José State has been preparing professional performers, composers and music educators longer than any other school in California. Its School of Music and Dance features ballet, jazz, hip hop, the internationally acclaimed Limón Dance Company, and university choirs, bands and orchestras. At the turn of the century, the School of Music included more than twenty performing ensembles, and its alumni populated the city-university arts scene.

Irene Dalis' lasting imprint on the West Coast is Opera San Jose. Unlike other companies, Opera San Jose hired young singers for a full year, offering them modest salaries, housing, benefits and coaching. Many San José State grads continue to have the leads in Opera San Jose, fill the choruses and perform various administrative functions, including director **Larry Hancock**.

Barbara Day Turner, who earned her master's degree in harpsichord from San José State, returned to conduct its Symphony Orchestra and founded the San Jose Chamber Orchestra in 1991, where she serves as its music director and conductor. This professional string orchestra provides chamber music to the valley, both classic masterpieces and new works. She also was conductor and artistic administrator of Opera San Jose for 18 years.

Janet Van Swoll earned her master's at San José State and after graduate work returned to teach dance, especially ballet, to SJSU students. She also helps with Opera San Jose, having choreographed many productions.

New works and innovative media also are an integral part of the music contributions of San José State. **Dan Sabanovich**, another master's degree holder from San José State who joined the faculty, directs the SJSU Latin Jazz Ensemble.

concert through their twenty-ninth tour, highlighted by their appearance at the World Symposium of Choral Music in Rotterdam, The Netherlands.

Archibeque taught, scripted, and conducted her students' performances through 12 European cities, with repeat visits to the cultural centers of the old world. In the off years, the San José State Choraliers went to Mexico, Hawaii, Australia, and even performed a Caribbean series aboard the *SS Ocean Breeze* cruise ship. She created a winning formula from which awards and recognitions followed as predictably as improvement sprang from practice.

Through the 30 years of continuous performance and touring, one 1991 award remained a highlight. That summer, the San José State Choraliers won the title "Choir of the World" at the Welsh International Music Eisteddfod in Llangollen, Wales. This was remarkable because the Welsh enjoyed their own rich choral traditions and normally carried off the best of the awards.

In a 1998 interview Archibeque said, "For students to know excellence, they must experience it. I want the university to provide students with the highest possible experience in choral music." On her 1999 Choraliers fact sheet, Archibeque listed the occupations of the 28 members of the group. Reflective of the working-class origins of most students, her choraliers were bank tellers, sales persons and goldsmiths as they pursued degrees in music, geology, and business administration.

Those students who partook of the magic of "Dr. A." cherished it. Alumna Wendith Lewandowski recalled, "I discovered that once I'd experienced and achieved excellence in this one segment of my life, I wanted to strive for it in other areas as well."

James M. Freeman

Professor of Anthropology, 1966 to 1999
President's Scholar, 1983-84
Outstanding Professor, 1985-86

SEPARATE COMMITTEES of faculty peers recommended Dr. James Freeman to President Gail Fullerton as their nominee for President's Scholar in 1983-84 and for Outstanding Professor in 1985-86 because his record in scholarship and in teaching was very clear, very focused, and very good. His research focused upon compelling social issues viewed from perspectives not previously considered. He examined life in India from the perspective of untouchables and life in Silicon Valley from the perspective of South Asian immigrants. He shared his early findings in academic journals and popular magazines. He published his mature work in three books that spanned the fields of anthropology, history, biography, politics, and psychology.

In preparation for his first book, Freeman lived for three years in India, learned the Oriya language and recorded the life stories of village residents through oral history interviews. In *Scarcity in an Indian Village*, he documented the widening economic gap between the wealthy and the poor. As with the university's best-published faculty, the quality of Professor Freeman's first book attracted major outside support. Both the Center for Advanced Study in the Behavioral Sciences and the Social Science Research Council advanced his work, and the latter did so twice.

The result was *Untouchable: An Indian Life History*, the first detailed life story of an illiterate in India, symbolic of the voiceless stratum of that society whose perspective had not previously been deemed relevant. The well-received, frequently cited volume focused on issues of injustice and deprivation of human rights. Published by Stanford University Press, the story was *Choice Magazine's* selection as "Outstanding Academic Book for 1979." *Untouchable* enjoyed wide and very favorable reviews in the outlets for new knowledge such as the *Times Literary Supplement*, which paved the way for additional inquiry through the use of Freeman's oral history methodology.

Multiple awards from the National Endowment for the Humanities, a funded community service contract, and Vietnamese language instruction sustained and inspired Freeman's third and most striking volume, *Hearts of Sorrow: Vietnamese-American Lives*, published again by Stanford. Freeman's oral history methodology allowed the story to be told in the words of the beholders. Through them, Freeman documented the effects that the fall of Vietnam had had on the lives of ordinary Vietnamese refugees who resettled in America. Freeman captured homeland memories and childhood environments, responses to the trauma of relocation, and adjustments to the first decade in the United States.

Recognition and honor came to Freeman and, therefore, to San José State from significant book reviews and from the national media, including Freeman's appearance on CBS Sunday Morning with Charles Kuralt. Freeman's scholarship received the American Book Award for 1990 as well as that year's Outstanding Book Award of the Association of Asian-American Studies. His sequel, *Changing Identities: Vietnamese Americans 1975-1995*, appeared seven years later.

Freeman taught his field methods for collecting life histories, and he liked to see students learn by doing. Under San José State's formalized assessment process, his instruction always earned highest evaluations. In a special supplement to the *San Jose Mercury News*, the editors identified Professor Freeman as one of the 10 best teachers from kindergarten through graduate instruction.

The advantage that came to the university and to the community from Freeman's teaching and publishing was unique, for both were socially and academically significant. His work positively impacted the lives of those from whom it was drawn and prompted his acceptance of advocacy and policy formulation roles. In this capacity he chaired the board of Aid to Children without Parents, Inc. That work entailed international inspections of the conditions of refugee orphans and abandoned children in Southeast Asia. His additional work with the U.S. Office of Refugee Resettlement facilitated language and job training for Highland Lao tribal peoples and their placement among high tech companies of the Silicon Valley.

Edgar Anderson

Professor of History, 1957 to 1989
President's Scholar, 1980-81
Outstanding Professor, 1973-74

Historian Edgar Anderson was among the exceptional recruits interviewed and hired for San José State by President John T. Wahlquist. Educated in Latvia, where he earned his master's degree in 1944 while the former independent state was under German control, Anderson migrated west through post-war Germany and completed his doctorate in history at the University of Chicago. Wahlquist immediately brought the cosmopolitan young scholar to San José.

Anderson believed that researchers had to understand the local languages in order to do primary historical research. He also believed that it was best to go to the places you were studying and about which you were writing. Upon his arrival in San José he spoke English, Russian, German, French, Latvian, and Swedish. Anderson's concept of himself, from his University of Chicago days to his untimely death in 1989 in a California highway accident, was simple. He was a scholar and a teacher. His subject matter was his first priority; his students were a close second.

His selection as the university's Outstanding Professor in 1973-74 and as President's Scholar in 1980-81 honors his abundant academic career. Before his career was cut short, Anderson had published 10 volumes of original work, which appeared in most of the languages he spoke. His life's work focused on Baltic studies, with his beloved Latvia as a focal point. The broader perspective included foreign relations, culture, military matters, Russian and Soviet history, English, French, and Scandinavian involvement in the Baltic region, plus a very interesting sidelight investigation of Caribbean and African history. He represented San José State at scholarly meetings in Russia, Latvia, Australia, Canada, France, New Zealand, Italy, Sweden, West Germany, and the West Indies. Anderson was sought out and invited to world congresses and other prestigious gatherings by the scholars and their governments who staged them. His most celebrated invitation came from Pope John Paul II.

The pontiff had read some of Anderson's earlier work that had been published in Polish. John Paul was impressed by the quality of the research and remembered it over the years. The papal archivist contacted Anderson, who happily agreed to address the papal conference celebrating the 800th anniversary of the Christianization of Eastern Europe. Anderson's original research astounded the Pope and the other conference attendees. Capable of reading even more languages than he could speak, and familiar with the archives throughout the region, Anderson correctly documented the error on which the papal conference was called. The history of Christian missionaries to Eastern Europe was not 800 years old. It was 1,000 years old.

Anderson's career sidelight, the early history of Trinidad and Tobago, provided his second celebrity encounter. It took the form of a lecture to an exclusive audience that included Queen Elizabeth II. The occasion was the opening of a combination library and historical-archeological exhibition in Tobago behind which Anderson had been the scholarly prime mover. His University of Chicago doctoral dissertation had been on the historically obscure and no longer extant country, Courland, located within western Latvia. The history of the Couronians, as Anderson called them, engaged the interests of Trinidad and Tobago officials because Courland had colonized eighteenth century Africa and the Caribbean. The Courland history offered the Caribbean island an interesting heritage that was distinct from standard British colonialism. Anderson's unique expertise offered him pleasant and interesting research expeditions to the Caribbean island.

On September 6, 1989, after the fatal highway accident, the celebration of Edgar Anderson's life of scholarship and teaching took place at the Spartan Memorial. His 27 graduate students contributed to the event, and the memorial program listed the multiple honors and awards received from each of the governments and worldwide scholarly societies that sponsored the San José State professor's original research and his publications.

Harry A. Gailey, Jr.

Professor of History, 1962 to 1995
President's Scholar, 1978-79
Outstanding Professor, 1971-72

HARRY A. GAILEY, JR. earned all of his degrees from the University of California, Los Angeles. He also had military experience. His first academic love was the history of Africa, for which he was hired to teach in 1962. In the '60s, the history department was booming with 50 faculty members, including temporaries hired as sabbatical replacements. Rich specializations included early Korean and Byzantine history, Canada, Iceland, science and technology, and immigration, as well as standard offerings in modern Europe, America (North and South), Asia and Russia. During those flourishing years, Gailey taught multiple sections in the histories of various African states and distinct groupings of peoples from the continent's earliest history. During the 1970s and 1980s, he established himself as one of America's leading scholars on Africa with the publication of the first 12 of his 17 books.

In addition to Gailey's record of fulltime teaching (with uncompensated graduate overloads), he centered his intellectual life primarily on West Africa, the Congo, Gambia, Nigeria, as well as colonial policy, and military affairs. Central to his permanent contribution to scholarship was his three-volume study of Africa from pre-history to the late twentieth century.

Two distinct movements, one regional and the other national, disrupted the professor's academic agenda. Decades of suburban school district expansion had ended, as did the need to prepare large numbers of history teachers. Almost simultaneously the original Black Power movement emerged and spawned a new interest in America's African heritage. But the promise of high enrollment in African history classes failed to materialize. Gailey methodically converted his professional focus from Africa to modern military history, a subject that had long commanded strong and enduring appeal at San José State. During his refocused career, Gailey produced five more volumes; three focused upon major Pacific campaigns of World War II; a fourth dealt with the U.S. Marine Corps. His summary treatment appeared in 1995 as *The War in the Pacific: From Pearl Harbor to Tokyo Bay*.

As a classroom teacher, Gailey was informative, orgnized, and supportive of students. He cared little regarding which course assignments he received within his area of expertise (African, military, English, European and colonial histories). He was willing to teach any classes assigned to him, just so that small graduate seminars would continue to be offered. Gailey's concept of a university and the role of a university professor required no less. In believing so, he demonstrated what was possible within a system that addressed the functional but celebrated the best.

Charles B. Burdick

Professor of History, 1957 to 1989
Dean of Social Sciences, 1983 to 1989
President's Scholar, 1974-75
Outstanding Professor, 1966-67 and 1978-79
California State University Outstanding Professor, 1967-68 and 1979-80

CHARLES B. BURDICK'S DISTINCTION, the most accomplished faculty member in the history of San José State, rested upon the official decisions of his academic colleagues, successive presidents of the university, and chancellors of the California State University system. The students had already proclaimed Dr. Burdick "King of the Classroom" when President Robert D. Clark awarded him Outstanding Professor distinction in 1966-67. President Gail Fullerton repeated this action in 1978-79, making him the only professor to be twice chosen for the institution's top teaching award. On both occasions, the CSU trustees doubly honored Burdick with their own unprecedented, two-time selection of him as the most outstanding professor within the university system.

Dr. Charles Burdick also was named President's Scholar in 1974-75 by President John H. Bunzel. That distinction, which Bunzel created to recognize published scholarship or artistic and scientific accomplishment, rested upon Burdick's library of published research and his international acclaim in the field of German military history.

Burdick grew up in San José, the oldest of six Depression Era children of Donald L. and Inez E. Burdick. After the conclusion of his under-age, 1944 enlistment in WWII (with parental permission), he enrolled at San José State College in 1946, completed his degree in three years, and began graduate studies at Stanford. While still in their undergraduate years, Burdick and Kay Lutz began a marriage that would endure for 50 years. Starting with his Stanford graduate years, he and Kay (and their four daughters as years advanced) enjoyed extended residences in Germany. At first Burdick introduced himself to the surviving leadership of the German military, interviewed them, and then collected original and manuscript materials dealing with post-1918 German history. His contacts and his gathering of source materials served as the basis of his and his students' subsequent contributions to twentieth century German history. Vast numbers of colleagues and students considered themselves the Burdicks' personal friends. Burdick always had time for them, for their problems and for their triumphs.

When his former San José State teacher Professor Dudley T. Moorhead recruited him back from Stanford in 1957, history did not yet exist as a department. This would take place under the leadership of H. Brett Melendy and Gerald E. Wheeler. Burdick's initial role was to design the comprehensive history curriculum, which he soon expanded into a graduate program. That reorganization, plus the huge and growing flood of new students, allowed Burdick to specialize in teaching European and German history. Each semester thereafter he was able to offer a research seminar or a master's level colloquium. The MA theses, more than 120 of which Burdick directed, became the prime requirement for the graduate degree.

In charge of instructional scheduling, Burdick assigned himself the European history lecture, that grew to an overflow attendance, at 7:30 a.m. every Monday, Wednesday, and Friday. For Burdick's students, failure simply was not an option. His students succeeded because he let them know that they would. They could not disappoint a professor who invested his faith and his valuable time in them.

Among his methods for bringing out their best was the individualized final examination. This exam had one section of general questions pertaining to the broad scope of the course, and a second section pertaining to each student's previously completed research project. This method allowed the diligent as well as the brilliant to perform even better.

Burdick zoomed through the promotion and tenure processes easily, enjoyed early Fulbright appointments in Germany, and became a most favored grantee of Germany's prestigious Alexander von Humboldt Foundation. The Humboldt sought Burdick out constantly with grants of extensive professional support, individual and family accommodations, research contacts and materials, providing the supportive and appreciative environment in which his scholarship thrived. In his retirement, the Humboldt struck a medal in Professor Burdick's honor and presented it in a lavish ceremony in Germany. The Federal Republic conferred upon him the Commander Cross of the Order of Merit in 1992.

Burdick himself had authored 10 books, mostly on German history, and had served as editor of 15 more. His former students (mostly well placed in education or government service) presented him with a *Festschrift*, a book of their original, scholarly essays, in his honor and at a campus banquet on the occasion of his 60th birthday.

When he was 72 years old, Kay's man and everyone's friend developed an inoperable tumor that first denied him sight, then life. During his decline, he and Kay received a steady stream of admiring friends and former students. As was his way, Charles never allowed a guest to feel anything less than happiness in his presence. When his friend, former chair and dean Gerald Wheeler visited Charles at his retirement residence in Ferndale, California, Charles joined the dinner party that Wheeler gathered at the town's quaint Victorian Village Inn. Though unable to see much beyond his dinner plate or to sense the once-familiar bouquet and taste of the German wines, Burdick made that evening one more among so many that had been charged with charm, wit, and enduring friendship. His friends received copies of his concluding act of scholarship, a well-researched examination of ordinary people caught in uncontrollable historical change. Burdick's final article and gift, "The Expulsion of Germans from Japan, 1947-1948," was a sensitive examination of evil's impact upon innocence. It was a twentieth century farewell from the best product of San José State's academic life.

Epilogue

IN THE THREE YEARS since the author completed the manuscript, the pace has only accelerated at Silicon Valley's metropolitan university.

At the close of year 2002, the campus was changed dramatically by the imposing structure of the new Dr. Martin Luther King, Jr. Library. On time and on budget, this library will open to the public in August of 2003. By then the first phase of the 6,600 bed Campus Village project will be underway in the area where three of the six red brick residence halls once stood. Phase One will include programmed suites for freshmen and sophomores, apartment-style accommodations for upper division students and graduate students, as well as housing for 200 faculty and staff. The mid-rise

Students take up residence in University House

AS A RAPIDLY GROWING CAMPUS absorbed surrounding city blocks during the Wahlquist years, the university purchased not just land, but also buildings. Many houses now part of the campus footprint were put to use as "temporary" offices. By the turn of the century, most had been replaced by campus revitalization south of Paseo de San Carlos.

One cluster of four residences at the corner of what used to be San Carlos and Fifth streets was the last to be transformed. The University Police Department vacated their "house" in exchange for new offices in front of the Seventh Street Parking Garage. The Alumni Association moved to other campus facilities, and its former house was demolished. Building X also was torn down. That left Building DD, also known as Scheller House, after one of its turn-of-the-century residents. Built in 1905, Building DD became a focal point for preservation buffs and neighborhood activists. In the early 1990s, Executive Vice President J. Handel Evans offered the house for sale — for $1 — to anyone who would move it off campus. There was interest, but no takers for the once-grand, now rundown residence.

In limbo for decades, Building DD's situation eventually took a turn for the better — a 90 degree turn so that it now faces San Carlos Plaza. The old house has young inhabitants — the Associated Students offices — and a new name — University House. Its renovation cost Associated Students $2 million. The new facility now houses AS administration, government, campus recreation, and special events offices.

When AS moved in on Oct. 18, 2001, renovation began on its former offices in the Student Union. Two months later, another AS project — a $1.2 million student Computer Services Center funded from an $18 per semester student technology fee — opened for business. Students daily fill more than 100 workstations with seven different operating systems and all types of software for various disciplines.

"University House was consciously renovated to keep most of its original beauty," says Alfonso De Alba, executive director of AS and a 1996 graduate of San José State with a degree in political science/public administration. "As a focal point for students on the Paseo de San Carlos, it may be the most beautiful building on campus, besides the Tower."

structures also will have two levels of below-grade parking.

More and more students park at the South Campus Park and Ride lot, taking advantage of lower prices and free shuttles to and from campus. The new city-owned parking lot across San Fernando from the new library will accommodate the community library users, as will the public transportation being built near the new San José City Hall, now under construction one block north of campus.

The Student Services Center, built to accommodate the staff and functions that were formerly housed in Walquist Library, has provided a central space where students can take care of a variety of tasks in one building. Now plans are underway to renovate the soon to be former Clark Library into Clark Hall, which will house the student success center, faculty offices, classrooms, the Metropolitan University Scholar Experience (MUSE), Honors College, the President's Scholars, learning labs and administrative functions.

In 1994, when I arrived to serve as president of San José State University, the California State University system was beginning to develop its expectation that presidents

Joint library says volumes about city/university cooperation

THE DR. MARTIN LUTHER KING, JR. LIBRARY, the nation's first joint library serving a major city and university, is set to open in fall 2003 at the corner of Fourth and San Fernando streets. The revolutionary library will be a nationwide model for city/university cooperation and for high-tech innovation.

The eight-story building will be 475,000 square feet of both public library and university research facility. With capacity for 2 million volumes and 3,600 seats, the library will include university special collections and dozens of group study rooms as well as a public browsing library and special children's areas.

The $177.5 million project is funded from a variety of sources: $70 million from the city of San José, $86 million from state higher education construction bonds, $5 million from university funds, and $16.5 million from private donors. The Dr. Martin Luther King, Jr. Library fundraising campaign is led by Silicon Valley leaders and philanthropists, with John Warnock as honorary chair. The committee's fund-raising goal is $16.5 million to be used to supplement the building's technology. The David and Lucile Packard Foundation contributed $1 million to the campaign.

Technology innovations will help create a resource center befitting Silicon Valley with access to a world of information through online remote access to reference services, computer labs, and even a children's electronic discovery area.

A *San Jose Mercury News* editorial (Feb. 4, 1997) called the joint library proposal "brilliant" and said, "...it may well be the main accomplishment for which (Susan) Hammer is remembered as major." It also forms a concrete foundation for President Robert Caret's vision of San José State as a metropolitan university serving Silicon Valley.

be external advocates rather than just internal managers. It has been a pleasure to actively participate in such key regional organizations as Silicon Valley Manufacturers Group, Joint Venture Silicon Valley, the Convention and Visitor's Bureau, Lincoln Law School, and numerous arts organizations. In addition, I am the immediate past president of the Western Athletics Conference and am active with national professional organizations such as the American Council for Education and the American Association of Schools, Colleges and Universities, where I serve on committees and as a presenter at local and national conferences. I attend dozens of community events each year in order to reach out to the region served by San José State University.

Provost Linda Bain retired in the summer of 2000, after providing five years of academic leadership. The search for a new provost brought Marshall Goodman to the campus in the spring of 2001. In relatively short order, Provost Goodman started the Survey and Policy Research Institute to provide survey research capacity to the campus and community. Its consumer confidence surveys are widely reported in business and

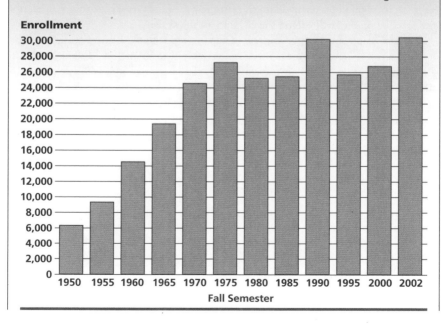

Enrollment on the rise through the decades

THE NUMBER OF STUDENTS attending San José State has been increasing steadily, with occasional fluctuations from year to year. Building more classrooms was paramount during President Wahlquist's era as the campus prepared for the coming baby boom generation, which arrived *en masse* in the 1970s. Enrollment hit a high point 1990, then trended down in the early '90s during the state's recession and budget woes, only to climb back up as more and more of the state's growing population looked to higher education as their first step up the economic ladder. Fall 2002 set an all-time enrollment record with 30,350 students attending SJSU.

Enrollment

Fall Semester

U.S. News & World Report Rankings

	Top Public Schools	Engineering	Electrical Engineering	Computer Engineering
2000	9th in the West	15th nationally		
2001	6th in the West	16th nationally	12th nationally	7th nationally
2002	4th in the West	16th nationally	7th nationally	6th nationally

popular media. By the fall of 2002, the provost had instituted a freshman seminar concept entitled MUSE (Metropolitan University Scholar Experience) for 1,000 incoming freshmen. These 15 student seminars, taught by outstanding senior faculty, engage students early in their college years in intellectual discussions and help them to adjust to a new academic life in college. Goodman is also active in the globalization movement, catalyzing groups to set up additional reciprocal agreements with universities abroad and encouraging more San José State students to take advantage of study overseas.

Enrollment began growing over the past two years as the economy in Silicon Valley cooled, freeing students to enroll in more units to complete undergraduate degrees or start graduate programs. As the campus nears its physical capacity, plans are in the works to create off-campus satellite centers where students can more conveniently take a portion of their courses. The location of these centers tracks the southern population growth into Morgan Hill, Gilroy and Hollister. Enrollment at most other California State Universities has jumped as well, with some campuses nearing or reaching their maximum capacities. Electronic course delivery, year-round operation and satellite centers will extend the capacity of the system.

San José State University is working in partnership with the University of California at Santa Cruz to develop an academic center with NASA-Ames at Moffett Field. The site, with a focus on technology, research and teacher preparation, will provide convenient access to students living in the northern part of San José State's service region.

In fall 2003 the first cohort of Urban Leadership doctoral students will begin their studies. The EdD will be offered with University of California, Berkley; University of California, Santa Cruz; and, CSU, Hayward. A second joint doctorate will be offered in Educational Leadership in partnership with University of California, Santa Cruz. Several other joint programs are under discussion to meet the needs of the region.

At the close of 2002 San José State was responding to a new challenge from the NCAA. All Division I-A football programs are required to a) play at least five home games, and b) document an average of 15,000 people in attendance for each of the five home games. San José State University currently fields six men's sports and ten women's sports. Scheduling the five home games has already occurred. A group of campus and community leaders met in June 2002 to focus on ways to meet the new standards. Out of the retreat came *Spartans First!*, a conceptual plan for reaching the new standards. Coordinated by the executive assistant to the president, the president's staff chairs initiatives (Marketing, Resource Development, Facilities, and

Athletics Programming) and includes community members to develop action plans.

From 2000-2002, Spartan Stadium was the site of the Silicon Valley Football Classic. This Western Athletic Conference post-season bowl game was played on New Year's Eve day as a festive precursor to welcoming a new year. Air Force was the victor over Fresno State University in the inaugural classic. Fresno State qualified to represent the Western Athletics Conference against Michigan State in 2002, and on its third SV bowl appearance, Fresno took home the trophy after an exciting contest against Georgia Tech.

Each year *U.S. News & World Report* publishes regional and national college rankings to help prospective students select a good match in higher education. San José State University's rankings have gone up in each of the past two years.

Such rankings, while not a perfect measure, are certainly moving in the right direction. The campus has a number of program jewels — some ranked, some not.

As San José State University approaches its 150th anniversary, the campus is actively influencing its future. In 2007, the university will serve a capacity student body preparing to power Silicon Valley with yet another wave of graduates. The campus will continue to offer green space in the urban core with new buildings rising higher rather than spreading across precious open space. Students, faculty and alumni will continue to be an integral part of the unique region known as Silicon Valley. Thank you for taking the time to learn more about the history of the oldest public university on the West Coast.

Robert L. Caret
President
San José State University

April 2003

Editor's Note

L ESS THAN A MONTH before *San José State University, An Interpretive History, 1950 – 2000*, was to be printed, the campus and its community learned that President Robert Caret had decided to accept the presidency at Towson University in Maryland. His decision to return to Towson, where he spent 21 years as a faculty member and administrator, caught many by surprise

The *San Jose Mercury News* published the news on April 3, 2003, and complimented Caret for his successful tenure. "Caret gets credit for laying out a strong vision for what is possible at a state university in Silicon Valley and for pushing the first joint city-university library in the nation."

Caret's deliberately symbolic act upon his 1994 San José arrival — ordering that the windows be washed for the first time since 1989 — also drew comment. "Caret not only had the windows washed, he also opened them to the community, airing out an institution that had become stale and insular. He built strong partnerships with valley companies. He offered a vision for a metropolitan university, a far cry from the gritty image of a commuter school. He acknowledged simmering racial tensions and created an atmosphere of trust."

Lastly, as the community reluctantly came to accept that Caret would be leaving San José mid-summer, the *Mercury News* on April 5, 2003, commented on his fundraising success. "Caret raised almost $90 million during his seven-year tenure.... Donations climbed from a 10-year low of $7 million in 1994-95, when he was appointed, to a high of almost $18 million in 1997-98."

Those who support the university and its extended community agree that President Robert Caret deserves gratitude for a job well done and that someone very much like Caret would be the best choice for his successor.

Carol Beddo, SJSU, BA, English, 1968
Editor
May 2003

Index

About the Author

JAMES P. WALSH is emeritus professor of history at San José State University. Born in San Francisco of Irish parents, he earned degrees from the University of San Francisco (BS and MA) and from the University of California, Berkeley (PhD). Dr. Walsh enjoyed a thirty-four year career at San José State as professor of history during which time he served as chair of the history department, dean of the college of social sciences, and academic vice-president. Punctuating these years were three foreign research and teaching appointments and the publication of seven books. The California Historical Society recognized Professor Walsh's career contributions to the interpretation of California history with its J.S. Holiday award.

James P. Walsh